DECONSTRUCTING PSYCHOPATHOLOGY

DECONSTRUCTING PSYCHOPATHOLOGY

Ian Parker, Eugenie Georgaca,
David Harper, Terence McLaughlin
and Mark Stowell-Smith

SAGE Publications
London ● Thousand Oaks ● New Delhi

ISBN 0-8039-7480-9 (hbk)
ISBN 0-8039-7481-7 (pbk)
© Ian Parker, Eugenie Georgaca, David Harper, Terence McLaughlin
and Mark Stowell-Smith 1995
First published 1995
Reprinted 1997, 1999, 2004, 2005

SAGE Publications Ltd
1 Oliver's Yard
55 City Road
London EC1Y 1SP

SAGE Publications Inc
2455 Teller Road
Thousand Oaks
California 91320

SAGE Publications India Pvt. Ltd
B-42 Panchsheel Enclave
PO Box 4109
New Delhi 110 017

British Library Cataloguing in Publication data
A catalogue record for this book is available from the British Library

Library of Congress Control Number: 95071356

Typeset by Photoprint Ltd., Torquay, Devon
Printed digitally and bound in Great Britain by
Biddles Limited, King's Lynn, Norfolk

Contents

Introduction

This co-authored book is not designed to operate as a textbook, but as a polemical and accessible 'counter-text' for students and practitioners. It develops a deconstructive approach to the practice of professionals and researchers concerned with 'psychopathology'. We will be doing three things in the course of the book. First, we will open up the notion of 'psychopathology' as it is conventionally used in psychology and psychiatry using a practical deconstructive approach to the language and institutions that hold it in place. Secondly, we will explore the implications of deconstructive ideas for the theories and practices that underpin clinical treatments. Thirdly, we will be describing alternative views of the language of psychopathology and models for critical professional work and good mental health practice.

Let us trace the shape of the book. We are concerned in the first part of the book with how forms of mental 'illness' or distress have become divided from mental health, and how professionals participate in 'dividing practices' in the present day. As we describe how these dividing practices work, we throw them into question by deconstructing clinical categories. Deconstruction in this book is used to unravel suppressed meanings in texts, and to provide a way of re-reading and re-working ideas and practices that are normally taken for granted. In Chapter 1 we review the way in which abnormal psychology has been divided from the 'normal' psychology that most people are supposed to enjoy. Chapter 2 looks at 'alternatives' from psychoanalysis, anti-psychiatry, family therapy and cognitive approaches. In Chapter 3 we look at how symptoms are constructed, and how they reinforce popular stereotypes and different forms of oppression.

We then turn our attention to the ways in which cultural images of psychological distress, which are so important a context for the development of psychiatry and clinical psychology, bear on the ways in which people who are categorized in the mental health system understand themselves. Chapter 4 explores cultural representations of psychopathology, and how those representations affect clinical practice. We look at the other side of the problem in Chapter 5, when we discuss pathological identity, and we trace the network of paths that lead people into the mental health system. This is all well and good, but we also want to ask what opportunities for change this picture presents to the professional reader who will want to know what theoretical and research alternatives our deconstruction opens up, and to the user of mental health services, who will be concerned with examples of better practice. In Chapter 6 we develop our account of 'psychopathology' as something that is embedded in cultural texts, and we look at research on language, and the ways in which traditional psychiatric work, which produces a circular argument confirming existing labels, can be challenged. The different practical challenges that have been developed are explored in Chapter 7, which covers the development of the alternative mental health movements.

Psychiatric texts, like many other texts, try to cover over the contradictions in the argument they develop and the assumptions they use. This book too is interlaced with contradictions, and so it is helpful, we think, to anticipate some of the objections that will be levelled against us, and some of the disagreements between us that will have found their way into the book. This book is not a closed system nor a complete solution, and so Chapter 8 reviews some of the dilemmas and contradictions that face those critical of mainstream psychiatry and clinical psychology, as well as providing a resource list of groups that are taking our academic discussion forward in the real world.

As we go through the book we show why it is necessary to 'deconstruct' psychopathology, and describe what we mean by 'practical deconstruction'. We have come together to write this book from diverse parts of the mental health system – from clinical psychology, psychiatric social work, psychoanalysis, psychology teaching and action research – and have no desire to replace the old jargon around mental health and distress with a new one. As we unravel, deconstruct traditional notions in the following chapters, we suggest strategies for change, and hope that you will be inspired to participate in building, reconstructing something better.

1

Madness and Modernity

This first chapter provides a historical review of the development of 'psychopathology' as the study of mental 'disorder' in Western culture. We give an account of Michel Foucault's work as it applies to clinical categories, and then describe how psychiatric and abnormal psychology texts and practices can be deconstructed. We also introduce the notion of 'deconstruction' and show how it can be made relevant to this history of categorization, and to the ways in which some people have been marked off as different, as 'other'.

Abnormal psychology

The notions of madness and abnormal psychology as we understand them are particular and peculiar to our culture and our time. That is the starting point for our historical deconstruction of psychopathology. However, this assertion on its own is no longer controversial or very radical. Many practitioners of psychiatry and clinical psychology would accept that the categories we use to understand mental distress are specific to our society. Even the terminology adopted in liberal American and British texts on the issue has moved on from the old oppositions of 'sane/insane', or even 'healthy/sick', to ones which try to escape a medical model. One popular opposition employed in psychology now, for example, is that of 'normal/abnormal'. As one recent text puts it, abnormal psychology is the study of 'The Problem of Maladaptive Behavior' (Sarason and Sarason, 1987). While madness is now commonly referred to in inverted commas, it is 'abnormal psychology' in these texts that is treated as a fact. The problem is that not only does the formulation 'abnormal psychology' belie the continuing power of medical models of 'illness', but it is doubtful whether simply adopting that polarity in preference to the others will solve the problems facing what are often now called the 'users' or 'consumers' of mental health agencies.

The words we use to describe 'maladaptive behaviour' are only part of the problem we want to focus on in this book, but they are an important part. The terms we use are loaded with assumptions, and those assumptions are reproduced moment by moment in the practice of psychiatry, in its poor cousin clinical psychology, and in its even more dependent relatives (in mental health nursing, social work and so on) struggling to make sense of distress in the community. Words do not only denote a phenomenon, but carry with them an array of connotations. These connotations – of pathology, incapacity or lack – funnel into the scientific definitions that are circulated in textbooks and medical manuals on the identification and description of types of 'psychopathology'. Each slot in the latest edition of the *Diagnostic and Statistical Manual of Mental Disorders* (DSM) produced by the American Psychiatric Association (1994) or the *International Classification of Diseases* (ICD) overseen by the World Health Organization (1992) becomes occupied either by those rare human exemplars who fit perfectly, or, more often, by the 'difficult cases' who spill over their assigned place and require a complex combination of names to pin them down. When the categories are used, they become charged with an emotional force which has far-reaching consequences for those who are labelled. Not only are 'patients' pathologized by the diagnostic classification itself, but they are further pathologized when they do not fit, because it does not work. The labels are not simply innocent counters available to the psychiatrist or clinical psychologist to be tagged on to a case and to point to an appropriate remedy. The use of medical terminology also affects those who are responsible for labelling. The power of psychiatry rests, in large part, on its ability to force psychologists, nurses and social workers who are not medically qualified to play only supporting parts in institutions. It is the power of medicine itself which sets the agenda (Stainton Rogers, 1991; Turner, 1987). Because clinical psychologists and the rest of the cast often aspire to psychiatric power we will need to look directly at that power and how it operates.

Choosing friendly euphemisms will not solve the problem, for the traditional oppositions that constitute the field of psychopathology can always be renewed, and will then hold the same cultural power of exclusion and institutional abuse. This problem has been emphasized by those working with learning disability, in which the use of hundreds of different terms fail to escape demeaning meanings (Sinason, 1989). In this sense, the shift to 'normal/abnormal' simply reconstitutes the opposition between 'healthy' and 'sick' or between 'sane' and 'insane', and the power of psychiatry is left firmly in place. At the same time, however, the move from one set of oppositions to another opens up new spaces for resistance, spaces for new voices to be heard. This is part of the work of 'deconstruction' which was elaborated in French philosophy by Jacques Derrida, and we have to link that work to practical changes to ensure that the new oppositions do not simply function to divide and oppress in the same ways as the old.

Derrida (for example, 1976, 1978) provides a systematic reading of philosophical texts which focus on the ways in which an argument is policed to guarantee a fixed reference point, an essential point of 'truth' which the reader then takes for granted and sees as the foundation for other less important things. A deconstruction, in this 'original' and 'purest' sense, identifies conceptual oppositions, recovers notions that have been excluded, and shows how the ideas that have been privileged are dependent on those they dominate. For example, when we speak, it appears as if all meaning comes from within our individual 'mind' and then travels through language which operates as a mere carrier. Forms of communication, such as writing, that seem out of the mind's control, are then relegated to a lesser place. Derrida (1978) draws attention to philosophical traditions that treat writing in this way as 'impure' speech. He then goes on to argue that because language is a system of terms that is always already out of our control, it could be seen as a variety of writing, and so, in his deconstruction of the opposition between speech and writing, 'writing' disrupts the opposition.

These matters are very important to psychiatric knowledge, of course, because psychiatry and other clinical approaches have been concerned with what goes on inside individual minds and bodies, and they have tried to brush away the role of language and society in the experience and treatment of distress. Deconstruction in the strict philosophical sense offers us a way of tackling the internal contradictions in psychiatric texts, but that is where we start, not where we want to finish. It is helpful to be aware of the origins of the term deconstruction, but we are using it in a less 'pure' way in this book. We will be linking our deconstruction of psychopathology with an analysis of the practices of power that hold traditional oppositions in place. To do that we need some historical account, and we will be locating our critical reading of texts in their institutional context. This is why we use the work of the historian Foucault, a writer who also had a clinical psychology training (Parker, 1995a). We will be adopting a looser form of deconstruction that connects psychological critique with political context (cf. Parker and Shotter, 1990). In its most radical form, 'postmodernism' in psychology is another codeword for the same type of challenge to the disciplines of the mind (Kvale, 1992). Attending to politics and power when you do a critical reading, and thinking through the effects of your critique on institutions and forms of knowledge is what we term *practical deconstruction*.

Deconstructing terminology

Deconstruction *is* abnormal psychology, for it looks at things askew, seeing things that do not at first glance seem to be there, it is very suspicious, and it breaks the rules to show that what is usually treated as normal is itself really rather odd. When we refer to our reading as 'abnormal' here, we risk reinforcing the 'normal' negative connotations attached to different behaviours and experiences, but we are also taking terms and using them *against* traditional systems of knowledge and power, acknowledging the necessity for suspicion and defying the routine way it is pathologized. Deconstruction is a process of reading which unravels the way insane categories are used to suppress different perceptions and behaviours, and it overturns the opposition between, for example, illness and health. It works with a strange, pathologically curious attention to language and practice to show that a measure of 'sickness' is needed to survive in this world, and to show that the division between sickness and health is *not* discontinuous, and, more than that, that the division is constructed in such a way that it produces those two ends of the continuum. At the same time, deconstruction recovers the subordinate term in a conceptual opposition and transforms it, to use it against the dominant team.

In political struggles, the terms 'black' and 'gay' were taken from the weaponry of prejudice and used defiantly by those who were labelled in such a way that they disrupted simple shorthand pathologizing in everyday language. The notion of 'health', for example, requires a description of 'sickness' to make sense. It could not exist without the opposite that defines it. The terms 'insanity', 'illness' or 'abnormality' are then put under erasure so that we do not use them in the simple way they are usually used and defined by their powerful partners ('sanity', 'health' or 'normality') but rather as conceptual levers to throw the language of modern mental health policing into question. To put something 'under erasure' is to question its taken-for-granted meaning, to mark it as a problem to be challenged. Moreover, we must challenge not only one set of oppositions, but also the way they are linked together in a set that constitutes the popular and professional definitions of the things that lie outside 'reasonable' society.

The practical deconstruction described in this book roots the conceptual oppositions that structure psychopathology in abnormal structures of segregation and regulation that have accumulated a pervasive and insidious power over the years in Western culture (the culture we refer to as 'ours', though 'we' are trying to keep our distance here). It is practical in the sense both that it focuses on the way language works in material apparatuses of medicine, the state and the community, and in that it is designed to be useful to critical practitioners and those struggling at the sharp end of the mental health system. Along the way we will be describing how other writers, such as Foucault (1977, 1981) who was centrally concerned with power, can be used in this critical struggle.

The language of abnormal psychology is enmeshed within institutions of mental diagnosis and surveillance. Three themes will run through this first chapter and then appear in the rest of the book. The first is that an understanding of language is crucial to a critical account of psychiatry and its sidekicks. The second is that we have to connect language with the institutions in which it is used. One of the most important ways of doing that is to see things from the standpoint of those who suffer psychiatry. The third theme is that we need some account of the 'irrational' or the 'unreasonable' in human experience which language excludes. It excludes what it deems to be irrational at the very moment it constructs it. This means that we have to think tactically about how to make alliances with such constructed and excluded phenomena at the same time as developing an understanding as to how they function. In this culture we will need some notion of resistance to accomplish that task.

When we appeal to the irrationality that is shut out of over-rational clinical knowledge we do not want to imply that we believe in that irrationality as a 'pure' source of liberation (in the same way as someone who uses a gun in a liberation struggle is using a weapon that is constructed by the system they oppose). And we are not only talking about things constructed in language, but, as Foucault (1977) did, about the construction of physical apparatuses of power and resistance (like prisons and guns, chemicals and bodies). To pursue these three themes it will be necessary to give a critical historical analysis of psychiatry and 'abnormal psychology'. This is where our deconstruction is given a further, even more radical turn, as we will see in the next section. We should ask how the commonly used indicators of mental 'illness' and the powerful institutions of mental health came into being. Psychiatry tells a story of progress to support its work, and its way of writing history needs to be challenged. What appears to be commonsensical must be rendered strange. When we put concepts under erasure, that does not mean that we will never use them again; we hold and transform them. We will use them in a different way. One thing we should not erase in a practical deconstruction is our memory, in this case as a 'counter-memory' (Foucault, 1977), of how this state of things came to be.

Three histories of abnormality

There are three types of historical account we could give of madness. The first is a fairly uncontentious account of the development of 'madness' as a problem in Western culture since the Middle Ages and of changes in diagnostic categories. The second is a more radical examination of the notions of mental health which lie under those categories, and the third is one which throws into question the very notions of reason and unreason which language forces into being. We will run, in turn, through these three accounts.

The historical specificity of diagnostic categories

There have, of course, been many different explanations of 'madness' over the centuries, and the radical and rapid shifts in definition testify to the difficulty we face in trying to decipher what it 'really' is. Take the links that were made in the Middle Ages, for example, between water and madness.

On the Continent the melancholy of the English was explained by way of our maritime climate: 'all those fine droplets of water that penetrated the channels and fibers of the human body and made it lose its firmness, predisposed it to madness' (Foucault, 1971: 13). It is in this context that images of the 'Ship of Fools' suddenly appeared in the fifteenth century. These ships, according to the contemporary popular representations (especially in art), travelled around with the mad to be occasionally sighted by the inhabitants of port towns. Although the historical accuracy of Foucault's description of these ships has been questioned (Gordon, 1990; Sedgwick, 1982), the symbolic importance they played in the popular imagination is the key point at issue here. According to Foucault (1971), up until the fifteenth century the great fear was death alone. From the fifteenth century *madness* makes an entrance as the ghastly scourge of the Western mind. Whilst death was a threat that came from without, and at the end of life, madness is something always present as a threat from *within* and as an everpresent possibility. People then realized that 'The head that will become the skull is already empty . . . Madness is the *déjà-là* [already there] of death' (Foucault, 1971: 16).

The mad then filled the space that was opened up by the closure of the leprosaria at the end of the Middle Ages. Lepers ceased to be the main problem on the outskirts of life, and the new diseased of mind occupied their place, but it was only after the confinement of social deviants in general that the mad became marked out for special treatment. The General Hospital of Paris established in 1656 first of all opened its doors to various vagabonds and was primarily a place of confinement rather than a place of treatment. What we now designate the 'mad' were thrown in with a mixed bag of deviants, and within a short time, by 1676, the King ordered that there should be such an institution in every city. These places were enormous. Paris, for example, saw one in a 100 of its population incarcerated in a few months. In England it was decided that 'houses of correction' should be set up in each county in accordance with an act of 1575. Confinement across Europe was a police matter, not one of medical care. That 'care' came later, in institutions and then, as an extension of the institutions now, out into the community again (an issue we explore in Chapter 7). It was common knowledge, Foucault notes, that until the end of the eighteenth century the mad were not seen as sick. The animality of madness 'protected the lunatic from whatever might be fragile, precarious and sickly in man' (Foucault, 1971: 74).

The bridge to the medical treatment of the mad was the moral treatment of the insane in special places, treatment which was provoked by popular fears that the distressed inhabitants of the large institutions in cities were contagious. The inhabitants of Paris near the Hôpital Géneral, for example, had long complained about the dangerous vapours which wafted out and which threatened to make them mad too. It was the reinterpretation of the issue as a moral one which set the way for releasing the mad from their chains. Samuel Tuke, one of the English Quaker reformers, founded a retreat at York in 1729, for example, and advocated warm baths and human kindness. One of Foucault's more controversial arguments is that the notion of 'kindness' as a cure was to mesh into medical models which would then in turn enmesh the mad in other more powerful invisible chains. Foucault's case is that the humanization of treatments of the insane encouraged the internalization of the difficulties they exhibited. The mad then had to take responsibility for cure, and the kind treatment which replaced the rods and whips would work its way inwards. The conscience of the mentally ill would act as a self-discipline all the more efficient than the social discipline of the general hospital. We will return to the implications of this internalization of treatment and responsibility for mental disorder when we look at a more radical way of historicizing psychiatric practice in a moment.

The moral treatment of madness was to give way eventually to medical approaches, but the rise of modern psychiatry followed a sustained period which lasted through the nineteenth century and into the twentieth until after the First World War, a period in which the medics were little more than helpmates in regimes of moral improvement. These regimes did often involve physical 'treatments' intended to bring the individual back into an engagement with civilized society, but since madness was seen as a combination of an inherited constitution and unfortunate life events, rather than any underlying disease entities, little medical intervention could be made. The moral regime during this time consisted of a mixture of notions, the two most important being organicism – inherited weakness – and hygiene – lack of cleanliness and social adjustment. This version of moral treatment was to lay the basis for modern full-blown medical psychiatry. The 'mad' were starting to be seen not so much as completely 'outside', but as problems 'inside' society: 'The paradigmatic subjects of the modernizing psychiatric apparatus posed a threat only in so far as they acted like grit in the institutional machinery of school, industry and elsewhere. They represented a source of social irritation, a loss of potential efficiency, and a future burden upon the state' (Rose, 1986: 52). It became increasingly important to monitor and regulate those who might fall into this condition and cause such irritation, and the observation and control of mental distress continued through to the 1950s when the so-called psychiatric miracle drugs allowed medical notions finally to triumph.

Not only did the release of the mad from the large anonymous prisons, in the eighteenth and nineteenth centuries and now in the twentieth century, treat them as special cases, but it also meant that they then, as special cases, needed to be observed carefully and classified. This classification has proceeded apace until the present day; the emphasis now is on the individuality of the 'patient' and the specificity of the symptoms they display. In hard-line medical approaches the emphasis is on the symptoms, and in the softer humanist varieties the person is valued as the carrier of the symptoms. However, these are two sides of a process which individual-izes distress, and treats it apart from social context. The categories in the various versions and revisions of the DSM or ICD have to be expanded and altered every time to give a supposedly more accurate, more carefully observed, set of categories. Since the observation is framed in medical terms, it always fails to work as a neat array of pigeonholes; people are never only 'patients' but complex thinking human beings, and so they just will not fit. This does not mean that a simple emphasis on the individuality of the sufferer will solve the problem, of course, because the rhetoric of individuality functions to wrench the person from the various social contexts that have contributed to the distress all the more. Medical language itself is rooted in social contexts, it is still framed by moral-political factors, and it is continually disrupted by them too.

The more recent changes in diagnostic categories still follow changes in moral reasoning in the surrounding society, and the decision to take out a category often reflects changes in morality. An example of this is the removal of homosexuality from what was to become the DSM-III-R (the third revised edition of the DSM). In 1973 the American Psychiatric Association Board of Trustees voted to take 'Ego-dystonic Homosexuality' off its list of mental illnesses (Wilson, 1993) and the American Psychologi-cal Association followed suit two years later. It should be noted, though, that 'persistent and marked distress about one's sexual orientation' was still given as an example of sexual dysfunction in the DSM-III-R (American Psychiatric Association, 1987: 296). It is also no accident that changing notions of sexuality should force the alteration of psychiatric categories. This is because definitions of abnormal and perverse behaviour and thinking cluster around sexual activities in this modern culture which is so saturated with sexualized notions of self and other (Foucault, 1981). These changes not only attest to the fragility of the current category system but also show us something about the assumptions which underlie it. The type of history we have traced so far allows us to see what the role of the discipline of abnormal psychology is in this society. But this is just the first step. We can go further than this, and we need to go further to link a historical account with deconstruction, to make it a deconstructive history.

Cultural changes in the experience of distress

Might our suspicion that the language we use to describe 'psychopathology' is culturally specific also be worth directing at the phenomenon itself? It is not only the terms that change, perhaps, but what we imagine to 'really' lie underneath them. Of course, mainstream psychiatrists like Roth and Kroll (1986) will see the 'reality of mental illness' as existing at every time and place, with different cultures simply having different words for 'it'. However, different cultures have such radically different conceptions of what we call mental illness that we have to consider the possibility that not only the talk, but also what is described is radically different. Take the case of notions of madness nearly 25 centuries ago in Greece (Padel, 1981). Here, the experience of distress was not of a turmoil inside the head of the sufferer but of a clash of wills outside. The activities of different deities demanding conflicting courses of action from a human subject would lead to contradictory and unreasonable behaviour.

In fifth century BC tragedy in Athens, for example, we have accounts of the mad as isolated from others because they are seen as particularly dangerous. But the great fear which animates those who have to deal with the mad is that the person who is mad is, in some odd way, close to the gods. Madness is the sign of this closeness. Each god puts pressure on the person to act in certain ways, and has a vested interest in that behaviour. While the gods often coexist peacefully, their interests may sometimes clash and this is where problems will arise. When the gods make mad those they wish to destroy, they can do so by a process of isolation, and it is here that one of the most interesting contrasts between conceptions of madness in fifth century BC Greece and our own time arises. It is precisely the contrast, the *difference* that we want to emphasize in this deconstructive history. We do not, for example, want to subscribe to traditional psychiatry's romanticization of ancient Greece, and to the notion that all the deepest truths about human nature were revealed there. We have chosen this example to demonstrate the *discontinuity* between that cultural context and 'ours'.

To take one example of the differences in language across the centuries; we should be aware that the English word 'idiot' which plays such an important part in the descriptive vocabulary of the everyday treatment of irrational or 'stupid' persons came from the Greek word '*idiotes*'. This Greek word means 'private person', and Greek culture at that time did not at all value notions of privacy or solitude. The consequence is that the wish to isolate one's self from others would be evidence of abnormality. It would also be a sign of a peculiarly close relationship with a god. More than that, the urge to isolate oneself would be experienced as abnormal. In this very different world, 'the mad and the ex-mad are distanced from other people further by feelings; both by the feelings other people have about them, and by those they have about and in their madness' (Padel, 1981: 114). The moral treatment of the idiots from the end of the eighteenth century in Europe in places like Tuke's Quaker asylum, on the other hand, required the 'retreat', the secluded 'reflection' of the person on their individual distress. Solitude here is a precondition for the solace moral treatment, and then medicine, would provide. How people understand 'solitude' and 'asylum', then, is culturally constituted.

Identifying the culturally specific popular representations of distress is not simply a matter of historical and anthropological interest. Popular representations do not float around ready to be used at will by whomsoever may wish, but are organized in material structures of power as *practices*. Popular representations are put to use in lay and professional practices that deal with individuals in distress, and professional discourses inform and change popular representations. Identifying the mutual relation between representations and practices does not only break the distinction between 'biased' lay knowledge and professional expertise, but it also contributes to unravelling the complex web of relations between professionals, institutions and the public. It is the linking of the different forms of knowledge about psychopathology and normality that sustains current theories and practices for the management of distress. Theories and practices today rest no less on popular representations of what is 'normal' and what is assumed to have gone awry when people do not act normally. Foucault's work has been invaluable in drawing attention to the way language is organized around different systems of meaning which offer positions of power to certain categories of people and disempower others. These systems of meaning are *discourses*. In recent debates inside psychology, critical writers studying structures of power in discourse have been taking seriously what oppressed people have long known, that the way we talk is bound up with privilege and, sometimes, resistance (for example, Parker, 1992).

Contemporary biological explanations of schizophrenia, for example, both draw upon and form popular representations and reservoirs of popular support. These representations are bound together in discourses, systems of statements about the world that create lived realities. The reason why the medical model has such power now is that people trust medicine and will be willing actively to assist the medical control of the mentally ill. Moment by moment the representation of what is wrong becomes a practice which creates the problem and its imaginary 'solution'. One example is the Schizophrenia Association of Great Britain (SAGB) which is an organization of lay people, many of whom are relatives of those diagnosed as 'schizophrenic'. It is currently trying to raise funds to build an institute to discover the biological basis of schizophrenia. The posters proclaim that the breakthrough is imminent, and the newsletters argue against social and family interaction explanations of the 'illness'. One poster says 'Schizophrenia is not all in the mind. It affects the body and the brain. It is a physical disease.' This message is directed at a non-medical audience. The questionnaire the SAGB send to members focuses on diet, other medical disorders and family histories, and consumers of medical treatments of schizophrenia are encouraged to interpret their distress in biological terms. This enthusiasm for medical treatment led the SAGB in 1994 to suggest that lithium be put in the water in Ireland and Bosnia to stem psychotic violence, and so end war.

The National Schizophrenia Fellowship (NSF) encourages this optimistic view of biological research too, and sets psychiatry goals, 'the breakthrough', which it cannot, of course, deliver. The practice of psychiatry is, in part, conditioned by consumer demand for the cure to a disease, and also, more so, by a more pragmatic symptom management agenda that is set by the drug companies. Each needs and fuels, and is under pressure from the other, though the drug companies seem to be doing best out of the deal at the moment (Breggin, 1991). The recent hype for the depression drug 'Prozac' also conveniently blurs the distinction between recreational drug use and medical drug abuse (Wurtzel, 1995). The large drug companies assign a marketing representative each to around six general practitioners, putting incredible pressure on already over-worked doctors in the process. Precise figures are difficult to obtain, as one would expect, but one report in 1989 estimates that US drug companies spent 2 million dollars on advertising to geriatricians (Pilgrim and Rogers, 1993). Many conferences and medical journals enjoy and suffer the patronage of the drug companies. It is also worth noting, as we consider the interplay between popular and professional representations of disorder, that other folk knowledges are heavily scientized too. (One example, which we discuss further in Chapter 5, is that of the notion of 'race'.)

Apart from the biological model which underwrites the medical control of psychiatry, there is the array of psychoanalytic approaches (and psychoanalysis itself has played a powerful role in the categories used in different versions of the DSM and ICD). Running alongside the UK psychoanalytic institutions such as the British Psycho-Analytical Society, the Institute of Psycho-Analysis and the Tavistock Clinic, are a host of other social work and counselling organizations and therapy centres which draw on, and popularize, psychoanalytic ideas. These ideas can then feed back into the institutions when 'patients' demand a particular treatment which accords with the model of the mind they use to understand themselves. Work in France at the end of the 1950s, for example, found the 'social representations' of psychoanalysis had percolated through the French population to such an extent that people described themselves in terms of 'id', 'ego' and 'libidinal' drives (Moscovici, 1976). The cure they then wanted was a 'talking cure' in which they could talk more about these things. In America and the United Kingdom too, in a variety of subtle ways which include advertising and fashion in disciplines like sociology and literature, popular notions of psychoanalysis have fed into the public mind and then are used by persons to describe, understand and experience their own inner mental lives. Popular family therapy has also helped to relay these notions to the general public (for example, Skynner and Cleese, 1983). There may not have been an Oedipus complex in Sophocles's day, despite the continual use of the rhetorical device which claims that the sources of all present-day knowledge about people were 'discovered' by the ancient Greeks; Freudian talk of such a thing may have created the problem *and* the cure.

If we unpick the oppositions that structure modern day discourse about mental health and sickness we will find that medical psychiatry does not stand alone as a pure system of thought. Not only is it rooted in many messy practices but it also creates, and is sustained by the many 'others' pitted against it. The fantasies of the final push that are presented by the Brain Research Association's 'Decade of the Brain' in the 1990s, for example, fantasies that are of a piece with biological psychiatry, also feed a consumer movement that feels that it has the right to speak about these hopes too. The spread of para-medical institutions offering psychoanalysis or psychotherapy as a treatment alongside or as an alternative to drugs gives psychiatry a human face, and then directs attention to the importance of 'talking things through'. This is not to say, of course, that either a biological miracle or psychoanalysis are good solutions to mainstream psychiatric and clinical practice (and we will be describing other more radical consumer movements in Chapter 7). What we need to understand now is how they have been constituted as alternatives *and* as part of the problem.

Reason and unreason

There is a further twist we can add to the history of madness, to give it its final 'abnormal' deconstructive character. What if the very act of dividing reason from unreason were a product of culture? Here we come to the third, most radical, of the historical accounts. This argument is advanced by Foucault (1971), and says that we need some understanding of the cultural production of the rational as a 'good thing' and the irrational as something which needs not only to be excluded but also to be rigorously policed. It is not good enough to shut out what is felt to be irrational, for we then have to guard repeatedly against the threat of its return. We need look no further than Descartes, writing in seventeenth-century Holland, for an example of the culturally potent split between mind and body which now rules Western culture. Descartes not only divided the human being from the rest of the animal species with the argument that cries of pain were mere creaks of a bodily mechanism in lower animals while the consciousness of pain was qualitatively different in the human mind, but he also put the mind at the pinnacle of earthly value. He did this with the argument that only one thing remains when a human being puts everything in doubt, the certainty that there is an 'I' who is doing that doubting, thinking. The baseline for the human soul for Descartes was the recognition that 'I think therefore I am', and this rhetorical device (for it is no more than a rhetorical device, as the French analyst Lacan was to show) – in Latin *cogito ergo sum* – marks rational human doubt off against the animality of the mad.

A necessary corollary of this picture of the self is the guarantee we give to the potential self-sufficiency of the human mind in its ability to doubt. For Descartes it is when we lose the ability to doubt that our rationality disappears, and it is Foucault's argument that the exclusion of madness as an irrational 'otherness' where doubt has disappeared is also then something that requires policing. It is no accident that Descartes makes a distinction between dreaming as a state we can draw back from and assess in waking life, and madness as a state which we cannot imagine leaving once we have fallen into it. It is as if when 'I' do not think 'I' no longer am. This is a conceptual policing which parallels, and is just as important as, the physical policing of the mad which the construction of the Paris General Hospital portended (D'Amico, 1984). This image of the self-sufficient mind is also now an image of the mind as something 'individual' (considered to be undivided and separate). It is interesting to note Derrida's (1973) critique here of the fascination in Western culture with the idea that there is an integrated self-conscious core to the human being, and that it must be possible to discover this 'presence' lying in every person and every text. However, we want to emphasize, with Foucault, that this fascination is a historical product.

One way of conceptualizing the birth of reason as embodied in a rational subject, the individual, is to raise the question of *modernity*. Whilst the confinement of the mad along with other labelled deviants took place, according to Foucault, in a 'Classical Age' before the turn of the eighteenth century, the care of the mad as pitiable mentally ill persons needing care and rehabilitation began as the Modern Age, or modernity – the representation of the world as organized by meta-narratives of humanized science, progress and individual meaning – came into being. It is also necessary to acknowledge criticisms that have been made of Foucault's account on grounds of historical 'accuracy'. Sedgwick (1982) argues that it is over-schematized and ignores or distorts information and data that is incompatible with the overall schema. The way it is presented in this chapter, at times, does also make it read like 'the truth', but we hope that you will read it like a guidebook, as helpful in orienting yourself. Descartes's work was a philosophical anticipation of modernity (that which is sometimes called the Enlightenment in Western culture). From around 1800 the medical approach was seen as part of science, and it was hoped that this supposedly progressive movement would reach a more accurate understanding of mental illness.

The individual in medical approaches is assumed to be responsible for aiding the process of cure and then to accept diagnosis and medication in suffering silence (Turner, 1987). The psychoanalytic version is that it becomes the responsibility of the individual to *speak* as they seek 'cure'. The common core of both medical and psychoanalytic variants of psychiatric practice, though, is that the abnormal is experienced as something which is *internal* to the person. This would also be true of the cognitive models of psychopathology which currently within the UK appear to enjoy, at least comparable, if not greater popularity than the psychoanalytic model (something we discuss in the following chapter). This individual experience of abnormality is such that it must be expressed, released, in order to be assuaged. Here we have the notion of confession that Foucault (1981) saw as central to modern practices of subjectivity.

Modernity is held together, then, by stories of progressive rational scientific discovery of the nature of the exterior world and the interior of individual people's minds. To break from that vision of the world is to be 'irrational'. What deconstruction has to do is to look at that irrationality and work with it in a radical empowering way; not to treat the 'irrational' as it is conventionally treated, as the dustbin concept for what modernity's rationality cannot handle, but as something that signifies resistance to the triple trap that our history in this chapter has traced so far. What these three historical approaches have allowed us to do is to turn 180 degrees and direct our gaze not at the mad but at the culture, institutions and language which make madness matter so much.

Abnormal psychology's others

What arises from these historical studies is the idea that the organization of language is crucial to an understanding of mental 'illness'. Language does not only organize reason but it also structures what we imagine to lie outside reason. It structures not only what we talk about but what we imagine we cannot talk about. Every time we put that experience into language, of course, we are necessarily speaking of it in the language of reason. To try to grasp it is to lose it. It is for this reason that some have objected to Foucault's study of madness as provoking a nostalgia for a time past when reason and unreason were not split apart (for example, Sedgwick, 1982). If the use of language requires that split, maybe the political consequences of Foucault's attack on psychiatry are not that radical, merely hopelessly utopian (D'Amico, 1984). What this warning draws attention to is the worry that simple opposition to the psychiatric system can sometimes end up being just as bad as it, or part of it. This is not to say that we can step outside any system of thought or practice completely. Deconstruction, Derrida (1973) points out, must use 'the stones of the house' as weapons, for there is nothing else available. What we need to keep in mind is that there are risks in doing that, and we must be suspicious of anything that looks like a too simple and easy answer. In the next chapter we will look at some of the other practices that have developed alongside and against medical psychiatry and clinical psychology. We will focus on psychoanalysis, the anti-psychiatry movement, family therapy and cognitive approaches. First though, in order that we are not heard to be naive idealists who want to wish the body away, we should say something about biology. Our deconstruction of psychopathology is not only concerned with the authority vested in certain concepts or in the power of language. We are also concerned with the material limits to what we are allowed to say, and the practical deconstruction of their role in clinical institutions.

The grounds and limits of language

Our counter-history raises questions not only about the relationship between reason and unreason but also about the relationship between meaning and biology. The keystone of the medical model, and of psychiatric practice, is that there is an organic foundation to the distress people sometimes experience. We cannot just wish away the influence of physiology by looking at the organization of language. We need some account of that, though in this book it will necessarily be all too brief. As a general rule we need have no trouble accepting that biological processes inform the sense we make of the world if we hold firm to the idea that human beings *attribute* meanings to those biological changes, and if we always attend to patterns of power that structure what we are allowed to attribute to what. Institutions of power and knowledge structure the way we understand physical health, and the ways in which we understand the relationship between bodily ills and mental discomfort (Stainton Rogers, 1991; Turner, 1987). Every appeal to theories of the body and its limits is itself saturated with culturally specific assumptions, ours no less so when we draw political lessons in a moment from Oliver Sacks's (1984) medical tall tales. The lesson we want to draw from the history of 'madness' is that the structures of meaning we use have changed, and will continue changing. We need also to go on to show how structures of language are embodied in clinical institutions and by virtue of that enjoy a certain type of power.

As we pointed out earlier, the stress on language does not mean that biology does not often insinuate its way into the way we act and speak. There may be physiological correlates for experiential phenomena which seem, to an extent, to delineate a 'problem' and make it understandable. Work on aphasias, for example, can open up areas of mental variation without explaining them away. Aphasias are understood in psychiatric texts in a number of different ways, and cover a variety of difficulties that people have in understanding and producing language. Work on aphasias often functions to turn problems of meaning into biological problems in the person. It is still possible, however, to link a biological account with a more humanist approach. Take the case of reactions of 'aphasia' and 'tonal agnosia' patients watching a political speech, a case reported by Sacks (1984). The patients are sitting watching a speech by the American President (whom we guess from the context must be Ronald Reagan). The aphasics were puzzled and silent in the ward of a New York hospital, and the tonal agnosics were laughing. Why?

Sacks provides an illuminating account of the manifestation of these disorders which contrasts the ability of the two types of patient to pick up messages in the speech. For the aphasics the 'loss' is purportedly in the left hemisphere of the brain and in the ability to understand the literal meaning of each word. These patients concentrate on the expressive, emotional, metaphorical aspect of communication. The words are baffling because they are, strictly, literally speaking, nonsense, and so they watch in silence. For the tonal agnosics, on the other hand, we are told that the disorder lies in the right hemisphere, and this results in a failure to understand the emotional tone. They attend to the literal word meaning. The tonal agnosics are creased up with laughter at the incongruities in the language of the broadcast. A conclusion is that in the speech 'so cunningly was deceptive word-use combined with deceptive tone, that only the brain-damaged remained intact, undeceived' (Sacks, 1984: 80). This is an interesting case for a number of reasons. Here we have a psychiatrist who attributes the difficulty to an organic disorder in the brain. In this respect he is following the medical model. At the same time, however, he seeks meaning in the patients' experiences. The account need not necessarily *reduce* that experience to biology.

Language and power

We should not forget that the attribution of meaning is bound up with power. The question of power which has often fallen into the background in critiques of the 'medical model', but which is there implicitly in the accounts of the institutionalization of the insane, now needs to be fore-grounded. Psychiatric institutions operate as power structures which operate regardless of the individual intentions of power holders (Miller and Rose, 1986). We can give an account of their growth which need not involve conspiracy theories about nasty psychiatrists, and we should be clear that psychiatry itself is not the originating cause but an *effect* of regimes of power. We sometimes use the term 'psychiatry' as a shorthand term in this book, but reader beware when it seems as if larger historical and political structures are being let off the hook. We are caught in a historical process that positions psychiatrists, clinical psychologists and other mental health professionals in relations of power over 'users' or 'consumers' of services, and the best we can do is to identify the fault lines in that power, to open up new spaces of resistance for those working in and against the clinical apparatus.

This brings us up to the present and to the accumulated effects of debates over the nature of madness and unreason over the centuries. The operation of power accords rights to speak to certain persons and takes them away from others. Take the following response by Ronald Reagan in a press conference when he was asked whether he would be prepared to raise taxes:

> But the problem is the – the deficit is – or should I say – wait a minute, the spending, I should say, of gross national product, forgive me – the spending is roughly 23 to 24 per cent. So that is in – what is increasing, while the revenues are staying proportionately the same and what would be the proper amount they should, that we should be taking from the private sector. (Observer, 25 October 1987)

This is, of course, nonsense. This time, however, a psychiatrist specializing in language disorders is not on hand to tell us what the meaning of it may be, and lock this man up.

There are issues here about the organization of language, and how the rights to speak, define and display rationality are apportioned. The problem stretches beyond the meanings of each individual word or phrase to the ways these meanings are held in discourses that run through the practices of power in modern medicine, psychiatry and clinical work. We are confronted with assumptions about the rationality we expect of people in different positions in everyday life. Certain persons in certain positions and situations could conceivably be pushed into the categories of the DSM or ICD for the response Reagan gave. For some, however, it counts as 'normal'. Here there are also directly political considerations as to the function of psychiatry (Sedgwick, 1982). Class, race, gender and age issues should be at stake in any analysis of the structure of language and culture, and they certainly must be if we want to have a *critical* understanding of psychiatry and abnormal psychology. The structure of psychiatry operates, as we will see in the following chapters, as an apparatus which can be extremely oppressive to women and to black people. We will also look at attempts to break out of that language in the work of the anti-psychiatry movement. Deconstruction leads us to look more closely at a 'borderline' case in the psychiatric institution, how language accomplishes and reproduces the split between reason and unreason in the individual subject. The deconstruction of the various oppositions that hold psychopathology in place can then lead us to a practical political assessment of the ways in which subjects and providers of services can develop some 'unreasonable' and useful progressive alternatives.

2
Alternatives to Abnormality

In this chapter we review some of the alternative ways of looking at psychopathology that have developed alongside mainstream psychiatry. Psychoanalytic, anti-psychiatry, family therapy and cognitive approaches each provide spaces of resistance and form curious alliances with psychiatric models, and we review some of the advantages and disadvantages of these in the course of the chapter.

Psychoanalysis: psychiatry's rival and twin

There is a close historical link between moral and medical treatments of mental distress. Foucault (1971) argues that this entails bringing into being mental chains which the person weaves for him- or herself as they take on board attributions of responsibility for their abnormal state of mind and for the progress of their cure. This link between morality and medicine has been obscured in traditional psychiatry, and responsibility *appears* to pass over to the doctor. There are certainly some advantages for the 'patient' in the sick role which is advocated by the medical model. You put yourself in the hands of the doctor, and, by following the prescribed treatment to the letter, you can appear to shift responsibility for the cure into the hands of an authorized person. In psychoanalysis the link between the moral and medical notions of the abnormal is reinforced. We want to focus on the assumptions which underlie the approach, and draw attention to the powerful role of language in the psychoanalytic account of problems and their cure.

There are three reasons why we need to devote some attention to psychoanalysis in this book. First, psychoanalytic theory is very different from the caricatures painted of it in most traditional psychology textbooks, and it actually differs from much academic and popular psychology in its emphasis on the self as something that is *constructed* rather than being an essential pre-given thing. Instead of personality being seen as wired into biology, psychoanalysis looks at the way the family environment and the surrounding culture *produce* different forms of subjectivity. Secondly, there is a peculiar contradiction between psychoanalytic theory and practice that needs to be addressed. Precisely because psychoanalytic theory offers an interesting and attractive constructionist view of the self, it seduces many radicals in mental health work into accepting, at the same time, reactionary therapeutic practices carried out in its name. Although psychoanalytic theory deconstructs traditional ideas of sexual orientation, for example, many psychoanalysts and psychoanalytic psychotherapists still treat gay identity as pathological. Thirdly, psychoanalytic notions of repression and hidden needs underlie most therapeutic practice, and that includes much humanist counselling which mistakenly sees itself as being fundamentally non-psychoanalytic. When Anna O, a patient of Freud's colleague Josef Breuer, called her experience the 'talking cure', she inaugurated a tradition of inward reflection and talking to experts that practitioners as varied as Fritz Perls (1969) and Carl Rogers (1961) elaborated.

Psychoanalysis is a stark manifestation of the split between unreason and reason which has proceeded with increasing intensity since the fifteenth century. Not only does it split these two sides of experience apart, in the process of splitting it *constructs* irrationality as something 'other' – whether that is felt to be threatening or appealing – to the way we understand ourselves. As such, it is preoccupied with the relationship between the cure of mental distress and *language*. In order to attain a cure, the 'analysand' (the patient in analysis) must put the unspoken distress into words, and yet the analyst always looks beyond those words to explore unconscious meanings.

Psychoanalysis is characterized by two fundamental notions. The first is the idea of the unconscious running alongside the rational, conscious mind. When we say 'the unconscious', that use of a definite noun treats 'it' as if it were a thing, a separate thing or being with its own desires and intentions. This is one of the traps of language, and we should be aware that Freud's understanding of what was unconscious was more subtle than that (1984 [1915]). The unconscious is a 'second system', and continually affects what is occurring in the conscious mind. The second notion is that of infantile sexuality. Again, it is easy to caricature Freud, and to imagine him saying that infants have sexual desires and motives in the same way as adults do. Rather, it is the other way round according to Freud, and we have sexual desires and motives, at some level, that repeat and modify those we experienced in infancy. Infantile sexuality is different, but because of the experience of growing up and repression; it has to be overlaid, and re-formed by culture, but the early desires do continue and inform the way we experience our sexuality now.

There are, broadly speaking, two different lines of emphasis in psycho-analysis. The traditional models will stress the biological, natural scientific and medical character of psychoanalysis. This would appear to be the mechanistic variety so influential in American 'ego-psychology' (Hartmann, 1958) which came in for so much criticism in the 1960s from radicals concerned with the power of psychiatry. Then there is the more humanistic, human science and lay analytic approach which warrants the

contemporary take up of psychoanalytic ideas into psychodynamic psychotherapy (Bettelheim, 1986). The demand that psychotherapy should be
available as an alternative to drug treatments is still a radical demand.
There is a sense, though, in which this humanization of psychoanalysis
could be making things worse. It may not be the solution radicals were
hoping for. We can go a little further into the psychoanalytic approach, and
draw on these notions of human science and the importance of meaning to
show how language is crucial to the whole of Freud's project. In the
process of retrieving this non-medical version of psychoanalysis from
psychiatry we can do more deconstructive work to see whether it really is
good enough as a radical alternative to traditional visions of psychopathology.

Aphasia to hysteria

If we trace the emergence of psychoanalysis we will see that it was closely
tied to biological theories, and it is not surprising that it should have played
an important part in traditional psychiatric classification systems. At the
same time, Freud tried to break from a purely biological model of
hysterical distress. Well before the development of psychoanalysis, Freud
was interested in 'aphasia' as a biological and mental phenomenon, and as
a problem to do with structures of language in the individual subject
(Forrester, 1980). Freud saw the difference between aphasia and hysteria
as lying in the link that was set up between causation and cure. In hysteria,
the cause is not a physical lesion, but, as it were, the 'lesion of an idea'. The
hysteric symptoms were formed when an unpleasant experience resonated
with repressed memories from the past infant state. The contemporary
idea joined with the repressed ideas and so lost touch with the moderating
influence of verbal consciousness. They were thus lost as 'word presentations' and existed underground as 'thing presentations': 'What makes the
patient ill is silence' (Forrester, 1980: 31). Freud spoke of the process of
cure as if the repressed memory dissolved when it was returned to
consciousness, that is, to the 'word presentations' level. Freud says, 'Once
a picture has emerged from the patient's memory, we may hear him say
that it becomes fragmentary and obscure as he proceeds with his description of it. *The patient is, as it were, getting rid of it by turning it into words*'
(cited in Forrester, 1980: 31). So it was that psychoanalysis was dubbed
'the talking cure'.

Continuity and 'otherness'

Psychoanalysis does not see the mental distress of its analysands as a
discrete, special state. We have, rather, a *continuum* between those who

are very unhappy and those who are relatively well adjusted. At the extreme end of the first group are those suffering from psychosis who are unable to make much connection with language at all. (A limitation of much psychoanalysis is that because these people are unable to speak about the problem, unable to recognize that there is a problem, psychoanalysis is unable even to start.) At the other end of the continuum are those of us who suffer from the repression of painful experiences and repeat those memories in our dreams and slips of the tongue. An advantage of psychoanalysis is that it allows even the most 'normal' of us to empathize with the distressed by experiencing to some extent the same processes. The Hollywood versions of psychoanalysis, where the analysand goes 'aha, now I remember, I'm cured' is quite wrong (though American analysts who are captured by the medical model sometimes seem to believe it themselves). French analysts (such as Lacan) argue that psychoanalysts in America have adapted to that culture; not only do they medicalize problems but they also individualize them all the more (Roudinesco, 1990). A characteristic of European psychoanalysis is that it is more sensitive to the role of language and more suspicious of psychiatry (although it must be pointed out that it still uses the same diagnostic categories). We will see this difference between American and European psychoanalysis again when we look at the development of anti-psychiatry.

European varieties of psychoanalysis have been important to feminist writers who have wanted to reclaim some account of the unconscious from the patriarchal story presented by Freud (Mitchell, 1974). In recent years feminist psychotherapy has blended some of the more progressive aspects of Lacan's work with Anglo-American 'object relations' theory (for example, Ernst and Maguire, 1987), and these debates have found their way into feminist counselling (for example, Chaplin, 1988). In practice, the particular *feminist* dynamic in this psychotherapeutic reworking of Freud's ideas has been the most important and progressive aspect, and the discourse of 'feminist therapy' shows tensions between competing political descriptions and reductionist psychological explanations of distress (see Burman, 1995). Psychoanalytic theory on its own offers little that is progressive; only when it is linked to a critical account of structures of power in discourse and institutions does it become helpful to those without power.

Victim-blaming

But we should first consider questions about the value of psychoanalysis and the power it wields. There are conceptual problems in analysis which flow from the depth of interpretation which is demanded. As with slips of the tongue or of the pen, dreams could be interpreted by way of associations and similarities which are quite banal (Timpanaro, 1976). The problem is that the analyst is put into a position of power in which meanings can be imposed instead of being cooperatively reached. There may be an ideal psychoanalytic situation which is never actually attainable precisely because of that power imbalance. There are also deeper problems which emerge from the recent histories of Freud's discovery of infantile sexuality. The message of some recent accounts is that Freud engaged in a process of victim-blaming (Masson, 1984). The drive for prestige among the medical profession of Vienna at the end of the last century led Freud to abandon his seduction theory which he formulated after his time in Paris studying under Charcot in 1885–6. There was much evidence then that later hysteria and mental distress could be traced to actual instances of child abuse. It was, however, more convenient to Freud to adapt to the anti-child climate of Germany and Austria, and to claim instead that the fantasies of seduction were just that, *fantasies* constructed out of the desire of the child for the parents. According to Masson, this was then reinforced when Freud attempted to cover up for the malpractice of his friend Fliess after an operation on one of his patients. Although this came to public attention in the furore over Masson's revelations (Malcolm, 1984), there has been a long tradition of feminist critique which has drawn attention to misogyny and abuse in Freud's work (for example, Millett, 1977; Rush, 1984).

A contradiction runs through psychoanalytic practice, of course, in which the analyst is the expert, but will treat the patient as having a good deal of expertise in evading and 'resisting' interpretations. The attribution of responsibility to the person, however, may point to even deeper problems. The main danger of psychoanalysis could be that it binds the person into a relationship which requires absolute subordination. This is endemic to psychoanalytic practice, and we can see evidence of this in the repeated attempts by psychoanalysts to solve the problem of power; sometimes by insisting that therapists must 'learn from the patient' (Casement, 1985), sometimes by urging colleagues not to disregard patients' accounts (Hobson, 1986), and sometimes by abandoning the process of 'interpretation' altogether (Lomas, 1987). Despite these more cuddly proposals, the main problem remains, that it is not good enough to say what the analyst wants to hear, you must *believe* it. As psychoanalysis delves deeper and deeper, the analysand must give accounts which bring a different meaning to what they had originally said. This means that not only must patients speak, but they must continually recant, continually realize the falsity of what they had told the analyst just before. Hence Foucault's argument that psychoanalysis reinforces moral modes of confession (Foucault, 1981).

If this picture is true, of course, then the new humanistic readings of psychoanalysis which pretend to value what the patient says may be even more pernicious than the medical models. It is then all the more the responsibility of patients to account for their distress and for why they remain stuck in it. Instead of being an alternative to traditional psychiatry, psychoanalysis would then be seen as its supplement. It should be pointed out that the motives for Freud's development of psychoanalysis should not *necessarily* lead us to say that the theory is wrong. Despite, or perhaps because of, Foucault's (1981) argument that psychoanalysis is a deep part of our culture, we have reason to be ambivalent towards it – finding it repugnant and attractive at the same time. We find this ambivalence at work again when we look at the activities of the anti-psychiatrists.

Anti-psychiatry: medicine and its others

The psychoanalytic 'model' of mental distress often functions as a comple- ment to the mainstream medical model. It does not necessarily stand in opposition to it. At least, this is the position in Britain and America. Psychoanalysis as an institution is governed by the medics in the English- speaking world, and it is this which gave the so-called 'anti-psychiatry' movement which emerged in the wave of political unrest in the 1960s a particular form. The movement around R.D. Laing tended to also be hostile to psychoanalysis (even though Laing himself drew heavily on psychoanalysis in his writing). We are going to say something about that movement, but we then want to contrast it with the anti-psychiatry movement in France. There, psychoanalysis – the type of psychoanalysis which has gained favour in feminism and on the Left here in recent years (Frosh, 1991; Mitchell, 1974) – was seen as an *ally* of the movement. It is useful to understand why, and what their relationship to Laing was. (In Chapter 7 we will look at other practical radical alternatives to psychiatry which have been developed and which have been important to radicals in mental health groups.) Although the anti-psychiatry movement was far broader than the group gathered around Laing and David Cooper, issues tended to be personalized and reduced to Laing's own activities. The contribution of Cooper (1972), for example, was important, but was pushed into the shadows by the Laing cult. A review of this time, then, does also necessarily revolve around his activities. Laing's objections to the medical model of mental 'illness', and to the power of psychiatry, are often lumped together with those of Thomas Szasz. We should be clear, then, what the difference is between these two figures, and also consider the more radical version of anti-psychiatry which flourished briefly in France.

Laing and existentialism

One of the main tasks of a critical approach to psychiatry is to provide a historical account, to explain why medicine gained the stranglehold it did. Although Laing was content to leave this task to others – he was responsible, for example, for the publication of Foucault's (1971) *Madness and Civilization* in Britain – what Laing did was to attack psychiatry from within by refusing to employ medical categories. He insisted on viewing the patient as a person. This was from an existentialist position which was to lead him, in turn, to look to social relations, particularly to social relations in the family. Existentialism, which Laing took from the writings of the French existentialist philosopher Sartre (1969), works on the assumption that each person makes sense of the world, and knows what the best way of being-in-the-world is. A crucial part of being a secure person is the recognition we gain from others, the validation we receive. This being-in-the-world carries with it anxiety and the threat of 'ontological insecurity'. A person who retreats into schizophrenia does so because the threats to their existence as a person necessitate that retreat. Laing (1965) argues in *The Divided Self* that forms of anxiety suffered by an ontologically insecure person will involve experiences of engulfment (the loss of identity), implosion (with the world pouring into the self and destroying it) or petrification (being turned into a thing).

It is, Laing says, 'the task of existential phenomenology to articulate what the other's "world" is and ways of being in it' (Laing, 1965: 25). This led Laing to a number of conclusions, most of which he was more cautious about, but which his supporters in the anti-psychiatry movement enthusiastically took up. Laing suggests 'that *sanity or psychosis is tested by the degree of conjunction or disjunction between two persons where the one is sane by common consent*' (Laing, 1965: 36, emphasis in the original). A more extreme conclusion is that insanity may provide insight that the ostensibly sane are not able to achieve. So Laing claimed that 'the cracked mind of the schizophrenic may *let in* light which does not enter the intact minds of many sane people whose minds are closed' (Laing, 1965: 27, emphasis in the original).

Although Laing started off as a psychiatrist, it quickly became apparent to him that the anti-psychiatry movement required different institutions. This is why places like Kingsley Hall and the Philadelphia Association in London were set up. (The Philadelphia Association is still going, and was one of the first psychotherapy training organizations in the UK to use Lacan's work.) Laing always defined himself as a psychiatrist, and one of his complaints in recent interviews is not so much that his alternatives to psychiatry were not successful, but that textbooks ignore him and Szasz (Laing, 1986). The attacks from traditional psychiatry were, predictably, severe. They claimed that popularizations of Laing's writings could lead people, particularly adolescents, to try to 'let in' the light and become schizophrenic (Boyers and Orrill, 1971).

The situations which Laing's patients, who were often young people living at home, found themselves in were often family situations. Because of this the structure of the family started to loom larger and larger in Laingian work. Laing, writing with Aaron Esterson, had argued that attention should be directed to 'the family nexus' (Laing and Esterson,

1964). It should then be possible, Laing (1965) argued, to identify 'schizophrenogenic' families. However, while supporters of Laing have sometimes portrayed him as being critical of the Western nuclear family as an institution, his case studies dealt with the particular structures of the families which produced the patients he saw.

There is an issue here which flows from the turn from individuals to family interaction, to what could be termed in more mainstream psychiatric jargon a 'family interaction' model (Siegler and Osmond, 1977). This concerns Laing's relationship with psychoanalysis. On the one hand the work on family interactions drew on systems theory. We had 'systems' or 'structures' which were faulty, and we heard the cries of help from the victims of those systems. This approach owes little to Freud, and Laing was taken by many of his supporters and critics to be hostile to psychoanalysis.

On the other hand, Laing did use psychoanalytic concepts. The existentialism he took from Sartre was filtered through his own understanding of psychoanalysis, and in some senses Sartre (1974) himself was sympathetic to Freud. Unlike straight existentialism, Laing always argued for the importance of the unconscious. It has been argued that the existentialist position which Laing described was not a position which a practising psychiatrist (which he was) could ever adopt, but that Laing really always adhered to a variety of psychoanalysis; adherence to existentialist precepts – at being alone in the world and so on – was an expression of distress driven by the unconscious (Collier, 1977).

But what do you do with people in distress, people who have been messed up by their schizophrenogenic families and have good reasons for the behaviour they exhibit? One answer, which has longstanding historical resonances going back to Tuke's Quaker enterprise at York, is to provide a 'retreat' where they can follow their journey through madness (Foucault, 1971). A well-known example in the Laingian tradition is the case of Mary Barnes at Kingsley Hall. In 1965 this community of about 20 people was set up. Mary Barnes, a former nurse, who was labelled 'schizophrenic' regressed to an infant state. She went back to being fed from a bottle, to breaking things and to refusing to eat in her journey through madness. This journey is recorded in the Barnes and Berke (1973) book, and she gained some popularity in the anti-psychiatry movement through her exhibitions of paintings produced when she was at Kingsley Hall.

The problems with this approach, which has been termed by critics working in the medical model 'the psychedelic model' of mental illness (Siegler and Osmond, 1977), is that the mental health professional abandons responsibility for the safety of the person. At an extreme, the attempts to prevent a distressed person from committing suicide are abandoned. Suicide could be seen in this framework as a 'rational' way out of an impossible situation. The infantilization of the patient also produces an arena for professional abuse. Here we may also have come to some of the limits of the radical politics that Laing dabbled with in the 1960s. Laing published in left-wing journals and started to widen his objections to society in general, referring to a world gone mad and those labelled as mad being victims who saw the truth about social reality. The solutions, however, were often either simple individual searches for meaning and a way of being-in-the-world, or deliberate retreats from political activity into schizophrenia. Laing eventually disappeared from view for a while as he headed for mystical enlightenment in Sri Lanka.

Some of Laing's critics on the Left have always been suspicious about his radical pretensions, and have not been surprised at Laing's journey out of politics into mysticism and then back into psychiatry a humbler man. The old criticisms of schizophrenogenic families are overtaken by praises in his later work for 'normal families' as illustrated in some of his free verse which talks of *'cosy nests / where no eyes are pecked out . . . with a nice mummy and daddy'* (cited in Sedgwick, 1982, emphasis in the original). It is also argued that only one type of narrative of a schizophrenic career is described by Laing, that of an acute psychotic episode, and the clientele of the Philadelphia Association were a highly motivated self-selected group. Perhaps it is necessary to be realistic about the value of medical approaches in order better to challenge their abuses of power (Sedgwick, 1982).

Psychoanalytic feminist objections to Laing in this country which draw on the French readings of Freud have also viewed his radical statements with a jaundiced eye. Juliet Mitchell argues that Laing's 'driven-mad-by-the-family-nexus schizophrenic is every adolescent writ large' (Mitchell, 1974: 279). The experiences Laing describes are bound up with the trauma of leaving home, and have always carried the message that the family was potentially a place which should be repaired. There are also echoes here of the traditional psychiatric condemnations of Laing which accuse him of pandering to impressionable adolescents who could read his descriptions as prescriptions for liberation from social rules, particularly from the rules of the family (Boyers and Orrill, 1971).

Szasz and libertarianism

While Laing was attacking psychiatry in Britain, Thomas Szasz was carrying out a quite different assault on medical models in America. Szasz (1961) reasoned that organic damage could lead to the absence of particular mental functions. It would be quite unproblematic, for example, for him to read Sacks's (1984) work on aphasia as requiring some medical account. However, the problem lies at the boundary between obviously organic disorders and the anxieties and experiential pain which are commonly seen as 'mental illness'. For Szasz, to turn to medicine here is to look to the modern day equivalent of secret demons. Medics never find the problem, but they pretend it exists. Meanwhile, they treat the person as a 'patient', and the sick role inhibits recovery. It is also dependent on a conception of medicine as being objective and value-free. It should be borne in mind that in some ways a diagnosis of physical ill-health is as much a moral and political judgement as psychiatric diagnosis (Illich, 1976).

Szasz was, and is, a psychiatrist. However, his criticisms of the medical model were always more conceptually radical than Laing's. This is paradoxical, for the political conclusions of Laing's work inside psychiatry were a good deal more radical than Szasz's. For Szasz, there is no place for any concept of mental illness. Psychiatry is just ideology. This is, in large part, to do with the alternative model he subscribes to, and the political consequences of his position. It is perhaps symptomatic that while Laing tried to include Szasz in his attempts to reform psychiatry, Szasz has been hostile to any such alliance, declaring that 'the anti-psychiatrists are all self-declared socialists, communists' (Szasz, 1976: 4), and that Laing in particular was 'a preacher of and for the "soft" underbelly of the New Left' (Szasz, 1976: 5).

Szasz adopts a moral position which requires the individual to take responsibility for treatment. In most cases this would consist of behavioural programmes. Here we may see, perhaps, why Szasz's position is so congenial to psychology. He falls out of medicine into the warm embrace of behaviourism, into a view of distress which treats individuals and which operates on a strict distinction between what is normal and 'abnormal', between what is appropriate behaviour and what is, in the phrase of a mainstream textbook on abnormal psychology, 'maladaptive behaviour' (Sarason and Sarason, 1987). It should also be pointed out, and there is another layer of paradox here, that Szasz, for all his vituperative, arguably anti-semitic attacks on Freud and psychotherapy (Szasz, 1979), also practises and writes as a psychoanalyst.

The political upshot of this individualistic moral position is very different from that of Laing's supporters in Britain. Szasz attacks psychiatry from the libertarian Right. He has no objection to people choosing to pay for medical treatment, and he has even proposed a legal procedure whereby individuals can decide what treatment they would prefer when they are in a good state before a breakdown. His objection is to the state providing mental health on the welfare, outside the private sector. Now we do not want to reduce Szasz's complaints about medical psychiatry to these political matters in a crude way, but it is as well to be aware that his conception of individual responsibility free from the sick role is a bit like insisting that people should stand on their own two feet and stop being molly-coddled. After all, if it is true that they can 'take responsibility', why do they need help anyway, except as an exercise of free choice?

Lacan and existentialism

Over on the continent, the objections to the power of psychiatry have been given a different twist by the existence of a more radical form of psychoanalysis. First of all the work of Lacan, who was expelled from the

International Psychoanalytic Association in 1963, has always been critical of psychiatry, and secondly the influence of Foucault's ideas on the historical production of 'madness' has been felt by some radical psychoanalysts. While Lacan's doctoral thesis published in 1932 was ostensibly in mainstream psychiatry, psychoanalytic themes were already appearing there. Symptomatically, these ideas were closely linked with the popularizations being spread by the surrealists. Lacan himself wrote in the 1930s for surrealist magazines, and Dali was a close friend (Macey, 1988).

One of the central concerns of the Lacanian readings of Freud is with language. Lacan (1977) saw language, and meaning in general, as comprising a 'Symbolic order'. We use the language of a culture to think and communicate, and formed within that ordered realm are the desires and wishes of the unconscious. Equating the unconscious with the Symbolic allowed Lacanian psychoanalysis to break from the individualism of modern psychiatry and of other psychoanalytic trends (Roudinesco, 1990). The unconscious is not what lies within the individual before socialization. On the contrary it is the *effect* on the individual of the culture in which she or he is born. The unconscious, the core of the subject, is, then, both individual and collective. The subject in Lacanian psychoanalysis is split between the unconscious and consciousness. The idea that the subject is unitary and coherent is only an illusion that covers up and denies this split. In this way Lacan subverts the certainty of Descartes's doubting 'I' as a unitary being that could reflect on itself from a single position. Consequently, Lacan breaks apart the distinction between reason and unreason, a distinction upon which modern psychiatry is based. Lacan's (1977) cryptic and allusive statement 'I think where I am not, therefore I am where I do not think' expresses exactly that split. 'I am' is the closest expression to the truth of the subject which resides in the unconscious. 'I think' is the illusory work of consciousness. 'Being' and 'thinking', the unconscious and consciousness, are two positions that can never be unified.

The family is seen as part of the Symbolic order. In fact, Lacanians argue, there is always a traumatic realization awaiting the child, that the father wields all the power in the family and in the culture by virtue of him being man, and this is driven home during the Oedipal conflicts that accompany the acquisition of language. A rather grim consequence is that politics is also seen here as part of the Symbolic order. You could either see a Lacanian position as being ultra-left (where the individual is necessarily opposed to every aspect of that order) or conservative (because opposition is probably fruitless). At least these were the two options perceived in the 1960s. Nowadays, those who adopt Lacan's interpretation of Freud often see it as pointing to the importance of culture and the importance of attending to the way ideology operates in culture to place people in different positions – and most crucially gender positions – where they have, or do *not* enjoy, power (Grosz, 1990).

Lacan's psychoanalysis did not go far enough. It tended to be the conservative lesson that was drawn from his account of the Oedipus complex and the power of the Symbolic order, the power of language. The work of Foucault, on the other hand, while more cautious about psychoanalysis, stimulated an even more romantic view of the unconscious as the repository of 'truth', or 'the body and its pleasures' (Foucault, 1981). In reaction to any social order or meaning, the unconscious repressed body was seen in the work of Foucault and his followers as a collection of 'desiring machines' (Turkle, 1981). From this followed the instantly and massively popular work of Deleuze and Guattari's (1977) *Anti-Oedipus*. For Deleuze and Guattari it was a mistake ever to have said *the* 'it' or 'id', and they turned to 'schizoanalysis' as a celebration of the controlled delirium in which one finds personal truth and desire. What Deleuze and Guattari effectively did here was to out-laing Laing. The nuclear family itself was now seen as constitutionally schizophrenogenic, and psychoanalysts who structure 'normal psychology' around the Oedipus complex reproduce that madness-inducing structure. The terms of the debate about psychiatry and anti-psychiatry were so much more radical in France. In a commentary on the case of Mary Barnes, Guattari (1984), who started off as a Lacanian psychoanalyst, makes a distinction between 'a real schizophrenic journey and a familialist regression along petty-bourgeois lines' (Guattari, 1984: 54).

In some senses the extreme anti-psychiatry movement in France has collapsed along with the post-1968 Left. There were still grass-roots groupings through to the 1980s, however, such as *Gardes Fous*, which were not so much concerned with psychoanalysis, and were closer to contemporary radical health movements in the UK (Turkle, 1981). It is as well to review this débâcle in 'radical' mental health, its collapse into psychoanalysis and then back into psychiatry, because the traces of these ideas are still around in those wanting to challenge traditional notions of psychopathology today. We want to turn now to another promising arena, a direct intervention into the politics of the family, a place in therapy where radical ideas are still going strong.

Family therapy: the identified patient

Laingian anti-psychiatry meets the mental health system, for good or bad, in family therapy. When Laing argued in the 1960s that we should stop trying to identify schizophrenogenic, madness-inducing mothers and look to the overall family structure, he participated in a dynamic which could be resolved in two ways. Family therapy changes our conceptions of what normal and abnormal psychology looks like because it locates all the symptoms of a 'psychopathology' in the family unit rather than in the individual. This is the first consequence of looking at family interaction.

The second way of looking at the structure of the family treats that structure as a problem rather than as something to be patched up. Family therapy is concerned with patterns of meaning. We can focus on that meaning in two ways. One way looks at the particular patterns which mesh families together. Here are those communication patterns that can keep a normal family going, or make an abnormal family hell for one or more of its members. The other way links in the meanings with the structure of language as a whole, and the way language 'positions' people in families. It is the former concern with the communication patterns internal to the family which provides the basis for much family therapy.

Communication

Schizophrenia was first treated as a problem of family patterns by the Palo Alto Mental Research Institute in the 1950s (Poster, 1978). It was here that Gregory Bateson (1972) looked to cybernetics, systems theory, and communications theory to provide the basis for adequate psychotherapy. Schizophrenia, in this 'First order cybernetics' model, was seen as a result of distorted communication. Certain communications, 'double-binds', were seen as especially dangerous. There are three defining characteristics of a double-bind: first, there is an intense emotionally significant relationship which exists between the participants; secondly, there is a sender of the 'double-bind' message who sends two orders of message in which one denies the other; and thirdly, there is a receiver of the message who cannot comment on the disparity between the two orders. Take a child who is continually told to show affection to a parent, and then is met by coldness, and then is blamed for their confusion about the messages. Such a victim of a bind may then be unable to untangle the different levels of message sent outside the family, or to attribute meaning to their own feelings. Such a victim may then show the dissociation of feelings from thoughts that characterizes 'schizophrenia'.

This view of the causation of schizophrenia was extended by Theodore Lidz (1963) who defined what a healthy 'essential dynamic structure of the family' might look like. Lidz, who also anticipates some of the worst normative structural notions of ideal family functioning, argues that it is the failure of the family properly to define gender roles and to maintain a distinction between generations in the family which gives rise to problems. Lidz goes on to argue that in the ideal family men have 'instrumental' roles, and women 'expressive' roles. He is then able to explain how the weakness in one role can affect the whole family structure. Here it is deviation from the Western nuclear family structure which is seen as the problem. This is the context, then, in which Laing boosted interest in the schizophrenogenic function of families. Although supporters of Laing were critical of families, family therapists generally operated on the assumption that the family was essentially a good thing.

Structural Family Therapy

Like Bateson, Lidz and Laing, Minuchin's (1974) version of family therapy sees the person with the problem as being the 'identified patient' (or 'index patient'). The cure must be directed to the family of which that patient is an integral part. Each family member relates to the others through ritualized activities which carry meaning. These ritualized activities are the 'transactional patterns' which the family therapist will try to uncover. The family as a system contains within it many 'sub-systems'. An individual may be a sub-system, and will belong, in turn, to other sub-systems. The parents, for example, will constitute a sub-system with specific enclosed interactions, and the children another. The boundaries define who participates in different sub-systems. An elder child may be given responsibility as part of the parental sub-system to look after the others when both biological parents are out of the home. This may then lead to something more than a simple 'alliance' between the mother, say, and the child. This alliance may then become a 'coalition' against other family members. Such a coalition may then be confusing to the child because the boundaries between the different family sub-systems are unclear. You may have appearing what Minuchin would term 'a cross-generational dysfunctional transactional pattern' (Minuchin, 1974: 62).

The therapist's job is to restructure the family, to engage in tactical alliances with family members to, in Minuchin's words, 'facilitate the maintenance of sub-systems that promote healing and growth' (Minuchin, 1974: 256). Minuchin is careful to warn family therapists against viewing the extended family as necessarily 'pathogenic'. Such families, he says, may function perfectly well. However, in practice, the family therapist will often have to adopt a model of the 'good' family, or, at least, of the good family member. While this is not spelt out as explicitly as in Lidz's work, it has to involve a view of the 'good father' and the 'good mother'.

One of the arguments against structural family therapy is that the systems and sub-systems that the therapist concentrates on are assumed to operate regardless of social context. This social context intrudes into the structure of individual families by way of the structure of language. Particular binds are not produced by individuals, but the material for those binds is provided by the surrounding culture. We will see a clear example of the way such binds can be reproduced by psychiatry in the next chapter when we look at the way diagnostic systems operate in psychiatry, clinical psychology and allied professions.

'Post-structural' schools

Another dominant influence in work with families is the 'strategic' tradition which picks up Bateson's (1972) ideas and employs them pragmatically in the work of Jay Haley (1963) and Milton Erickson (for example, Erickson and Rossi, 1979). Here too, there is a notion of a charismatic therapist using their power tactically to achieve certain effects in families. This is the tradition that brief 'solution-focused' therapies such as de Shazer's (1985), also come from. Whereas in both structural and strategic family therapies the therapist did certain things with families (for example, giving them certain tasks and so on), a group of Italian family therapists began to emphasize the importance of the actual conversation with the family as the unit of therapy. The Milan Systemic model, described, for example by the Milan associates (Selvini, Palazzoli, Prata, Boscolo and Cecchin; Selvini et al., 1978, 1980) focused almost exclusively on the power of words to produce change in families. Sometimes therapists said that the prospects for change seemed so slight that they actually instructed families not to change. Such suggestions were termed 'paradoxical interventions' and increasingly such techniques began to be used for their strategic effect. Later the Milan team tried to distance themselves from such technique-based approaches and began to focus much more on the importance of questions, particularly 'circular questions' (questions designed to elicit an understanding in the therapist and the family of the systemic nature of the problem, that is, how it was tied up in the family's relationships). Eventually, the team split into two groups; Selvini, Palazzolli and Prata on the one side and Boscolo and Cecchin on the other, with the latter group being more open to postmodern influences.

Family therapy's critics

Although family therapy had always been open to criticism from outside, particularly from more individually focused psychodynamic therapists, the late 1970s and the 1980s saw a period of sustained criticism from within its own ranks. In particular, the work of feminist family therapists like Virginia Goldner questioned the dominant family values (of patriarchal hierarchy and structure) endemic in much family therapy (Goldner, 1993; McKinnon and Miller, 1987). Therapists working with violent and sexually abusive men found that challenging such values was actually part of their therapeutic work. In addition, a number of other commentators questioned the epistemology underlying family therapy. Many felt that Bateson's ideas did not fit easily with a naïve realist view of the world. Writers turned to the likes of Maturana (Maturana and Varela, 1980) and others in their attempts to demarcate 'second order cybernetics' which examined the wider systems in which therapy was located. Increasingly, family therapy's use of expert power – hiding behind one-way mirrors, sending out 'paradoxical' messages and so on – came into question. Instead, workers like Gianfranco Cecchin (for example, Cecchin, Lane and Ray, 1993) invited therapists to be 'irreverent' of theoretical dogmas,

Tom Andersen (1987) suggested that family therapy teams should have their discussion in front of the family, which also implied a more respectful kind of conversation, and David Epston and Michael White (White and Epston, 1990) strove to inculcate an explicitly political view of 'psychological problems'. It is in the latter strand that some have seen the possibility for a 'deconstructive therapy' and this is something we will discuss in Chapter 6. Family therapy has tried to show how people in distress are caught in a machinery beyond their control. We also need to be aware of a fourth major tradition operating in tension with psychiatry that looks to a machinery inside people's heads that is causing the problem, and we turn now to these cognitive approaches.

Cognitive approaches: the mechanics of the mind

In the post-war climate of therapy for the masses, behaviour therapy appeared to rule supreme. Increasingly, psychologists and small groups of nursing staff trained in behaviour therapy proved their therapeutic mettle in applying operant conditioning, often to marginalized groups like autistic children, people with learning disabilities and so on to the point where, in the case of learning disabilities, most other therapies were totally discounted. Where the likes of Azrin (for example, Azrin and Holz, 1966) was doing this in American institutions, writers like Wolpe (1958) and Rachman (for example, Eysenck and Rachman, 1964) devised behavioural programmes for obsessional and other anxiety-related problems in the UK. However, the crudity, mechanistic and sometimes (especially in institutions) punitive nature of many of these therapies led to therapists looking into the so-called 'black box' that mediated behavioural responses and so behaviourists were forced to return again to the mind. Indeed, today even some 'radical behaviourists' will be willing to discuss phenomena previously regarded as mentalistic. The therapy literature soon began to talk less of operant responses and more of cognitions and attributions. However, the status of the 'cognitive revolution' of the 1960s has been questioned, with some like Lovie (1983) arguing that cognitive research had never disappeared and that talk of a revolution was simply a powerful rhetoric for helping to found a new paradigm in psychology.

The marriage of behaviour therapy with cognitivism; from neurosis to psychosis

The welding of cognition onto tried and trusted behavioural therapies was politically useful in the UK in the 1970s – a time when clinical psychology was struggling to create an autonomous identity separate from psychiatry and trying to move on from psychometrics and the odd ward-based behaviour programme or token economy. A working compromise saw psychologists dealing with 'neurotic' problems like anxiety, obsessions and the like with psychiatry dealing with 'psychotic' problems (Pilgrim and Treacher, 1992). However, cognitive approaches were soon being used with people who were depressed, with them actually proving more 'effective' than medication. By the late 1980s and early 1990s, the cognitive paradigm was taking over in realms previously regarded as psychiatry's own. Two groups of cognitive-behavioural workers focused on 'schizophrenia'. The first group was characterized by works like Birchwood and Tarrier's (1992) and Fowler, Garety and Kuipers's (1994) texts, and broadly accepted the validity of the diagnosis of schizophrenia. The second group, exemplified by Bentall's (1990) *Reconstructing Schizophrenia*, questioned the validity of 'schizophrenia' but accepted that 'hallucinations' and 'delusions' did exist and that cognitive-behavioural interventions were effective in reducing them. Although still a small force, some of these workers seem grandiose in their ambitions for cognitivism; Bentall (1992a) for example, has talked of devising a cognitive version of the periodic table for psychopathology. Increasingly then, the battle over therapies has reflected political battles and psychiatry faces a threat, albeit in its infancy, similar to the one which saw it lose control of services for people with learning disabilities, services which, since the 1960s have increasingly become managed either by social workers or psychologists.

The tension between psychology and psychiatry in the UK over cognitive approaches was curious, not least because some leading cognitive-behavioural therapists are psychiatrists (Aaron T. Beck (1976) – famous for his work on depression – in the US, and Isaac Marks (Marks et al., 1977) – well known for his work on obsessions and phobias – in the UK, are psychiatrists). Clinical psychology as a discipline thus proved flexible in taking on ideas from therapeutic traditions like cognitivism and from other professions and then laying claim to the territory. Increasingly, however, other professional groups caught on so that in the new NHS marketplace in the UK psychologists competed with community psychiatric nurses and occupational therapists in providing cognitive-behaviour therapy.

Critiquing cognitivism

But is cognitive therapy a radical approach? Many proponents have argued that it is and that it carries few of the human rights issues which made many behavioural techniques ethically dubious and little of the dodgy theoretical assumptions of psychodynamic work. (In their defence, many behaviourists would claim that behavioural methods could be used across cultures and that they carry few culturally specific assumptions). Cognitive therapists have argued that it is an approach which is face-valid, can be explained simply to clients and which is less dependent on experts: it can be 'given away'. Eclectic therapists can therefore use cognitive techniques in a mix-and-match fashion. However, such optimism fails to acknowledge some of the theoretical and political tensions which have become increasingly evident. Cognitive approaches come half-way down the postmodern path in acknowledging that we can never be in direct contact with 'reality'. However, they are ambiguous about the existence of one reality and the subject's relation to it. Thus it could be said to be 'constructivist' rather than *constructionist*.

In the therapy literature these terms are often used interchangeably, even though it is important to keep clear the distinction between 'constructivist' approaches which are simply concerned with the way individuals view ('construct') the world and their problems in different ways, and 'constructionist' approaches which look at the way culture and social structures construct a reality which individuals then have to operate within. Naïve realist assumptions are widespread in the cognitive literature where clients are said to have irrational, distorted or biased cognitions – not surprisingly, there has never been a thoroughly plausible account of what a 'cognition' is. Moreover, clients are faced with therapists asking for empirical evidence for their beliefs. Characteristically, cognitive therapists would claim their approach was value-free. However, as others have noted, cognitive approaches are based on an individual/social dualism in which what happens inside people's heads frames what is happening in the social world (as if these sides of the same coin were necessarily two separate phenomena). Moreover, it maintains an opposition between scientific fact and common sense (with the latter routinely derided). It also lays itself open to mechanistic and hierarchical interpretations with terms like cognitive 'architecture', 'structure' and 'schemas' abounding. These difficulties have presented a number of challenges for cognitive psychology: How can it respond to persons who are apparently inconsistent in their beliefs, are as concerned about values as reality, and who seem to think dynamically rather than hierarchically? In practice, therapists might encounter clients who felt that keeping diaries of their behaviour or challenging their cognitions was not enough to cope with their distress, and increasingly cognitivism has come under fire by writers like Miller Mair (1989) and David Smail (1987).

In recent years, cognitivism has proved its flexibility again in the blending of cognitive approaches with psychodynamic concepts in Anthony Ryle's (1990) 'Cognitive Analytic Therapy' (CAT). As an approach that has become increasingly popular it is interesting for a number of reasons. First it combines a tradition focused on explicit definitions of terms (cognitive) with one that is often obtuse (analytic). Secondly, it blends a tradition founded on dynamic relationship issues (analytic) with one that is relatively new to therapy (cognitive). Thirdly, it combines an emphasis on detailed psychological formulations in the first few sessions of 'assessment' with an eclectic disregard for the therapeutic orientation in the following sessions. Fourthly, CAT incorporates the text of the session into the therapeutic process as if that text simply encapsulated bits of the external world. Finally, its emphasis on a brief period of work (approximately 16 sessions) renders it palatable to service managers at a time when longer therapy contracts are increasingly coming into question.

Concluding comments

We explored the historical emergence of traditional regimes of psycho-pathology in Chapter 1 as part of our deconstruction of the notion, and then looked at how the 'others' or opposites of psychiatry (psychoanalysis, anti-psychiatry, family therapy and cognitive approaches) have arisen alongside it. The opposites have often operated as subjugated and subversive forms of knowledge, but we have wanted to show that it is not good enough simply to appeal to one or all of these as a full-blown progressive alternative. What may also be significant is the way in which a more practical, progressive impetus is given to each of these forms of knowledge when they are influenced by structuralist and poststructuralist ideas (Lacan, Foucault and Derrida), the ideas that inspire our decon-struction of psychopathology. For all its faults, psychoanalytic ideas, particularly Lacanian forms, emphasize the role of language in the creation of different forms of rationality and irrationality. Anti-psychiatry has benefited from Foucault's history of madness and civilization and the argument that psychiatry is part of a wider system of surveillance and regulation. Family therapy has now started to take up Derrida's elab-oration of deconstruction to show that what has been constructed can be unravelled, unravelled as a form of self-understanding and empowerment. Eclectic practitioners using cognitive approaches have also been able to take techniques and use them in a postmodern spirit in a mix-and-match fashion as part of self-help without subscribing to any correct underlying model.

Each of these ostensibly radical forms of knowledge is so heavily conditioned by what it opposes, marked by it, that it folds very quickly into a form of psychiatric practice itself when it is tempted or put under pressure to do so. Nevertheless, in line with the deconstructive argument that you have to use the 'stones of the house' to attack a dominant system, we will be drawing cautiously and selectively, radically and transforma-tively upon these oppositional forms of knowledge in later chapters.

3

Whose Symptoms, of What?

This chapter focuses on symptomatology, on the ways in which people today are understood according to particular categories of distress. We describe the ways in which the American Psychiatric Association's *Diagnostic and Statistical Manual of Mental Disorders* (DSM) and the World Health Organization's *International Classification of Diseases* (ICD) are used to produce different pictures of the individual as 'abnormal'. We then look at the demarcation disputes between different disciplines, particularly between clinical psychology and psychiatry, over the nature and treatment of mental distress. We also describe the way in which other professionals are affected by this dispute.

We open this chapter with a set of puzzles. These puzzles concern the failure of the DSM or the ICD adequately to represent the diversity of human experiences of distress and the role of these category systems in practices which intensify the distress of certain groups in society. The practices themselves are the problem, of course, and we will review the way in which they impact on those already oppressed to make things worse. We have to lead into our deconstruction of psychopathological categorization in this way, in part because we are more concerned with material oppositions, contradictions in actual treatment, than mere conceptual untidiness. The chapter is divided into four main sections then. The first lays out a history of how the present system of classification came about. The second explores the gendered, racialized and classed battlefield which is mental health care and the problems this poses for category systems (DSM and ICD). The third looks at the ways in which the category systems represent the issues, respond and fail. The fourth section turns to warring tendencies within mental health disciplines.

Enshrining abnormality

A powerful rhetorical device the DSM and ICD routinely employ in their understanding of distress is to individualize it, so it no longer seems to make sense to consider the gender or race of someone who is being diagnosed. This should be borne in mind as the backdrop to each of the main categories in the diagnostic systems that we describe in this section.

The two competing systems are formulated by professional bodies: the *Diagnostic and Statistical Manual of Mental Disorders*, which is now in its fourth version (DSM-IV), is overseen by the American Psychiatric Association (and the American Psychological Association follows suit); and the *International Classification of Diseases*, now in its tenth edition (ICD-10), is the baby of the World Health Organization (and so is more European-based). It is worth noting that these manuals are relatively recent developments. Boyle (1990), for example, has talked of early attempts at diagnostic classification being chaotic. Later attempts appeared more scientific but were bedevilled by circular arguments (for example, with categories being asserted and evidence being found *post hoc* to back them up). Moreover, diagnoses serve a wide variety of interests – research, legal, administrative – and are supposed to reflect a consensual view, thus some decisions are voted on. Wilson (1993) has provided a history of the DSM which is sensitive to some of these power disputes. Numerous critiques have been made of these classifications: that they reflect commercial interests (Kirk and Kutchins, 1992); that they are individualistic (Tomm, 1990); that they simply reflect dominant conceptions of the Western self (Gaines, 1992); that they are social constructions (McNamee and Gergen, 1992); and that they are empirically invalid (Boyle, 1990).

The scientificity of diagnostic classification was aided by the development of what Berrios (1988) has described as the 'anatomo-clinical view' in medicine in the nineteenth century. In following medicine as its guide, psychiatry focused on the 'form' rather than the 'content' of signs of madness. At this point the history of psychiatry changed and 'the technology of madness changed from negative to positive, from being binary to being complex and multiform. There came into being a vast technology of the psyche' (Foucault, 1980: 185).

Anyone looking at diagnostic manuals will be struck by the wide variety of categories included. DSM-IV, for example, covers 'disorders' across the lifespan relating to substance abuse, schizophrenia and other psychoses, mood (including depression), anxiety, sexual and gender identity, eating, sleeping, impulse control (including gambling and fire-setting), adjustment and personality. ICD-10 follows a similar pattern. What is also surprising is how very different categories of behaviour are grouped together. Nuckolls (1992) asks us, for example, to consider whether the behaviours 'reckless driving', 'casual sex' and 'shoplifting' belong together. They do, he notes, because, according to the DSM they are all instances of 'borderline personality disorder'. Similarly, according to DSM-IV, gambling, fire-setting (pyromania) and pulling one's hair out are all examples of 'impulse control disorders'. Moreover, although the manuals would like us to believe that each category is a pure form of pathology, the experience of practitioners is often of someone who seems both anxious and depressed, of people whose problems seem ambiguous and messy, not at all scientific. Indeed, it is unclear how often diagnoses are actually used in everyday clinical practice – often their only purpose seems to be administrative (like being recorded on hospital discharge forms).

What then are we to make of all this? We would argue that we will continue to run into problems if we believe that such diagnoses are simply descriptive of reality 'out there'. Rather, these categories are *constitutive*. In other words, the existence of these categories actually creates these problems. Thus Hepworth and Griffin (1990) have argued that the 'discovery' of anorexia nervosa in the late nineteenth century was constructed by a number of discourses (of science, medicine, of femininity and so on) in order to medicalize self-starvation, presenting it both as a typically feminine condition and as a natural corollary of feminine irrationality. Rose (1990: 106–10) has noted how such categories make a new sector of reality 'thinkable and practicable' in that forms of subjectivity become translated into objects to be regulated through the 'systematic government of the psychological domain', by managing subjectivity 'according to norms claiming the status of science'.

Following such an analysis, we could see diagnostic categories as discursive complexes. Discourses can be seen as sets of statements that construct objects and an array of subject positions, and discursive forms contain specifications for types of object and shapes of subjectivity (Davies and Harré, 1990; Stenner, 1993). Thus particular diagnoses set up certain positions which people may place themselves in (for example, by feeling that they are anxious and going to their doctor for help) or in which they may be placed by others (for example, the young person who is reported by their parents to their doctor after talking about hearing voices). Even though we live in a culture which claims to be liberal, abnormality is still powerfully defined with reference to what is considered to be normal behaviour and relationships. Indeed, although dimensional models have been proposed as alternatives to the current categorical system (see for example, Goldberg and Huxley, 1992), they simply act as a softer version of pathologization since there are still individuals at the ends of the dimensions who are perceived as abnormal.

Diagnosis and discrimination

What happens to people who are pushed to the edges of what is considered normal, or to the ends of a psychiatric dimension, is that they are *positioned*, a place is marked out for them and a set of behaviours and experiences is defined for them. The concept of positioning becomes useful when we look at some of the contradictory ways psychiatry classifies people according to their gender, colour, class and so on and it is to this that we now turn our attention. We will discuss the way positioning works in relation to gender, race and class, and draw attention to some common processes of marginalization and oppression.

Sex, lies and statistics

It is a truism that mental health services are discriminatory and a wide variety of statistical sources testify to this. UK Department of Health statistics from 1986 show that women are more likely to be diagnosed with affective psychoses like depression (twice as likely), and neurotic disorders like anxiety (twice as likely). Men are more likely to be diagnosed with alcoholism (twice as likely) and slightly more likely to be diagnosed with schizophrenia and personality disorder (Pilgrim and Rogers, 1993).

The DSM-IV (American Psychiatric Association, 1994) reports a wide variety of gender differences in diagnoses. Women are three times as likely to be diagnosed with panic disorders and twice as likely to be diagnosed with depression. Ninety per cent of those with anorexia and bulimia and 75 per cent of those diagnosed with borderline personality disorder are women. In comparison, men are more likely to be diagnosed with pyromania, gambling problems (two-thirds are men), paranoid personality disorder, anti-social personality disorder (three times more likely) and obsessive compulsive disorder (twice as likely).

How do we account for the disparity between men and women in their encounters with psychiatry? The classic text for work on the treatment of gender by psychiatry is Phylis Chesler's (1973) *Women and Madness*. Ussher (1991) also provides a useful polemical review of these issues. Chesler argues that women are caught in a type of 'double-bind'. The meanings which attach to behaviours of men and women in families are given by the wider social context, and Chesler describes the bind as follows. On the one hand, the classic female role demands a set of behaviours and experiences which, judged against an ungendered norm, are clinically neurotic. Female psychology is 'abnormal psychology' and brings with it as a matter of course 'anxiety', 'depression' and 'paranoia'. On the other hand, resistance against that norm is liable to be interpreted as deviation. Here women again express the symptoms of an 'abnormal psychology' which could be labelled as 'schizophrenia', 'personality disorder', 'promiscuity' or 'lesbianism'. In sum, *'What we consider "madness" whether it appears in women or in men is either acting-out of the devalued female role or the total or partial rejection of one's sex-role stereotype'* (Chesler, 1973: 53, emphasis in the original). This then, of course, also adds a particular weight to the oppressions of lesbians (and gay men) in psychiatry and psychotherapy (Burns and Newnes, 1994).

Sociological writers attempting to explain these differences tend to resort to a fundamental dualism linked to the fact that society is discriminatory: that it is discrimination that causes mental distress or that it is this that leads to biased diagnoses. On both sides of this opposition there are plausible reasons put forward, and fierce objections. However, it should be noted that the objections to each of the explanations rest on an idealized and essentialist view of what a woman is, and what her experience must be like. We could perhaps save each of these explanations as a partial explanation, applicable in varying measure to particular individuals, if we take seriously the idea that all experience is contradictory.

What the cultural representations of women and mental disorder may point to is not so much the function of internalized stereotypes but the existence of different historically constructed discourses which carry with them certain positions for individuals to adopt and play out. A discourse is a set of statements about an object which allows people to define and speak about things (Parker, 1992). Foucault (1971), whose work we discussed in Chapter 1, was concerned with the development of a medical discourse about madness. Perhaps what we have here is the linking of discourses about femininity with that medical discourse. Discourses always entail relations of power, and the power present here is distributed according to the structures of patriarchy. Patriarchy can be defined as that set of social arrangements in which men dominate women and older men dominate younger men (Millett, 1977).

There are further problems with traditional concerns about gender and diagnosis which reflect the contradictory nature of culture. The first is that most of the work quoted is based on figures of those in contact with formal services. When we talk about distress as it is explored through community surveys the picture becomes more complex. Thus Goldberg and Huxley (1992: 19) argue that men experience similar rates of psychological distress to women but that women 'are more willing to acknowledge illness, to make contact with a doctor, to present psychological complaints, and to remember having had psychological symptoms'. This point might lead us to examine the discourses which position women (and within which women may position themselves) as those who seek help within a psychological framework. This both brings them into contact with services when they are vulnerable *and* it positions them as more prone to distress. A second contradiction is opened up by the fact that, as we noted, women are not over-represented in all diagnoses. Thus we see that men are over-represented in rates of drug and alcohol problems, and this may reflect dominant patriarchal discourses about appropriate conduct for men. Some writers have argued that men deal with their distress through turning to drink and drugs or crime and are also more likely to come to the attention of psychiatry involuntarily, for example through being sectioned under the Mental Health Act (something often associated with a diagnosis of schizophrenia) or through forensic psychiatry after being convicted of a criminal offence. A third contradiction is whether we accept the use of these diagnoses to reflect the differential experiences of men and women or whether we challenge the 'truth' of the categorical systems themselves as systems of knowledge that simply reflect the preoccupations of our culture at a particular point in time.

Turner (1987) describes how the treatment of women's mental distress has historically been bound up with the medicalization of women's experience. Hysteria was a psychosomatic expression of an emotional problem which resulted from 'the division of the social world by a public arena of authority and a private world of emotion and sensibility' (Turner, 1987: 106). Note here how the distinction between reason and unreason has been used to draw a line between the public sphere in which men act, and the private sphere in which women work. Now, according to Turner, conditions like anorexia, which was originally described as a hysterical syndrome, have stepped in to take its place. Each condition reveals something of the age in which they were described: while hysteria in the nineteenth century was bound up with the moral restraint of women's sexuality, anorexia in the twentieth century is bound up with the idealization of women's sexuality in public images of her body. Available social meanings condition experiences of normal and abnormal experience.

Showalter's (1987) work is on the way female insanity over the past 150 years has been suffused with sexual meanings. Hysteria, for example, has long been linked with female sexuality. The word 'hysteria' comes from the Greek *hysteron* (womb). In ancient Greek medicine the womb was thought to be a kind of animal that longed to generate children. If it remained barren, it became distressed and strayed around the body causing problems, affecting the respiration and tranquillity of the occupant. Once the reproductive urge of the womb was satisfied, the disturbances ceased. Showalter shows how the belief that a 'normal' heterosexual relationship could solve hysterical disorders persisted in psychiatry into the twentieth century. What is then at stake in psychiatric practice and in the representations of women's sexuality in literature is the normalization of women's experience. The cure involves her re-placement in a family structure with a man, producing children.

Here, there is an explicit agenda of positioning, where the treatment of the aberrant woman involves physically positioning her back in the home. The way this agenda plays its way out, though, is through the myriad discourses that identify the woman and her problems, draw her into the psychiatric system, and represent her madness to the outside world. We also see this close connection between what goes on inside psychiatry and the cultural representations that surround it in discourses of race and racism.

Race and identity

A glance at psychiatric statistics reveals the existence of institutional racism. Skin colour in the direct experience of racism is, of course, tremendously important. However, those who are not directly and immediately identified as 'other', such as Irish or Jewish people, do also suffer from racism and differences in their experiences of psychiatry. Greenslade (1993), for example, has shown that the rates of psychiatric admission for immigrants to England from the north of Ireland and Eire are higher than any other immigrant group. Littlewood and Lipsedge (1989) describe how Hasidic Jews can be spiralled into the psychiatric system when their lifestyles are misinterpreted by doctors.

A 1977 study revealed that West Indian first generation immigrants had higher rates of psychiatric admission than British people whereas Indian and Pakistani immigrants had lower rates (Mercer, 1986). If we turn to methods of admission, voluntary admission is the normal route of entry for white patients. Black people are more likely to be compelled to enter. Black people are twice as likely as their white counterparts (if you control for age, gender and class) to be held under section 136 of the 1983 Mental Health Act (Mercer, 1986). Moreover, temporary breakdown is more likely to be treated as chronic psychiatric illness, and there is evidence that chemotherapy (that is, psychiatric drugs) and electroconvulsive therapy is more likely to be given. The other side of the coin is, of course, that black people are less likely to be given non-physical treatments such as psychotherapy (Fernando, 1993). Black people are over-represented in regional secure units.

Once again, many writers return to a dualism to explain the over- and under-representation of black people. Again discrimination and racism are used to explain both misdiagnosis and high rates of psychological distress. This dualism finds itself expressed also in the activities of some working within the psychiatric system to try to address problems of race and racism. The implications of the statistics are disturbing, and the way this mistreatment resonates with racist stereotypes prompted some liberal psychiatrists to set up the Transcultural Psychiatry Society (TCPS) in the UK in 1976. The early work on transcultural psychiatry which sets the context for the work of Philip Rack (1982), who was the first chair TCPS, and Littlewood and Lipsedge (1989) does make a clear distinction between the underlying psychiatric problem and the cultural manifestations, and so both illness and culture are treated as real things that can then be juggled around in different ways in different medical accounts. In Kiev's work, for example, 'clinical manifestations . . . are colored by socio-cultural factors' (Kiev, 1972: 3). Different cultures and belief systems have different ways of understanding clinical disorders, and appropriate rituals for dealing with them. Transcultural psychiatry originally saw its role as describing and understanding culture-bound disorders.

For transcultural psychiatry, as understood by the founders of the TCPS, the underlying problem is seen as a problem of communication. Three main points mark transcultural psychiatry (TCP) out from traditional psychiatry. The first is that the doctor should know the patient's culture. The descriptions of immigration patterns in Rack's (1982) book also have the purpose of putting that understanding in a wider context. The point of the doctor knowing the patient's culture is that relationships between doctors and patients should be improved. It is hoped that then ethnocentric assumptions will be avoided in the making of a diagnosis.

The second precept of TCP is that the patient should not be viewed as 'being a problem'. In traditional psychiatry the black person is not only more likely to be labelled as psychotic, but the types of treatment offered also make it seem as if the person is to blame. Instead of 'being a problem' the patient should be viewed as 'having a problem'. Part of this shift of emphasis is reflected in the way TCP advocates psychotherapy and other non-physical treatments, as well as a great emphasis on the use of interpreters. The third point also sums up the overall aims of those involved in TCP today. Through understanding and communication more accurate diagnoses can be made. It should be possible for a psychiatrist versed in the cultural peculiarities of the patient to distinguish better between 'normal' and 'pathological' behaviour. Better diagnosis will then make for better mental health services, and make the existing services more accessible to black people (Rack, 1982).

There are objections, however, to these proposals, and some of these are voiced by Mercer (1986). It is significant that TCP ignores or evades talk of 'race', and substitutes for 'race' the notion of *culture*. It attempts to get away from the old biological definitions of 'race', but its use of the term 'culture' is, perhaps, not a useful alternative. There are two assumptions in TCP which are particularly problematic. The first is that simply empathizing with the black patient and respecting their 'identity' has the effect not only of individualizing the problem, but also individualizing cultural difference, making the person into a representative and exemplar of their community. It is made to seem as if the community in question was homogeneous, and, for the purposes of diagnosis and cure, not affected by gender and class divisions. The second problem is to do with professional interests. Understanding 'race' and 'difference' as a communication problem allows the good doctor to listen to the patient, but it ignores the fact that the problems of minority groups owe at least as much to structural racism as to communication problems. In addition, the preoccupation with cultural difference can reinforce stereotypes (of, for example, the Afro-Caribbean as aggressive and excitable, and the Asian as meek and docile). This has the effect of restoring credibility to psychiatrists who want to categorize disorders. Notice also that TCP discourse locates the white person as the doctor and the black person as the client 'having the problem'. This aspect of the discourse gives rise to justifiable suspicions that instead of making radical changes in the mental health service TCP is just concerned with making the same old service more accessible.

What the discourse of TCP does, then, is to replace 'race' with 'culture'. This 'culturalism' then plays a part in the surveillance function of the state. In the Foucauldian terminology which Mercer (1986) borrows, it becomes part of the 'gaze' by which the state turns its subjects into objects. The final twist is that when the individual person 'having the problem' turns up in front of the social worker, doctor, psychiatrist or psychologist, they are treated as if they individually contain all those characteristics which obtain to their community. This process is one of 'subjectification'. You will recognize the foucauldian theme here of the person in contemporary psychiatry being forced to take responsibility for their distress. The position that is made available to subjects of this psychiatric gaze is one where they must display appropriate cultural attributes to be normal. This makes it difficult for someone to speak outside of the place that liberal psychiatry creates for them as an individual with certain group characteristics. The individualization of the problem is also important in the case of class.

Class and social power

Class is a powerful arena of discrimination in diagnosis. Figures are harder to come by here since official statistics do not collect information on class. The Socialist Health Association's (1987) report *Goodbye to All That?* notes how research has continually illustrated class differences in mental health following Hollingshead and Redlich's (1958) work in the US which showed that members of social class V (unskilled manual) were three times more likely to be hospitalized than those from social classes I and II (business and professional). Goldberg and Huxley (1992: 19) have noted that 'with few exceptions, most studies show greater rates for common mental disorders in those of lower [sic] social class'. They go on to mention Brown and Harris's (1978) classic study which argued that working-class women had higher rates of depression because they had higher rates of severe life events and major social difficulties. It could be argued that class is related to experiences of unemployment, which Goldberg and Huxley state 'is associated with elevated rates of disorder' (1992: 21). Abramowitz and Dokecki (1977) have noted how studies have consistently found less favourable clinical judgements being made of 'lower' as opposed to middle-class patients. Moreover, they note: 'lower social-class has been associated with less acceptability for treatment, fewer outpatient visits, treatment by pharmacotherapy rather than psychotherapy, and less perceived similarity to admitting residents [psychiatrists]' (Abramowitz and Dokecki, 1977: 462)

Once again, explanations are haunted by the familiar dualism: it is class that both causes misdiagnosis by professionals (who are likely to be middle class) and causes psychological distress. In our discussion of issues of gender and race and distress we have traced some of the contradictions in culture and positions that are given to people. Nowhere, perhaps, are these contradictions more evident than around the issue of class. Although by its very nature a 'social' concept, implying a group, increasingly 'class' has become a term to be applied to individuals. Worse than this, classes are defined in the psychological literature without any reference to the exploitation of labour, alienation or oppression (Parker and Spears, 1995). Indeed class is heard of less and we now hear more of 'socio-economic status' – an individualized variable. Pilgrim and Rogers's (1993) *A Sociology of Mental Health and Illness* includes chapters on gender, race and ethnicity, and age but only a section on class. However, despite all this evidence, class is increasingly disappearing as anything other than a 'social factor' or yet another variable. Bromley (1993) has noted that the past decade has seen a dearth of research on class and psychotherapy (and it is noteworthy that even Bromley uses the term 'lower class' as well as 'working class' to define the problem). Goldberg and Huxley, whilst detailing the influence of race, class, unemployment, age, gender, and the physical environment on diagnosis, at no point theorize about why this is the case although obvious candidates include racism, sexism, working conditions and alienation.

Some therapies, in trying to deal with class, often reproduce class divisions. Thus Bromley (1993) quotes Freud in 1905 opining that 'those patients who do not possess a reasonable degree of education . . . should be refused'. Young (1988: 80–3) suggests that rational emotive therapists working with 'lower class' clients need to develop a 'position of command' through the 'use of a loud voice' (which, according to the text is one of the most effective ways of gaining the attention and respect of such clients), using 'commanding gestures', remembering to 'touch the client' (in a 'forceful, determined way'), through trying to 'establish and exploit a reputation' (by simply announcing 'in a firm, loud, self-assured voice that you are indeed an expert'), and through displaying 'superior wisdom and knowledge'. Although crass, Young's discussion provides some insight into the subtler workings and class assumptions of other therapies.

The positioning of people identified as being of 'lower' class, then, not only obscures the real nature of the problem, but also makes it worse at the very moment when it appears to be taken seriously. Well-meaning psychiatrists and psychotherapists have tried to put aside their class privilege, or the power that is given by gender or race, but often reinforce the oppression of those who suffer most from distress and from clinical abuse.

Abnormal categories: the materiality of distress

We have seen how differential diagnoses do not simply reflect the impact of gender, race or class as individual variables. Rather these diagnoses reflect the actual positions real people find themselves in, for example as young unemployed single mothers or unemployed black men. Each of us is multiply positioned in terms of these different characteristics and thus our experiences are sometimes similar, sometimes different but always contradictory. In contrast, the diagnostic measures against which we are compared by the psy-complex try to appear as objective truths, minimizing diversity and contradiction. Of course the operation of these categories is intimately related to culture and Chapter 4 will explore this relationship in more detail. Here, however, we wish to examine some of the tensions and conflicts in these categories in the way they are used.

If we are to deconstruct the ways that diagnosis fixes on our gender, race and class we need to understand more about how particular categories function. Our experience is always mediated through dominant discourses and the same is true of mental health talk and writing also. This is not to deny that there are people in distress. Rather it means asking more about the *mediation* of distress: how did our ideas of psychological distress become current and what are their implicit assumptions and implications. We will briefly mention six categories to illustrate how a deconstruction of the discourses that sustain 'disorder' might be useful to demystify the way psychiatric knowledge embraces people in distress.

Anxiety

Smail (1987) has suggested 'anxiety' is a position that people find themselves in when they become aware of the objectifying gaze of society. Hallam (1994) notes some of the ideological context of 'anxiety' including the key role that it plays in a system of social control based on self-regulation, that is, the idea that we must learn to 'cope' with the events of life rather than seek political change. It is interesting in this context that it is more likely to be women who are placed (and who may place themselves) in this position.

Depression

Wiener and Marcus (1994) have argued that the concept of 'depression' individualizes a social transaction: 'helplessness, powerlessness, and worthlessness do not occur in social vacua' (1994: 225). Allwood (1995) has also noted how 'depression' serves a number of societal functions: urging people to see the events of life as a matter of the psyche rather than the public domain, encouraging internal self-regulation, specifically of women, and as a potentially damaging form of liberal humanist therapeutic theory emphasizing personal responsibility rather than a need for social change.

Once again, it is no surprise that women are the most likely to be positioned in such a category.

Eating problems

In a sense, the eating 'disorders' are one of the clearest examples of the functions of diagnosis. Overwhelmingly women are the largest group to receive this diagnosis, yet the existence of this 'disorder' mystifies the relationship between culture and women's relationship with their bodies. The gendered nature of anorexia and bulimia nervosa is thus regarded as incidental rather than as essential and fundamental. Hepworth (1994: 181) has described how the 'discourse of femininity can show us the assumptions made in the construction of femininity when certain psychiatric categories are assigned mostly to women. This discourse can also tell us a great deal about the construction of masculinity.'

Schizophrenia

This is a diagnosis most likely to be given to black and working class patients and it has been argued that the very existence of this diagnostic category serves to mystify the relationship between race, class, poverty and distress. Our attention is directed on to mental phenomena rather than our position in the world. Yet at the same time the psychotic phenomena, the symptoms, are categorized as being beyond the world of normal human discourse or at least the 'talking cure'. This is of course the bitter legacy Freud left to both the radical therapist and the user of mental health services. We can observe a correlation by social class of the populations not eligible for psychotherapy and prone to schizophrenia. Yet at the same time Freud could demonstrate insight on the general question of diagnoses: 'They resemble the Scottish King's test for identifying witches . . . This king declared he was in possession of an infallible method for recognizing a witch. He had the women stewed in a cauldron of boiling water and then tasted the broth. Afterwards he was able to say: "that was a witch" or "no that was not one". It is the same with us, except that *we* are the sufferers.' (Freud, 1973 [1933]: 191). This enlightened anecdote reflects both the felt position of the schizophrenic patient, often on high doses of neuroleptic medication and the torturous path of the syndrome itself through the annals of psychiatry. It also reveals something of the no-win situation that a psychiatric patient is in once the doctor assumes that something lies 'outside the text' when they cannot find the signs of schizophrenia within what the patient says. The category of schizophrenia is defended as if it were the jewel in the crown of psychiatry and this defence has proved resistant to the most scientific and rational argument (Boyle, 1990, 1994).

Perhaps the irrationality of the diagnostic systems is more of a problem than the problem those systems seem so obsessed with.

Psychopathic disorder

Blackburn (1988) has described the repeated failure of research to define coherently a 'psychopathic' personality. Levenson (1992) implies that the search to identify a distinct personality type is always undermined by the fact that notions of anti-social behaviour are realized in a particular social context. Despite such attacks, both from within and without psychiatric orthodoxy, psychopathic disorder remains an integral part of the English medico-legal framework. Both historically and in the present day it is identified with a type of personality disposed towards perpetrating anti-social behaviour. One of the most peculiar things about the emotionless destructive images of self that are identified in 'psychopaths' is that these images are precisely those that are provoked and celebrated in capitalist society.

Paranoia

Traditional psychiatric epidemiological research indicates that those diagnosed as paranoid are more likely to be poorer, be from a 'lower' social class, have less education and be immigrants than those attracting other psychiatric diagnoses (Kendler, 1982). Here then, social structure has already constrained the choice of positions open to the subject. As Sampson (1993a: 1227) has pointed out, the ascription of identity in this manner is not simply mental, since the terms by which an identity is realized 'also describe the actual material realities within which those lives are lived'. Texts of suspicion circulate widely in Western culture and provide for their characters a sense of mission and purpose, a sense of unification against a perceived threat. It is no surprise perhaps that some people, particularly if their structural position offers them few other choices, may adopt such a location. They, however, might see themselves not as paranoid but, rather as persons who know what is *really* going on. At the same time, we exist in a panoptical culture which regulates our own and others' behaviour, and thus those living a text of suspicion become positioned by others as paranoid. Of course, this may well happen the other way around: the subject becomes marked out, the object of a covertly organized group (for example, malicious gossip, jokes and so on). As a result, the subject may be both positioned as paranoid (as soon as she or he comments on the situation) and may position themselves this way since this makes sense of a world where others really are out to get you. The position of 'paranoia' tends to be granted to those with little power such as fringe political groups or isolated individuals. Those in powerful social positions can adopt a discourse of distrust without fear of being called paranoid (at least by those who matter).

It is ironic that mental health professionals should have such power to define what counts as an excess of suspicion when it is an important part of their role to be intensely suspicious of their patients. In addition, if we turn to the state of the mental health disciplines, we find them to be marked by internal divisions and conflicts which reflect the contradictory nature of the whole modern clinical enterprise.

Disciplining mental health

Following our concern to look at psychopathology by examining the practices of the 'psy-complex' it is time to turn to the practitioners of mental health and turn the objectifying gaze of the complex back on itself. We can even use the language of psychopathology in describing the growth of the psy disciplines as symptomatic of internal tensions and contradictions. Indeed, Rose (1986) has noted how modern psychiatry is no longer monolithic but instead sites for its practice have proliferated both in terms of geography (for example, from 'the hospital' to 'the community'), in terms of classification (for example, the differentiation of 'new' problems), in terms of new 'techniques of normalization' and new therapies and in terms of new markets and a new distribution of professional powers. As we pointed out in Chapters 1 and 2, the mental health system operates under psychiatric rule, with a variety of different professions jostling for space, attention and independence. In recent years a fairly concerted challenge to psychiatric hegemony has been mounted by clinical psychology, and we turn to that discipline first.

Clinical psychology

The profession of clinical psychology gradually became established in post-war Britain. The 1950s saw the predominance of what Pilgrim and Treacher (1992) term the 'psychometric role' which posed no threat to psychiatry and, indeed, was of value to it in measuring the psychological characteristics of patients. Pilgrim and Treacher note three campaigns which saw clinical psychology trying to break from this control: the first was Eysenck's attacks on psychoanalysis (for example, Eysenck and Rachman, 1965); the second was a (failed) attempt to get psychologists in control of the Medical section (now Psychotherapy section) of the British Psychological Society (BPS); the third was the beginning of behaviour therapy which clinical psychology championed. Additionally, work at the

Tavistock Clinic and Tavistock Institute in London saw other attempts to use knowledge gained during the war effort in civilian life. Even at this early stage clinical psychology was torn between psychoanalytic and behavioural models. By the mid 1960s clinical psychology had moved into its behaviour therapy role. Here, the image of the 'scientist-practitioner' reigned supreme. Its advocates believed in the straightforward application of psychological knowledge to mental distress. By the late 1970s a more eclectic role had emerged and clinical psychology's self-image was of practitioners who drew on a divergent set of theoretical models. Pilgrim and Treacher quote from a 1990 study which showed that clinical psychologists borrowed from a variety of therapeutic traditions: Eclectic (31.6 per cent); Behaviour/learning (22.2 per cent); Psychodynamic (21 per cent); Cognitive (13.5 per cent); and Systemic (6.2 per cent).

The 1970s had also seen a key political event: the severing of clinical psychology's link to psychiatry. The Trethowan report (Department of Health and Social Security, 1977) ushered in an era where clinical psychology services increasingly sought and found referrals directly from general practitioners thus becoming less dependent on psychiatry. Essentially, this saw the emergence of a fourth stage of managerialism and professionalization in clinical psychology which was most clearly illustrated in the BPS encouraging the Department of Health to commission a 'greenfield review' of the profession in order to increase training places on clinical psychology courses. The subsequent report, published in 1989, argued that there were three levels of psychological skill. Level 1 included basic counselling skills. Level 2 included the cookbook use of certain techniques (for example, anxiety management). Level 3 involved the theorization of new problems by using a wide range of psychological models. Only clinical psychologists, it was argued, had level 3 skills whereas other professions might well have levels 1 and 2. Pilgrim and Treacher (1992) have argued that this was yet another example of clinical psychology trying to 'corner the market' in distress and have pointed to the voluntary Register of Chartered Psychologists as a similar attempt at professionalization.

Although theoretically it possesses some potential to challenge psychiatry (and, as we saw in Chapter 2 clinical psychologists are increasingly encroaching on traditional psychiatric terrain) clinical psychology is still a small profession (approximately 2,500–3,000 in the UK). Also, although the majority of clinical psychologists are women, management positions are disproportionately occupied by men, and Black people are under-represented in general in the profession (Pilgrim and Treacher, 1992). Pilgrim and Treacher also note its ambivalent class status: on the one hand a middle class group of meritocrat professionals (nearly all clinical psychologists are members of the BPS); on the other hand a group of trades unionists committed to the National Health Service (and nearly all clinical psychologists are members of the trade union MSF). This position means that clinical psychology as a profession could act both as an ally for and as an obstacle to radical change in practices around mental health.

Psychological interventions offered by clinical psychologists provide an alternative to neuroleptic medication and increasingly appear as more 'user friendly' and drawing unique individual capacities for self-healing and coping. It would be a mistake to forget that this was one of the principles on which Hippocrates founded medicine. This challenge then has the potential to rescue psychiatry from some of its current excesses as much as improving the lot of psychiatric patients. Herein lie the possibilities for new partnerships. At the same time, militating against this is the practice of taking research funding from drug companies and writing up research papers as if psychological treatments are complementary to the drugs, whatever might be said behind the scenes. But it is perhaps behind the scenes that such partnerships are made.

Psychiatric nursing

Nursing is involved with psychiatry at three levels: in-patient, day patient (in day hospitals) and in the community (CPNs). Johnstone (1989) has noted how often psychiatric nurses working on wards are the people most likely to experience how people's real lives do not fit psychiatric categories. However, she also notes how the power differentials between nursing staff and psychiatrists – paralleling the distribution of power throughout medicine – prevent anything progressive emerging from this clash. The increasing role of the Community Psychiatric Nurse (CPN) has allowed more space for an independent professional role to develop. Similar to clinical psychology, CPN services have increasingly accepted direct referrals from GPs therefore bypassing psychiatrists. However, CPNs are still required to administer depot medications and thus still continue to be pulled back to a 'handmaiden' professional style. Moreover, they are often inundated with referrals which means they are often unable to spend much time with their clients. Too often, the community psychiatric nurses are caught between psychiatry and the community. There are spaces for resistance here. Thus CPNs are increasingly becoming involved in monitoring medication and in providing 'psycho-social interventions' to patients diagnosed as psychotic but these activities are usually dependent on the existence of cooperative psychiatrists and are still founded on relatively traditional versions of psychopathology.

Psychiatric social work

Currently social work has a dual relationship to psychiatry. This duality reflects, on the one hand, its continued immersion in a modernist outlook, whilst, on the other, it indicates its movement towards a more 'post-modern' state of being. According to Howe (1994), social work first emerged in the nineteenth century and displayed a modernist concern both with the underlying causes and with notions of 'cure' and 'treatment'. Its time of 'high modernity' came in the 1970s when there were various attempts to synthesize disparate social work approaches into a common theoretical base, through which social problems could be tackled. Such concerns resonated with psychiatry's own modernist project and, to the extent that there are modernist remnants within social work, there is a basis of a particular type of alliance.

This alliance takes the form of social work extending psychiatry's gaze beyond the clinic and hospital and into the social arena. Barrett (1988) describes how social work feeds into an ecological perspective in which the psychiatric symptoms can be understood as part of a causal relationship between the patient, their environment and their relationship to significant others. In practice, this might take the form of social work focusing upon the family and delineating pathogenic family processes. The social work perspective might also diffuse the patients' symptoms into their social environment by uncovering a 'kernel' of truth in what, for example, might previously have been considered a wholly delusional belief or idea (Barrett, 1988). Each of these manoeuvres serves the purpose of increasing the reality status of symptoms and diagnosis.

The post-modern diversification of theory and practice and the notions of epistemological equivalence between competing theories and explanations, however, has had significant implications for social work. First, there is no overarching theory to explain the social world. Secondly, the absence of a comprehensive theory has undermined the status of social workers as 'experts'. Howe suggests that one effect of this process has been to refocus attention upon the *act* rather than the *actor*. If there is no technology available to manage the client or patient then their behaviour must be controlled: 'Today's emphasis demands that actors change their acts, not by curing faulty minds but by showing obedience' (Howe, 1994: 527). Social work's current collaboration with psychiatry in 'Care Management', a practice that leans heavily towards this control and surveillance model, seems to illustrate both its capacity to be accommodated within this new framework, and, furthermore, its continuing ability to work in tandem with psychiatry's regulative practices.

Occupational therapy

Occupational therapy has travelled a long distance from when psychiatric ward routines were punctuated by basket-weaving and similar activities. Although the role of the Community Occupational Therapist (OT) has developed, in-patient occupational therapy still struggles to break the links with the past. OTs tend towards a holistic philosophy but this is also punctuated by a functionalist approach to distress (local authorities employ OTs to assess whether people with disabilities need adaptations at home). Similar to clinical psychology in its small numbers and para-medical position and similar to nursing in its institutional history and location and adherence to medical models, occupational therapy offers some possibilities for change within the limits set by the psychiatric system but also suffers serious constraints which prevent it from moving beyond those limits.

Generic mental health workers

The 1980s and 1990s saw the emergence of a new breed of staff in health, local authority and voluntary services. This new generation of generic mental health workers were usually from a variety of backgrounds. These developments sprung from a number of political movements: the Conservative government's anti-profession stance; services' needs for cheaper staff; and the need for workers to reflect the flexible needs of service users rather than the needs of the institutions. Although they provide a potential for political change, the lack of formal organization has so far limited their influence. Support workers are, though, likely to share the same trades union organization as clinical psychologists (MSF). Although the trades unions and the Left in general have been traditionally silent and un-radical on issues of mental health, a re-politicization (such as we attempt in this book) could place these issues firmly on such agendas.

However, where support workers characteristically differ from psychologists is in the intimacy of relations with medical discourse; whilst they are expected to provide special skills of 'communication' with mentally ill clients, their academic qualifications are generally outside the pathologizing disciplines. This sets up a special and potentially subversive relationship with the client, provoking issues of power, boundaries, professionalism and compliance, challenging those in the more regulated careers. The question is whether such potential can be managed out or become a source of alternatives and innovation. Such workers occupy a position reminiscent of that in a therapeutic community (one positive vision of care in the community), but at the same time in a quite different political context. The potential might reside in the development of a paradigm for research which activates and empowers such workers and clients in relation to the established forms of psychopathology. The issue for us is whether deconstruction can provide such resources.

Dividing practices and symptoms

We opened this chapter by looking at the puzzles that are set up by the messy systems of categorization offered by American psychiatry and the

World Health Organization, and we have turned our focus towards the end of the chapter onto the mental health professionals that try to administer these categories. The question of 'whose symptoms' are at issue is an important one, and it is possible to deconstruct the ways in which different clinical disciplines pose the question. Individuals are usually treated as the carriers of symptoms, and, in the medical model, their symptoms are an expression of an underlying disease entity. If we look closer though we discover that particular groups are targeted, and the language, the psychiatric discourse that is used to understand them says more about those with the power to define than those who are defined. We want to argue that the discourses that run through modern clinical practice are symptomatic of deep problems, and that we need to locate these seemingly scientific bodies of knowledge in the surrounding culture. They usually do the positioning, but we need to position them. We explore that issue further in the next chapter.

4

Representations of Madness

In this chapter we examine cultural representations of psychopathology, and the way in which images of 'illness' and 'abnormality' are structured in language, since in order to understand the practice of psychiatry it is necessary to understand culture. In the first section we show how cultural concerns and the concerns of psychopathology are not separate, but interwoven. We problematize the distinction between 'lay' and 'professional' knowledge, discuss the notion of madness as a cultural representation and show how traditional histories of psychopathology are flawed. We also describe the importance of language in representing madness and introduce Foucault's notion of panopticism to help us understand how representation is not a mental matter but something that is regulated and inscribed into our lives. In the second section we illustrate how we can deconstruct clinical categories by paying attention to implicit oppositions. We note that such a deconstruction is not simply a matter of privileging individual subordinated terms but, rather by transforming the oppositions themselves. In the third section we explore the two-way traffic between popular views of psychological distress and clinical practice. We look at the ways in which shared structures of language, or 'discourses' that are available in culture affect professional judgements about different forms of distress, and also how theories that have been developed in clinical work feed into popular culture. The final section suggests some of the interests served by notions of psychopathology, particularly that of governance.

Culture and madness

So far we have argued that a deconstructive approach to madness necessitates a critical understanding not only of the history of psychiatry but also of the history of cultural experiences of mental distress and of the cultural meanings of reason and unreason. We have also claimed that there is a need to analyse the language and institutions which construct madness as their object. We have used these considerations in order to provide a different account of 'symptomatology'. Throughout our analysis we have continually referred to the importance of culture. Some readers might wonder what 'culture' has to do with the study of psychopathology and believe that there is a strict distinction between popular and professional views, so that it is possible to distinguish 'lay' from properly scientific accounts of psychopathology. In this chapter our aim is to problematize this distinction and argue that it is impossible to separate different realms of knowledge since all are thoroughly embedded in cultural practices of one kind or another. Such an analysis has distinct implications which we will develop further in later chapters.

'Lay' and 'professional' knowledge

Pilgrim and Rogers (1993) begin their *Sociology of Mental Health and Illness* by sketching out five different perspectives: the lay view; psychiatry; psychoanalysis; psychology; and the law. In their account of the 'lay' view, they argue that although there are cross-cultural differences most cultures have some notion of mental distress. Thus, they suggest that commonsense 'folk' notions both of one's own mental health and of the behaviour of others prefigure professional and technical psychiatric terms. They go on to demonstrate the importance of cultural factors like class, gender, race, ethnicity and age on psychiatric treatment. These issues interest not only sociologists but also social psychiatrists (such as Goldberg and Huxley). However, as others have pointed out, the notion of 'social factors' influencing an entity called mental illness diverts attention from its socially constructed nature (Banton et al., 1985).

Representing 'madness'

Texts such as these demonstrate the acceptance of some cultural influences on our understanding and experience of mental distress. But which comes first: a 'lay' or a 'professional' notion? Can a certain emotional state or behaviour be said to have existed if there were no terms to discriminate it from other states and behaviours? Harper (1994a), for example, notes how seventeenth-century alienist Richard Napier had 42 patients with symptoms categorized by MacDonald (1981) as 'suspiciousness'. Did these people – remember, this was 100 years before the first psychiatric usage of the word paranoia – have paranoid delusions? And in what sense did 'anorexia' exist before doctors wrote about it in the nineteenth century (Hepworth and Griffin, 1990)? Might there be some truth in the view that the delimitation of a psychiatric concept actually 'creates' cases which fit its description? One cannot say that someone is depressed or anxious unless these words are culturally available (that is, we have access to these words and know what they mean). Thus the identification and categorization of others is at least dependent on, if not entirely created within, language.

When we talk about cultural representations, however, it is important to bear two points in mind. First, such notions can seem very vague – almost as if these representations are floating around in cultural space. Here, when we are talking about representations we are talking of clusters of practices of various kinds. These could include the institutional practices associated with psychiatric diagnosis or the accounting practices dominant in our society (for example, the image of the mad and dangerous individual requiring confinement currently conjured up by the Conservative government in the UK). Practices which reproduce social representations include the media and the way people talk about madness, the way 'mad' people are stigmatized and excluded.

Secondly, these representations are not uniform, rather they are fragmented and varied. It is a commonplace in political rhetoric to see apparently contradictory discourses and representations called upon by the same speaker to pursue a variety of political interests (Edelman, 1977; Edwards and Potter, 1992). It is therefore necessary to give an account not only of dominant cultural representations of madness but also to account for the way they and more subjugated representations are called upon to fulfil certain political interests. Thus different representations are adopted by dominant or oppressed groups (think of the debate between those who say they 'hear voices' and those who say they have 'auditory hallucinations'). However, at the same time the same representation may by used by groups with different, occasionally opposing, interests. Hence, in the UK, discourses asserting that those diagnosed 'mentally ill' are violent, or, at least, potentially so, are used both by right-wing proponents of draconian legislation (compulsory community treatment orders for example) but also by charities like MIND to campaign for better funding of community care. A multiplicity of representations are often found in the internal inconsistency of psychiatric categories (for example, the image of the hostile paranoid patient versus the image of the patient who is 'right' and has legitimate and realistic fears).

The past revisited

The varying cultural availability of certain terms leads some commentators to construct particular versions of the past: a history where, even though different words are used to denote a thing, the meaning is held to be the same. As soon as new concepts are described, experts then 'discover' cases of it in the past in case descriptions of famous political, literary and religious figures. Such an approach betrays an essentialist and acontextual view of history. It ignores the existence of discontinuities in history and the fact that words may have very different meanings in different historical contexts (Danziger, 1990; Smith, 1988). Depression, for example, is not the same as melancholia was. Psychopathy and paranoia do not mean now what they meant when they were first used. Even those who tend towards an essentialist history routinely note the different meanings the same word has over time (for example, Lewis, 1979). Moreover, such views of history ignore the way that psychopathology is situated in wider cultural and political contexts. We noted in Chapter 1 the varying ways in which homosexuality has been dealt with by the APA's DSM.

Language, representation and reality

Rose (1990) has argued that the vocabularies of the professions allied to the 'psy-complex' are 'languages of government [which] do not merely mystify domination or legitimate power. They make new sectors of reality thinkable and practicable' (Rose, 1990: 105–6). Psychiatric cases are thus 'brought forth' by the availability of a language to describe them in ways that differentiate them from similar cases (Méndez, et al., 1988). In this respect the practitioners of the 'psy-complex' are no different from other experts privileged by our societies at other historical moments. History provides us with other examples of excluding practices which draw on a language of social regulation but which are not now part of the 'psy-complex'. Although it is a crude example which has been subject to historical debate, the work of Roman Catholic clerics in dealing with the European witch-crazes of the Middle Ages provides an instance of this kind of operation. The marking out of others, comparison with diagnostic procedures and rules of evidence (such as the *Malleus Maleficarum*: Kramer and Sprenger, 1971) can be seen at work then, as they can now, in the modern mental health care system. Hence it is not just the 'psy-complex' which excludes. Rather, it is professional elites and the reality which is constructed by them through language. Then, witches were widely held to exist while now they are widely held not to exist. The difference here is that these new elites are employed by the state rather than the church and employ new technologies in which are contained older excluding and dividing practices.

Popular and professional knowledge and panoptical culture

We want to move on now to elaborate Foucault's vision of modern culture and to locate a deconstruction of psychiatric categories in that cultural context. Rabinow (1984) notes, in a resumé of a foucauldian view of surveillance in culture, 'through spatial ordering, the panopticon brings together power, control of the body, control of groups and knowledge . . . it locates individuals in space, in a hierarchical and efficiently visible organization' (Rabinow,1984: 19).

The surveillance necessary for the judgement of whether one's actions are normal is crucial here. In Foucault's (1977) work *Discipline and Punish* he described a device which he saw as symbolizing the kind of constant monitoring which occurs in modern society. This was Jeremy Bentham's Panopticon which was a structure affording maximum surveillance from a central location. The notion of the circular prison requiring only a warden at the centre to observe cells springs from this concept. The fact that the observer might be unseen increases the power of this form of observation since those observed will behave as if they are being watched just in case: discipline thus moves from something inflicted on others to something which becomes internalized and we move from regulation by others to self-regulation. Rabinow (1984) notes how 'discipline proceeds from an organization of individuals in space, and it requires a specific enclosure of space' (1984: 17). Thus panoptical space is a material organization of things such that we become regulated not only by others but, increasingly, by ourselves. This is not only achieved through the crude use of architectural space but, in the technological age, through the material organization of 'cyberspace', in the information stored on us on computers throughout the world (Gandy Jr, 1993). The experience of surveillance, Sass (1987) argues, in his analysis of the Schreber case (Freud, 1979 [1911]), may lead to the reification of self-scrutiny to the point where one becomes a 'quintessentially panoptical being', paralysed by paranoia. Within the field of mental health the notion of surveillance by others and by the self has aroused increasing interest (for example, Smail, 1984; White and Epston, 1990).

It is important to bear this context in mind when we look at the way culture seeps into every clinical judgement that a mental health professional makes. Clinical categories operate by excluding the contradictoriness of culture, but each attempt to protect the purity of the categories collapses under pressure. We can identify six points at which the categories can be deconstructed.

Deconstructing clinical categories

Harper (in press) has given an example of how deconstruction can be used positively to examine the implicit contradictory assumptions or oppositions in the diagnostic category of paranoia. That analysis can be broadened to other psychiatric categories. In such an examination, it is useful to regard a category as a discursive complex – a form of discourse where a system of statements constructs an object. Here then, we are self-consciously stressing the discursive nature of a diagnosis. Although there are a wide range of such statements for different categories it may be helpful to focus on six particular oppositions around which most psychiatric diagnoses are constructed. Each opposition works in conjunction with the others and we will see that simply attempting to subvert one without the others does not resolve the problem but merely reconstructs it.

The individual and the social

The first opposition, of the individual/social, reproduces the dualism inherent in modern Western culture. The 'psy-complex' has been one of the network of institutions which has served to individualize problems. It is easy to forget that this dualism has only been with us since the time of Descartes but it became politically useful at the birth of the modern state when the individual became a unit of governmental concern. The notion of problems being located in an individual removes any responsibility from society, although there is a need for a concept of the social (the 'normal population') to compare the 'abnormal' individual with. One response to this opposition might be to privilege the social over the individual. In a sense this happened with the rise of the family therapy movement. However, recently family therapists seem to be returning to the notion of the individual as the locus of change (Jenkins and Asen, 1992). Thus to attempt to fix meaning at the social end of the pole breaks down since 'society' becomes too abstract to operate (and thus is seen as constituted by 'individuals'), but privileging the individual itself continually breaks down since the individual only exists against the background of society.

Reason and unreason

A second opposition closely traces the steps of the first since rationality is as central to the modern Western concept of the self as individualism. Psychiatry celebrates this self and aims to focus on those who do not possess reason. Foucault and Derrida debated whether it was ever possible to talk about 'unreason' since, Derrida asserted, any attempt to do so colonized unreason and transformed it into reason (Boyne, 1990). Once again in this opposition we see contradictions creeping in. Modern cognitive psychology which leans heavily on a rationalist model has great difficulty understanding why people are not rational and are often inconsistent and so on. Yet simply to privilege unreason might be abnegating ourselves of the responsibility to help and understand others and, besides, ignores the constructed nature of the opposition.

Pathology and normality

A third opposition aims to police a firm distinction between what is normal and what is pathological. As with the previous opposition, for those who diagnose others as pathological a position of normality is secured and grounds are provided for questioning the legitimacy of the other's views. Moreover, this can work the other way with us deciding that, in comparison with other 'normal' people, there must be something wrong with us. Thus, once again one pole is dependent on the other for its meaning. Claiming that the pathological is really normal does not help us escape this though, since we need to challenge the cluster of other oppositions.

Form and content

Diagnostic schedules always pay much more attention to the form of distress than its content. Mental health professionals are often more concerned to know *if* someone is hearing voices or having strange thoughts than to find out *what* the voices are saying or *what* the thoughts are about. In part this is due to the medical paradigm's search for abstract general rules, from which psychiatry emerged. However, this aping of medicine becomes contradictory since many of the decisions about form are dependent on considerations of content (is a delusion persecutory or grandiose? Does the thought come from the person or outside? and so on). One cannot privilege content alone since it is always mediated in some form and it is not simply reification which is the problem (since it may often be helpful).

Pure categories versus messy real life

As with the form/content opposition, psychiatry's obsession with delineating detailed kinds of cases is closely allied with the desire of the psy disciplines to follow medical science in claiming the authority of the natural sciences. To discuss a pure pathology means one avoids discussing the inevitable ambiguities of the individual patient. There is a gate-keeping mechanism of requiring certain symptoms before being assigned a category which allows the psy gaze to decide whether the case is, for example, typical or atypical. Many professionals will know that for any one person a number of diagnoses will have been entertained. This is rarely a problem since diagnostic manuals are both highly detailed and yet also flexible enough to cover a number of eventualities. Such ambiguities are seen by journal editors as 'confounding variables' and research is thus only published if researchers maintain the practice of separating different clinical groups. The problem is not one of refining diagnostic systems but of acknowledging that the practice of diagnosis is not appropriate to human difficulties.

Professional versus popular, 'lay' and 'patient' views

These oppositions can be seen at work in a variety of psychological and psychiatric texts, yet the texts themselves form part of a final opposition since they are always produced by professionals. The knowledge that is used in diagnosing others is cut off from those others since they do not participate in the production of that knowledge. In saying this we are not arguing that the views of service users are necessarily homogenous or 'true', but we are noting that they are rarely heard. Indeed, many times they are de-legitimized. Pilgrim and Rogers quote one reviewer of research as having stated 'since some of the patients were suffering from paranoia, and others from depression, it would have been a basic precaution to check the objective value of statements with the medical records or the responsible psychiatrist' (Jones, 1962, quoted by Pilgrim and Rogers, 1993). Autobiographical accounts are often only published in scientific journals when they agree with dominant psychiatric concepts (see, for example, the 'First Person' section of *Schizophrenia Bulletin*), yet attention to a full range of autobiographies reveals there exists a diversity of explanations for people's unhappiness (spiritual, parapsychological, economic, political and so on). One option here might be to privilege the views of service users. However, since we all exist in culture, these views often echo dominant cultural stories and may not help us escape the trap. What is needed is more interchange between the two. As this occurs we would begin to see there is no real distinction between professional and lay knowledge. We will see in the next section that professional knowledge too is deeply embedded in wider cultural stories.

Transforming oppositions

As we noted above, it is not enough simply to privilege one side of one opposition. Doing that creates two problems. First it continues to fix meaning at one side and simply excludes the other. Rather we need to get at the conceptual policing which aims to keep the two sides apart. Why, for example, do we need a separation between the individual and the social? Secondly, if we only deal with one opposition by transforming the opposition (for example by using a concept that implies the individual and the social like 'positioning') but fail to deconstruct the other oppositions the problem is simply reconstructed. To use family therapy as an example again, therapists might wish to avoid individualization by stressing the interpersonal and systemic context of a problem. However, if it does so without questioning the notion of pathology or of expert professional knowledge (or the other oppositions noted) the problem reasserts itself in a different form.

Popular culture and the professionals

Our deconstruction has demonstrated that each 'pure' clinical category is dependent on cultural material. Now we want to move on to consider how that cultural material represents images of madness, and in particular the way it de-legitimizes suspicion by viewing it as a psychopathological state of mind, a state of paranoia.

The embeddedness of knowledge in culture

Social constructionist researchers have demonstrated how 'scientific' concepts are embedded within the taken-for-granted knowledge of the culture and within theories about reality. Thus Beryl Curt (1994) has argued that 'even a cursory glance through the literature of our collectivity reveals that many of the ideas we have about madness are informed by, and inform, a rich and varied collection of presentations of the mad – in painting, photography, film, popular fiction, theatre and song' (1994: 151). Cartoons are one illustration of this – for example the late Mel Calman's (1979) *Dr Calman's Dictionary of Psychoanalysis* and Barnes's (1986) collection of Punch cartoons (*Shrink Rap: Punch on the Analyst's Couch*). Such cartoons have also been an object of professional interest (Walter, 1992).

Contemporary cinema has had a vast influence on cultural representations of madness. It has portrayed the institutional life of asylums: *Bedlam* (1946, director: Mark Robson), *Shock Corridor* (1963, director: Samuel Fuller) and the liberatory *One Flew Over the Cuckoo's Nest* (1975, director: Milos Forman). But, more usually, it has projected an image of the mentally ill person as a violent and threatening figure in films like *Psycho* (1960, director: Alfred Hitchcock), *Play 'Misty' for Me* (1971, director: Clint Eastwood), *The Shining* (1980, director: Stanley Kubrick) and *The Silence of the Lambs* (1991, director: Jonathan Demme). Occasionally, there has been an attempt to understand some of the dynamics which produce unhappiness, for example *Family Life* (1971, director: Ken Loach).

Images of madness preoccupy not only the cinema, but the news and entertainment media also. Philo (1994) reports on a study examining television news and press reporting, popular magazines, children's literature and fictional TV (such as soap operas, films and drama). A content analysis produced five main categories: 'violence to others'; 'harm to self'; 'sympathetic coverage'; 'criticism of accepted definitions of mental illness' and ' "comic" images'. Overall in the coverage, 'the category of "violence to others" was by far the most common, outweighing the next most common, "sympathetic", by a ratio of almost four to one. We also found that items linking mental illness and violence tended to receive "headline" treatment, while sympathetic items were largely "back page" in their profile, such as problem page letters or health columns' (Philo, 1994: 173).

Scott (1994: 490), in an analysis of national newspaper coverage of mental health issues, found that article content suggested a 'preoccupation with forensic issues' and these 'frequently promoted the view that dangerousness is synonymous with mental illness'. This despite the findings of the

1994 Boyd committee that only 22 of approximately 700 British homicides were committed by people who had been in touch with psychiatric services in the previous 12 months (Mihill, 1994a). Such coverage is in stark contrast to the lack of public concern about the estimated one death a week caused by psychiatric drugs according to MIND (Mihill, 1994b). Philo (1994) has noted how media presentations are also 'a very powerful influence on beliefs about the nature of mental illness' (1994: 173) and that this often over-rides people's personal experience, something which is extremely unusual in media research.

The influence of popular culture on professional judgements

Professional accounts, then, cannot be separated from the wider cultural context. How might such representations influence professional accounts of madness? There are at least three possible ways. First, as we have noted, they affect the categories of behaviour which are considered pathological, removing them from being understood in relation to the broader social context. Secondly, they affect the interpretation of behaviour (and what is considered to fit a category). Thirdly, they affect the kinds of interventions offered (for example, there is considerable evidence that black people receive more 'physical' and punitive psychiatric treatment – Fernando, 1993). In this chapter we will largely examine the first two of these effects.

One of the most powerful examples of this is the area of psychiatric diagnosis or the process of 'identification' of 'pathological' behaviour. An enormous amount of work has shown how diagnosis is context-dependent (Rosenhan, 1973, 1975). However, research also points to the importance of earlier punctuations in mental health careers. For example, Smith (1978) has described a process of 'cutting out' which occurs when someone's behaviour is regarded by others as inexplicable according to normal social rules. This is, first and foremost, then, a social and cultural, not a professional process as are the numerous decisions made at later points (for example, whether to consult a public agency for help).

'Cutting out' occurs in the wider cultural context also. Witness the media response to the two-day conference in January 1993 entitled 'The first international conference that exposes a Global Deception' where a wide variety of speakers argued that world-wide conspiracies were in operation. Here, newspapers used a number of rhetorical strategies to de-legitimize the views of the conference organizers by suggesting they were paranoid (Harper, 1993). Of course, such marking out and excluding practices are engaged in, not only by journalists, but also by a person's friends, relatives and mental health professionals. Goldberg and Huxley (1992) have described the wide range of factors which determine why someone approaches their general practitioner (GP), how psychiatric 'illness' is recognized by the GP, what determines if a referral is made to a psychiatrist and how such a referral is dealt with. As a result of such cultural influences (often informed by particular cultural representations) fewer and fewer people get through the 'filters' between these stages.

As the individual reaches the attentions of a mental health professional they become objectified by a clinical gaze which supposedly records 'symptoms' and compares them with diagnostic criteria. However, a number of workers have suggested that this process is not so straightforward. Barrett (1988), in his study comparing the medical record of a diagnostic interview with a transcript of the interview, demonstrated how medical 'facts' are rhetorical constructions from often ambiguous and ambivalent interview responses. These facts were produced through the use of terms which bridged lay and professional realms. Hak (1989) has done similar, though more technical work, coming to much the same conclusions.

Barrett (1991) noted that, when talking about patients, professionals made use of an 'informal scheme of classifying patients based on "lay" concepts of madness' (1991: 8). In informal discussions mental health workers sometimes talk of clients as 'odd' in some way. In case records, however, Barrett reported that psychiatric interview conversations were transformed through the use of 'intermediate typifications' which were 'words or phrases which bridged "lay" concepts of mental illness and "professional" concepts of schizophrenia' (1991: 7). Elsewhere, Barrett (1988) has described how, in a psychiatric interview, the psychiatrist framed questions to a patient's relative in terms of lay understandings of mental illness. He has pointed out how 'this tacit network of meanings underlay the intersubjective agreement shared by the participants to this interview, yet it was little evident in the written account' (1988: 273). The account, then, was a form of writing which 'demanded that clinicians capture patient's private and personal mental experiences in codified idioms that could easily be reduced to a publicly available numeric discourse' (Barrett, 1988: 268).

Rather than straightforwardly 'recognizing' psychiatric disorder, professionals could be said to bring forth or construct psychopathology by recourse to a language with which to point to disorder. Thus diagnostic criteria could be said to be justificatory arguments rather than objective signs. Interviews with mental health professionals would seem to confirm this. Harper (1994b) has demonstrated how professionals move between both empiricist (that is, scientific and objective accounting) and contingent (that is, subjective and personalized accounting) discourses in explaining diagnosis. Moreover, the use of a criteria discourse affords professionals a good deal of flexibility in, for example, dealing with challenges to a diagnosis by reinterpreting contrary evidence or by introducing new criteria (Harper, 1994b).

This position is not something that psychiatry or other disciplines like clinical psychology can avoid by becoming more 'scientific' (for example, through the use of more formal interview protocols) since this simply leads to more stylized and artificial formulations. Indeed, psychiatry is currently under attack from researchers strongly espousing scientific (as opposed to simply ideological) values (Bentall et al., 1988; Boyle, 1990).

Is professional knowledge, then, simply a representation of popular knowledge, a more formal manner of 'cutting out' which goes on in everyday life? The situation does not appear to be as straightforward as this. For example, Curt (1994), discussing Gleeson's (1991) work, notes that although some of the 'mad' characters identified in her Q-sort study of representations of madness mapped neatly on to psychiatric diagnostic categories, many did not. For example, the general population do not draw a sharp distinction between those considered to be 'mentally ill' from those considered to have 'learning disabilities'. The fact that professional accounts do not simply mirror folk accounts can be seen as an attempt by professionals to demonstrate, through the distinctions they make, that they have specialist expertise and have a distinctive contribution to offer (Bourdieu, 1984; Bowers, 1988). Indeed, professionals often seem to be anxious to stress the expert contribution they have to offer. For example, the American Psychiatric Association's *Diagnostic and Statistical Manual of Mental Disorders* (DSM-III-R) states that 'because the ordinary English meaning of the term 'paranoid' suggests only suspiciousness, the more nosologically descriptive term "Delusional Disorder" is used' (American Psychiatric Association, 1987: 420). In stressing their specialisms it is no surprise therefore that there are territorial disputes between professions, as we saw in Chapter 3. Indeed, Barrett (1991) has described the results of how such a division of labour affects professional judgements.

The percolation of professional knowledge into the popular domain

Of course, this is not all one-way traffic. Gleeson (1991) notes that, instead, the relationship between traditional, new and old folk beliefs and professional views is a dialectical and interactive one. Thus current popular beliefs become the 'new' traditional beliefs. Moreover, although professional beliefs are heavily shaped by popular notions, professional views percolate back into popular culture and hence are constitutive of our current popular social reality. Handy (1987) points out that 'the findings of the social sciences are not only produced within a wider cultural milieu which influences their form but may also feed back into and influence that culture . . . psychologists should examine the effects which their theorizing may have on society . . . looking at . . . the influence of particular modes of construing reality on social life' (Handy, 1987: 165).

Examples of this can be seen in TV talk shows. Hardly an edition of the US Donahue or Oprah Winfrey shows goes by without the appearance of a psychotherapist of some sort and this phenomenon is on the increase in Britain (Livingstone and Lunt, 1994). We see Bart and his popular TV cartoon family, *The Simpsons*, attending for family therapy – in 'No disgrace like home' (1991, directors: Gregg Vanzo and Kent Butterworth, Gracie Films/Twentieth Century Fox) – as have families in the BBC radio serial *The Archers* and the BBC TV series *EastEnders*. Increasingly newspapers and magazines feature mental health professionals as expert commentators (for example, building up offender profiles, the results of post-traumatic stress on children and so on) or as writers for 'problem pages'. More and more magazines feature various kinds of 'personality' questionnaires helping us to rate anything from our aggression to our sexual lifestyles. To take psychologists as an example, we find that the 'Media Watch' page and 'On the air' columns in the British Psychological Society journal *The Psychologist* show the wide range of media psychologists are involved in. Further, many writers note the seepage of mental health professional discourse into everyday life. Thus Burman (1995) has described how discourse analyses of representations of the self can seem banal because of the 'permeation of therapy-speak into everyday ways of describing experience' (Burman, 1995: 487). Some have claimed that such seepage is perhaps a sign that Western culture has become a 'psychiatric society' in which 'people's problems are increasingly conceptualized in medical or psychological terms and in which medical judgements have an expanding influence on the way we live' (Handy, 1987: 165).

However, such a focus on negatively valued psychiatrization diverts us from considering the social consequences of the governance of the self and aspirations to an idealized 'free' and 'genuine' self reminiscent of the more positively valued counselling, psychotherapy and personal growth movements (Burman, 1995; Rose, 1989). The extent of such seepage can be seen in the way technical terms get taken up in everyday life. For example, the concept of paranoia is widely used in popular culture and we can see how it has had a vast influence on writing (O'Donnell, 1992), film (Barker, 1992), history (Graumann and Moscovici, 1987), politics (Billig, 1991) and everyday conversation (see, for example, work on gossip: Rosnow and Fine, 1976). Such popularity is frowned on by psychiatric figures like Lewis (1970) who argues that the 'literary and vernacular use of "paranoid" as meaning "resentfully distrustful" is as inexact as the corresponding use of "hysterical" ' (1970: 9). Despite this we call each other paranoid if we feel someone is being overly suspicious or if we want to remove legitimacy from someone's views. In doing this we thus bring to bear the stigma of psychopathology on the other. Calling someone 'paranoid' is likely to have more of an effect than calling them 'overly suspicious'.

An example of the permeation of this technical term can be seen in a cartoon from the back cover of *Freak Brothers* (Shelton/Rip Off Press, 1985), a comic detailing the escapades of the Fabulous Furry Freak Brothers (see Figure 4.1). Funniness is overdetermined, and we can see

Figure 4.1 *Feeling paranoid lately? (Reproduced by permission, Knockabout Comics)*

that the cartoon is humorous for a number of reasons. First, we can see the operation of what Gilbert and Mulkay (1984) have termed the 'proto-joke' where contradictory discourses are used simultaneously producing an incongruous and humorous effect. In relation to paranoia, the proto-joke would be 'just because I'm paranoid doesn't mean they're not out to get me'. In other words, on the one hand, the assertion of paranoia is a claim that you, the reader, are being pathologically suspicious (thinking that the 'secret police' have a file on you) whilst, on the other hand, there is a recognition that there is a good deal of surveillance carried out on us by both state and private agencies (Campbell and Connor, 1986). Thus, in providing the term 'paranoia' with multiple meanings, a basic 'rule' of language is broken and, at once, re-marked (Purdie, 1993). This effect is heightened if we know that the Fabulous Furry Freak Brothers are three men who indulge in a wide variety of illicit drugs. In this case the term 'paranoia' is provided with at least two further meanings. Thus, one effect of certain illicit drugs is to make the user (one of the brothers, or, possibly a reader) feel suspicious or 'paranoid'. Appleyard (1993) notes 'the particular controlled substances then [in the 1960s] widely available – dope, speed and acid – were all paranoia inducing' (1993: 16). Moreover, users would have grounds to be suspicious in case of police surveillance and drug raids or if involved in political action.

'Madness', governance and culture

It no longer seems sensible to talk of 'professional' and 'lay' concepts as separate things since the distinction between them is not so much in the kinds of discourses used by speakers but rather the position from which they speak. A professional may use a 'lay' discourse and a lay person may use a 'professional' discourse. In the same way as mental health staff may say a psychiatric patient is 'off' or 'settled' (Barrett, 1991) so a lay person may speak of 'clinical depression' or deliberately use technical terms rather than popular ones (for example, 'schizophrenic' instead of 'mad', or 'anxious' instead of fearful). White and Epston, for example, note that 'at times, especially when persons have been encouraged to use "scientific classification" to describe their concerns, persons offer problem definitions in terms that are informed by "expert knowledge"' (1990: 53).

We have argued that madness and its contents are located within discourses of difference which serve to regulate sectors of society and that this concept is historically allied with a number of politically dominant institutions and their practices (medicine, the welfare state and so on). Certainly it appears that socially valued phenomena like happiness are not included within diagnostic systems, although a case consistent with psychiatric theory can be made (Bentall, 1992b). Within supposedly democratic states the only way in which to conduct such a 'governance of the soul' is through the creation of a professional class and language which appears to provide objective help when people vary from an idealized norm – this not only occurs coercively (through the referral of people for psychiatric treatment following arrest by the police, for example, cf. Rogers, 1990), but also voluntarily (Rose, 1989). Thus the diagnosis of madness through the use of differentiated various sub-classes can be seen as a form of regulatory practice which operates a form of governance of the soul all the more subtle since it is driven not only by coercion but also by a desire to be normal (Rose, 1989; Smail, 1984). Such a position is extremely useful for a democratic state (Castel et al., 1979).

The creation of psychiatric categories can serve many cultural and political interests. Terms like 'anxiety' and 'depression', for example, locate the sources of fear and unhappiness within the individual by blaming biochemical changes or 'thinking errors' rather than the things people have been subjected to emotionally, physically and economically through their lives (Smail, 1984, 1987, 1993). The concept 'paranoia', enables suspicion to be pathologized. Thus the views of those we find uncomfortable and bewildering can be de-legitimized by locating them within a discourse of madness. Such categories are not used unproblematically in a one-way fashion, however, since many individuals and groups adopt 'paranoid' or 'conspiratorial' rhetoric to serve particular political ends. Thus, during her time as Prime Minister, Margaret Thatcher talked of the trade unions as 'enemies within'. Concepts like paranoia, then, delineate a discursive position in which one can locate oneself and, more importantly, locate others (Davies and Harré, 1990). It is in the creation of these subject positions that identities are created and transformed and it is to this that we turn our attention in the next chapter.

5

Pathological Identities

In previous chapters we have considered how 'madness' can be historically located and constituted within discourses of difference. In this chapter we want to consider the way in which types of identity are constructed in relation to psychopathological categories, and here we will be examining the identities that are constructed around the legal and clinical category of psychopathy. We will trace the category of psychopathy as it emerged in the context of the UK and locate its origins as part of the succession of typologies that followed the discursive construction of the issue of dangerousness (Foucault, 1978). In this way we will be tracing the evolution of the category as a set of texts and will be focusing upon some of the contradictions contained within them – contradictions which, we will suggest, reflect an attempt to integrate conflicting sets of clinical and legal discourses.

We will then move on to consider these textual realities as the material through which particular types of 'psychopathic identity' are formed. Through an account of how such identities are lived out within the discursive arena of the Special Hospital, we will illustrate the way in which contradictory or paradoxical forms of identity connect with underlying textual contradictions. Additionally, through an examination of the types of subjectivity that are implied by the inter-textual relationship between discourses about race and psychopathy, we will argue that language is significant in determining the individual's position and passageway through the mental health network. The deconstruction of the discourse of psychopathy, then, leads us to consider how psychiatric and prison institutions provoke and contain abnormal identities.

Language and identity

One way of considering identity is to see it as 'a theory about the self to which no ontological status is necessarily ascribed' (Kitzinger and Stainton Rogers, 1985: 168). We will argue that such theories are always conveyed in language and that they may take the form of something akin to *autobiography*. Harré (1983) argues that it is through autobiography, a linear structure that permits past, present and future to be bound together, that forms of personal and social identity take shape. In this chapter we

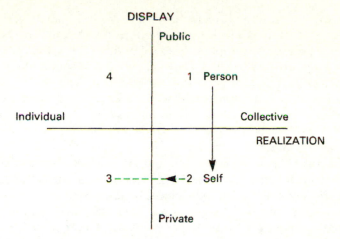

Figure 5.1 *Harré's dimensions of psychological space*

wish to employ Harré's 'Grid of Psychological Space' (1983) as a means of conceptualizing the way in which clinical discourses impact upon individual autobiography, thereby influencing both the types of subjectivity and identity that are brought into being. The grid of psychological space is represented in Figure 5.1.

As can be seen, the grid comprises four quadrants formed through the intersection of two poles. The first pole runs along an individual–collective continuum, where the person represents idiosyncratic characteristics to themselves at the individual end and the collective contains shared character-istics. The second pole runs along a private–public continuum, the former being a domain in which activities are carried out alone, and the latter in which activities are enacted in the presence of others.

Harré contends that quadrant one, the public–collective domain, con-tains the material from which psychological paraphernalia, such as the self, is constructed. Within this quadrant the self remains undifferentiated and in Harré's account it emerges as it passes into quadrant two, via a process of 'psychological symbiosis' (Newson and Shotter, 1974). In this process the child is developed as a cognitive, emotional and social being and comes to see itself as having both a point of view and as being the locus of action. In quadrant three the child reflects upon itself as the originator of action and point of view, being enabled to do this through, *inter alia*, having acceded to the personal pronoun. This serves a cognitive function, facilitating the organization of experience around a central point, the 'I', whilst simultaneously acting as a signifier that facilitates reflection upon and 'ownership' of that experience. Harré (1983: 257) argues that the movement from quadrants one to three involves the creation of 'personal being' through the 'transformation of one's social inheritance', that is through the assimilation and transformation of a network of signifiers, discourses, theories and metaphors. (There are parallels here with Lacanian theory in as much that the subject is 'located' by being fixed within a pre-existing conceptual system (Burkitt, 1991).) In quadrant four 'social being' evolves when, through a process of 'publication', idiosyncratic material is brought into the public arena. This might involve the publication of self as represented in a variety of ways, for example by specific signifiers, including proper nouns such as 'I', 'me', 'us', or proper names. Alternatively it might be through the publication of a particular discourse, metaphor or narrative.

Within this schema it can be seen that language is of central importance to the self and identity. Both are deeply enmeshed in the material structure of language and this enmeshment closes off the possibility of 'accessing' or 'discovering' a 'true' self that exists outside of language. Lovlie brings out this point by discussing the futility of Rousseau's attempt in *Confessions* to give a portrait of himself 'in every way true to nature' (1992: 127). He makes the (also Lacanian) point that the very process of writing (or speaking) takes Rousseau away from the quest for the fantasized 'true self' in that his attempt to describe this self, to unearth and delineate some kind of 'deep-structure', is distorted by the pre-given structures of, for example, metaphor and metonymy that are already embedded in the text. In a similar way, Middleton (1992) rejects introspection and confessional narrative as a means of finding out about the 'deep-structure' of modern masculine identities. He argues that to employ narrative is to enmesh oneself in pre-existing structures over which the writer has no control. These impose upon the story or account 'a more worked-out view point', and bias readings and understandings in a particular way. For example, 'the more self critical the tone of such writing, paradoxically the more virtuous the narrator will appear' (1992: 21).

The relevance of metaphor

The relevance of metaphor to our relationship with the world has been described by a number of writers (for example, Lakoff and Johnson, 1980). In relation to the self, Lovlie (1992) suggests that Western forms of subjectivity are constructed out of a complex of metaphors (and we can see such metaphors as being contained within Harré's public–collective domain). These act as a set of building blocks, from which particular types of selfhood are made possible. Lovlie cites such metaphors as the 'thread of life', which stresses continuity from the beginning to end of life, the 'circle', which emphasizes perfect harmony and integration and the 'core' – the idea of there being a centre, or soul, from which things grow and unfold. So fundamental is the material described by Lovlie in relation to the self, that it can be seen as acquiring the status of a 'root metaphor' (Pepper, 1942). The root metaphor is a linguistic device which provides the basic analogy around which whole systems of knowledge are organized.

Within a particular culture root metaphors acquire a taken-for-granted status as people become increasingly submerged within them. As such it becomes difficult to retain a reflexive understanding of such devices as metaphor, so that what were once tentative 'as if' ways of conceptualizing the world become reified and literalized.

The power of linguistic material, such as the root metaphor, emphasizes one of the challenges to a deconstructive approach. In exploring phenomena, such as identity, deconstruction might seek to expose the contingent and fragile nature of the linguistic material upon which identity is founded. However, in unmasking this relationship, real and tangible effects continue to be associated with their existence. In part, this results from the fact that the material is fixed within culture as both permanent and ubiquitous. The difficulty of moving beyond these structures is captured by Cixous who states that 'there are living structures that are caught up and sometimes rigidly set within historico-cultural limits so mixed up with the scene of History that for a long time it has been impossible (and it still is very difficult) to think or even imagine an "elsewhere" ' (Cixous, 1975: 83). Later on in this chapter we will consider the way in which the clients of psychiatry succumb to clinical discourse about psychopathy and how the ubiquity of particular types of discourse makes it impossible for their subjects to 'think or even imagine an "elsewhere" '. We cite Cixous here also as someone who has engaged with psychological theories in order to deconstruct them, and in order to present an image of the self which is something akin to a permanent deconstruction of identity.

Psychopathy, forensic psychiatry and disciplinary society

The roots of psychopathy can be traced back to the emergence of a set of practices – within modern assumptions about the nature of knowledge – in both the disciplines of legal psychiatry and the philosophy of law. Both of these arenas can be seen as reproducing and contributing to a reconceptualization of subjectivity.

Within the law, a significant shift can be identified in the abandonment of the 'classicist' tradition of punishment in which the scale of penalties was set in relation to the degree of perceived social harm (Foucault, 1977). This model adhered to the 'logic of retribution', discounting the need to pay attention to the individual's mental state, as the 'criminal was no more than the person to whom a crime could be attributed and could therefore be punished' (Foucault, 1978: 2). However, by the start of the nineteenth century, modalities of punishment had come to be focused upon 'rehabilitating' or 'treating' the criminal rather than punishing the crime *per se*. This shift is symbolized by the movement away from the body as the target for punishment 'to be replaced by a punishment that acts in depth on the heart, the thoughts, the inclinations' (Foucault, 1977: 16).

Within this new paradigm it was necessary, as a precondition for effecting treatment, first to *know* the criminal, 'his reasons, his motives, his inner will, his tendencies, his instincts' (Foucault, 1978: 9). It therefore became necessary to open up the mind of the criminal and a number of commentators have described how the nineteenth century saw the proliferation of theories postulating universal truths about the criminal, and the 'criminal mind' (for example, Forshaw and Rollin, 1990).

Knowledge of the criminal psyche was further supplemented by what Foucault (1978) has termed the construction of the issue of dangerousness. This issue was associated with the conceptual problems posed by a series of a-typical, horrific offences, occurring in the early decades of the nineteenth century. The offences linked with these cases were problematic in that they could not be attributed to either logical reasoning or existing conceptions of insanity. The latter were based upon the notions of *furor* and *dementia*, conditions that were identifiable by their external manifestations (excesses of passion, rage, anger etc.). In respect of these cases, however, the behaviour appeared to arise from a 'zero state of insanity' (Foucault, 1978: 4). That is, they struck without any prior warning in the form of external signs of disturbance on the part of the perpetrator. Foucault argues that they were explained through the creation of the concept of 'homicidal monomania' – 'the danger of insanity in its most harmful form; a maximum of consequences, a minimum of warning' (Foucault, 1978: 7). Foucault implies that this conceptualization significantly redefined existing notions of subjectivity by permanently inscribing the *possibility* of 'dangerousness' into the social body: 'The fiction of "homicidal mania" entails that the spectre of dangerousness permanently inserts itself into social life in that visible normality ceases to be a guarantee against the presence of a monstrous pathology' (Owen, 1991: 239).

Whilst the category of homicidal monomania has long since been abandoned, it can be seen that the definition of psychopathy that has emerged from the English medico-legal tradition, in which the condition is approximated to the notion of 'moral insanity', has much in common with it.

Psychopathy as moral insanity can be traced to Pinel who in 1801 described '*manie sans delire*', a condition characterized by bouts of violent, anti-social behaviour occurring in the absence of psychosis. Pinel suggested that this condition could be attributed both to early environmental experiences and to constitutional factors ('*instinct de furie*'). A similar elaboration is given by Esquirol in 1838 who coined the term '*folie morale*' to describe a condition characterized by 'impairments of the will and feelings, intelligence retaining its integrity' (quoted in Pichot, 1978: 56). Within English psychiatry in 1835 Pritchard described the concept of 'moral imbecility', the main indicators of which were the occurrence of irresponsible behaviour in the absence of any discernible mental illness. Maudsley supported this notion and, in an often quoted passage from 1874 here reproduced by the Eysencks, described it thus: 'As there are persons who cannot distinguish certain colours, having what is called colour blindness, so there are some who are congenitally deprived of moral sense' (quoted in Eysenck and Eysenck, 1978: 197).

All of these accounts emphasize psychopathy as a distinct clinical entity, which, despite the absence of clear biological or psychological correlates, is strongly associated with patterns of anti-social behaviour. This association has continued throughout the course of the twentieth century, being enshrined in successive mental health acts from the 1913 Mental Deficiency Act through to the Mental Health Act of 1983 where it is defined as follows:

> Psychopathic disorder means a persistent disorder or disability of mind (whether or not including significant impairment of intelligence) which results in abnormally aggressive or seriously irresponsible conduct on the part of the person concerned. (HMSO, 1983: 2)

Psychopathy takes as its object a particular type of pathological self. Following in the tradition of Pinel and Esquirol, numerous theorists have attempted to elaborate a satisfactory definition of the psychopathic self that can be accommodated within an orthodox, clinical framework. An initial observation, however, is that within this framework the notion of psychopathic disorder remains a contentious construct. Significantly, the term has no place in either of the major diagnostic systems (DSM, ICD); however, it does have analogues in the category of 'anti-social personality disorder', as specified in DSM-III-R (American Psychiatric Association, 1994), and in the ICD-10 category of 'dissocial personality disorder' (World Health Organization, 1992).

Roth (1990) suggests that it is rarely possible to encapsulate the traits of an individual within a single diagnostic category provided by either ICD or DSM. He, along with other theorists, delineates a fuller 'clinical' picture which includes features such as pathological egocentricity, immaturity, an inability to learn from experience, and an inability to display or receive affection. Some of these elements are incorporated in Cleckley's (1964) influential diagnostic criteria, which are themselves further reworked by Hare (1980), who suggests that a common thread to run throughout these criteria is an absence of 'interpersonal warmth', a quality which he sought to identify in his own 'Psychopathy checklist':

1 Glibness/superficial charm.
2 Grandiose sense of self worth.
3 Need for stimulation/proneness to boredom.
4 Pathological lying.
5 Cunning/manipulative.
6 Lack or remorse or guilt.

7   Shallow affect.
8   Callous/lack of empathy.
9   Parasitic lifestyle.
10 Poor behavioural controls.
11 Promiscuous sexual behaviour.
12 Early behaviour problems.
13 Lack of realistic long-term plans.
14 Impulsivity.
15 Irresponsibility.
16 Failure to accept responsibility for own actions.
17 Many short-term marital relationships.
18 Juvenile delinquency.
19 Revocation of conditional release.
20 Criminal versatility.

Culture as a problem for positivist accounts of psychopathy

Common to all of these descriptions is a tendency to employ existing norms of socially acceptable behaviour as a benchmark against which to measure or diagnose psychopathy. In part this is justified on the grounds that a marked disparity between the individual and society may be deleterious to both. For example, the psychopath's emotional detachment, shallowness, manipulativeness, egocentricity and impulsivity are traits that lead to the devaluation of the other, thereby potentiating anti-social behaviour.

However, the relationship between social norms and psychopathic personality has been a particular concern to positivist exponents of the psychopathy concept on the grounds that research has consistently failed to identify a particular personality type with which particular forms of disordered behaviour, emotion and cognition can be associated. In reviewing existing literature, Blackburn (1988: 511) points to the fact that previous studies have failed to identify 'a single type of abnormal personality which is prone to chronic rule violation' and have made the 'taxonomic error' of confusing social deviance with personal deviance. In a separate article, he concludes that 'Psychopathic disorder or anti-social personality are simply umbrella terms which cover a mixed group of people who have in common only a history of socially deviant behaviour' (Blackburn, 1990: 57).

Herein lies a major difficulty in the diagnosis of psychopathic disorder: in the absence of clear aetiological factors – no proven biological substrate exists and there is ambiguity as to the psychological causation (Blackburn, 1988) – a tautological inference occurs in which the disorder has come to be deduced from the behaviour which it is supposed to explain.

This problem has continued to dog psychopathy throughout its history. Levenson (1992) highlights some of the absurdities to which this can lead.

He concurs that, in practice, psychopathy is linked with socially deviant behaviour and adds to this by arguing that social deviance is itself defined by a failure to conform to the prevailing social norms. Hence: 'opponents of Nazi rule in Nazi Germany, opponents of segregation in the American south and Apartheid in South Africa and, currently, Americans who are not devoted to increasing their consumption display "a psychopathic trend" ' (Levenson, 1992: 54). He also argues that what is defined as pathologically anti-social behaviour also reflects a commitment to prevailing social values and points out that DSM-III-R criteria for Anti-Social Personality Disorder make no reference to: 'such practices as "despoiling the environment and destroying other species for personal profit", "manipulating others to their detriment in the conduct of management", "destroying the long term productive capacity of an economy in the interest of short-term profit" or "using deceptive practices to obtain public office" ' (Levenson, 1992: 55).

Discourse, race and psychopathy

A further illustration of the association between normative, culturally based judgements and, supposedly objective clinical categories is provided by the relationship between ethnicity and psychopathy. This is an area that, hitherto, has received little attention within the theoretical literature. We have focused upon it here since we regard 'race' as a powerful political and discursive phenomena and therefore see the inter-textual relationship between race and psychopathy as a cogent example of how linguistically based realities can determine both the individual experience of mental health and the individual's location within the mental health system.

Statistical differences in the frequency and severity of mental distress and the rates of psychiatric diagnosis within ethnic groups are now widely known and have already been considered in Chapter 3. In that chapter we saw that patterns of 'over-representation' within in-patient psychiatric settings have been described amongst Asian and black people, the latter generally characterized as being more likely to be diagnosed as suffering from mental disorder (in particular schizophrenia) than their white counterparts. Additionally we saw how black people were more likely than white people to be coercively introduced, and maintained, within the psychiatric system through the use of compulsory detention procedures.

There is general agreement that black people's experience within the criminal justice system parallels their experience within psychiatry, in that ethnic minority groups are heavily 'over-represented' at all levels. The net result of this trend is a disproportionately high percentage of black people in the prison system. In total, ethnic minority groups comprise 15.5 per cent of the male prison population, the majority of these (10.7 per cent) being drawn from the West Indian/Guyanese/African subgroup. This is a striking statistic given that the latter group constitutes only 1.2 per cent of the total UK population, with ethnic minority groups, as a whole, comprising between 4 and 5 per cent of the population (NACRO, 1991: 11).

Given the association between the diagnosis of psychopathy and anti-social behaviour (Blackburn, 1988) and the allegedly arbitrary distinction which is often made between the presentation of 'ordinary' offenders in the prison system and people detained in hospital as 'treatable' psychopaths (Allen, 1987; Collins, 1991), it might be assumed that out of this confusion significant numbers of ethnic minority groups, who had committed anti-social offences, displayed histories of anti-social behaviour – leading to their receiving custodial prison sentences – might, in time, find themselves receiving a diagnosis of *psychopathic* disorder, leading to their detention in secure psychiatric settings. If, however, the patient data for Regional Secure Units and Special Hospitals is examined – the institutions most likely to undertake the care and treatment of such people – the *reverse* of this pattern is seen to be true.

In respect of Regional Secure Units, a number of studies have demonstrated that despite an excess of black patients, there is a corresponding absence of black patients detained under the legal category of psychopathy (Cope and Ndgewa, 1990; Jones and Berry, 1984). Within the Special Hospitals a similar discrepancy exists. Whilst ethnic minority patients form a disproportionately high percentage of the overall patient population (according to the Special Hospital Data Base) there are comparatively few ethnic minority patients detained under the legal category of psychopathy. Norris's (1984) study of the discharge and integration of patients from Broadmoor noted an association between ethnicity and diagnosis: 64 per cent of white British patients were diagnosed as schizophrenic and the majority of the remainder as psychopathic whereas for the 'non-white' population, 92 per cent were diagnosed as schizophrenic and only 8 per cent as psychopathic.

One way of accounting for this contradiction is to consider the commensurability of discourses about psychopathy and the types of object that racial discourse constructs. In this way Stowell-Smith (1995) considered how there appeared, on the one hand, a crude fit between what was commonly defined in theoretical literature as both the 'core' features of white, male subjectivity and the core features of psychopathy and, on the other hand, an antagonistic relationship between these same core elements of the psychopathy concept and the psychological features attributed to the black male.

We have already noted some of the key elements in theoretical discourse about psychopathy. Historically, these discourses gave rise to a particular typology – that of homicidal monomania – in which anti-social behaviour was identified with a particular model of mind. In the present day, the 'mind' is substituted for personality but there is common ground in that the existence of this mental entity is again linked with the occurrence of anti-social behaviour. The previously described study by Stowell-Smith (1995) sought, amongst other things, to explore the relationship between pro-fessionals' pragmatic application of the psychopathy concept and their formulation of the black 'psyche'.

One association noted in this study was that psychopathy was more loosely identified as an individual pathology expressed as what were construed as an exaggeration of 'normal' traits. Normal traits included the need for autonomy and mastery. When expressed in their exaggerated form they were described as leading to a 'misalignment' between the individual and their community. In order to remedy this, psychothera-peutic intervention was deemed necessary. This was focused at the level of the *individual*, an objective of treatment being the encouragement of responsible individualism as a precondition of living a more satisfactory life within the community.

Race as discourse has been considered by a number of theorists. Miles (1989: 10), for example, argues that racial discourse can be conceived as a system of signifiers which emerge in a 'dialectic between Self and Other in which the attributed characteristics of Other refract contrasting character-istics of Self, and vice versa'. Sampson (1993a, 1993b), writing in the United States, considers race another manifestation of this self–other relationship, arguing that definitions of racial minority groups emerge against the background of the absent standard of the white, 'United Statesian', norm. Both Mercer (1986) and Wetherell and Potter (1992) offer similar accounts, arguing that 'race' and the related concepts of culture and ethnicity, can act as a linguistic resource through which various forms of subjectivity are brought into being.

The introduction of discourse about race and culture into the clinical domain is usually seen as having the benign motive of relativizing difference and facilitating understanding of other cultures. In the study considered here, it was apparent that whilst discourse about race and culture might, at one level, be offered as having a potentially universal application, at another level they remained firmly focused upon *black* patients, evoking images of difference and otherness.

These images were particularly apparent in transcultural accounts of mental disorder. These accounts appeared both as a coherent network of statements in themselves and as a code term for that of 'race'. For the black patient, culture was presented as a source of psychological sustenance or need. A corollary of this position was that, whilst dislocation from the native culture was conceived as being potentially pathogenic, relocation within its nurturing presence appeared to hold out therapeutic opportuni-ties. In this sense, discourse about culture provided a theoretical gloss (postulating group identification as a psychological need for black people) which reinforced some of the cruder images, directly elicited from interview participants, concerning the communal aspects of the black 'lifestyle'. An effect of this type of discourse is that idiosyncratic features of the black subject were not visible: the 'healthy' black subject was seen as one who was perfectly intertwined with his or her culture, to such an extent that they could almost be regarded as a cipher for that culture.

Accounts which defined the white subject, however, were organized around a quite different set of themes. Most conspicuous amongst these was the emphasis upon the existence of intra-psychic qualities, such as 'the unconscious' and 'cognitions', and 'morbid' individual qualities, such as 'dangerousness'. These seemed to create a pre-given 'inner-world' for the white subject, setting him *apart* from the socio-cultural context and endowing him with a sense of *individuality*. The white subject was located as an intact part of a dichotomous relationship between the individual and the external world. The 'healthy' white subject was the one who was able to attain mastery and autonomy over the threats of the external world. The type of perverse individualism associated with the notion of psychopathy, therefore, seems quite incompatible with normative assumptions made about black, male subjectivity. Hence, Glenn (1967, quoted in McCord, 1982: 89) might not mention skin colour in describing the psychopath thus: 'The hero of our age is the psychopath . . . Free from responsibility, free from guilt, free from anxiety, he pursues his goals. Corporation presidents, statesmen, educators, physician: his calling is irrelevant; his features are everywhere the same.' However, we intuitively realize that the psychopath which he ironically describes here, could not be anything other than white.

The psy-complex and the enduring appeal of psychopathy

In previous sections we have considered some of the pessimism concerning the possibility of coherently defining psychopathy as a clinical entity. This pessimism is reproduced in attempts to specify and implement appropriate forms of treatment.

Pessimism about treatment can be dated back to the 1960s when a consensual view emerged that the 1959 Mental Health Act had been over-ambitious in the role it had extended to psychiatry in the 'treatment' of psychopathy. This trend was acknowledged by the appending of a treat-ability requirement to psychopathy in the 1983 Mental Health Act, something which limited the number of NHS clients: Dell and Robertson (1988: 127) report that in 1984 there were only five such men detained in NHS hospitals under section 3 of the 1983 Mental Health Act.

The results of research examining the effectiveness of treatments for people defined as having a psychopathic disorder is, in general, either equivocal or disappointing. A general impression is gained of an attitude of scepticism towards the possibility of successful treatment. Dolan and Coid

(1993: 267) acknowledge this attitude but add that researchers have repeatedly failed to develop strategies for either proving or disproving the effectiveness of treatment with psychopaths, and they suggest that scepticism about the 'treatability' of psychopaths 'may, in part, result from the professionals' inadequate assessment in the first place, followed by an inability to develop, describe and research and adequately demonstrate the efficacy of treatment strategies'.

Some of this scepticism is contained in the belief about the psychopath's facility to display a level of institutional adjustment which conceals their underlying propensity for further anti-social behaviour. Faulk (1990), for example, discusses studies which have evaluated Grendon psychiatric prison (an institution which contains inmates broadly categorized as being psychopathically disordered). He suggests that when compared to a comparable prison population they showed a greater degree of adjustment and reduced neurotic symptomatology; however, levels of anti-social behaviour – reflected in rates of reoffending – at both a two- and ten-year follow up, showed no difference. As a specific example of this trend, Roth (1990: 447) cites the case of Graham Young who poisoned three people, passed through Broadmoor but soon after being discharged committed similar offences, this time poisoning a group of workmates, and Roth writes that having been arrested, 'At home were found Nasi [sic] emblems, drawings of graveyards and other objects affecting sadistic fantasies. In his many years of confinement in Broadmoor he had been quiet, inoffensive and well behaved.'

Doubts about the usefulness of treatment, allied to the previously described difficulties in offering a satisfactory description of psychopathy, underpin the debate as to whether the category of psychopathy might be removed from the mental health legislation. Ramon (1986) argues, however, that neither elasticity of definition nor difficulties with treatment are sufficient to dislodge psychopathy from its place within the mental health system. She points out that up until the 1940s psychopathy received little attention within mainstream English psychiatry and argues that events during the Second World War changed this. Two factors are particularly significant. First, the need for cohesion and productivity during the war led to an expansion of the 'psy-complex', and to the psychologization of several types of socially undesirable, non-productive behaviours. In this sense it reflected the increasing association between psychology and productivity in which 'the adequate and . . . the optimum functioning of the individual's subjectivity has been redefined in terms of its relation to production' (Miller, 1986: 173). As evidence of this association, Ramon points out that, during the war, the death penalty for desertion was revoked and deserters were more inclined to be treated as having definable psychological needs – needs which could possibly be met by the work of Foulkes, Bion et al. on the treatment and resocialization of psychiatrically disturbed soldiers (a category which was assumed to include psychopaths) through the use of therapeutic community. Secondly, there was a need to account for atrocities committed not just by the enemy but by the allies. Ramon suggests that the concept of psychopathy provided a useful means of promoting a psychological explanation that shifted blame away from wider social influences and on to individual psychopathology (Ramon, 1986).

Ramon, therefore, argues that psychopathy continues to provide yet another conceptual location within disciplinary society through which particular forms of subjectivity come to be inscribed, positioned and regulated. Its enduring appeal is based upon those features which provided the impetus for its increased popularity during the Second World War, namely its capacity for providing a medico-legal basis for accounting for and organizing persistent offenders whose anti-social, non-productive behaviour could not be readily understood or dealt with either by the existing criminal justice or welfare systems.

Legal and clinical elements in discourse about psychopathy

We saw earlier how both historical and contemporary applications of the category of psychopathy integrated elements of both legal and clinical discourse, the former pertaining to issues of control, the latter to issues of pathology and treatment. This is particularly apparent when the position of patients detained in Special Hospitals under the legal category of psychopathy is examined. We also described how psychopathy has received limited attention within mainstream psychiatric institutions and that, in general, the containment of psychopaths has been restricted to forensic institutions. This trend reflects the need to provide a degree of control over the anti-social behaviour of the psychopath no longer available in general psychiatric settings, whose movement away from segregative control effectively meant that only secure institutions had the facilities to manage the particular set of problems posed by this group (Pilgrim and Rogers, 1993: 143).

For a variety of reasons, the treatment of psychopathy is something which has been focused upon in the three English Special Hospitals – Broadmoor, Rampton and Ashworth. The most recently available statistics have shown the population of psychopathically disordered patients to stand at 386, comprising 24 per cent of the total Special Hospital population. In all but two cases each person was detained under sections of the 1983 Mental Health Act (Hamilton, 1990).

Critical historians, who have eschewed the traditional narrative of enlightenment and progress within which conventional accounts of the 'rise' of psychiatry are often written, have noted how, from their earliest origins, segregative regimes, such as Special Hospitals, have always embraced issues of control. The issue of control is made explicit within the

Special Hospital, its legal foundation – the 1977 National Health Service Act – requiring it to provide both 'treatment' and 'security'. Richman and Mason (1992) comment upon the way in which Special Hospitals employ a vocabulary laden with terms such as 'care' and 'treatment' which has many similarities to that employed in other medical establishments. However, in the context of the Special Hospital, these similarities may be illusory. Hence medical concepts, such as 'care' and 'treatment', are imported into the Special Hospital but, when linked to those criminological and custodial concepts which are more indicative of the need for control, they acquire a quite different meaning and purpose. Tensions emerge when patients have successfully completed their 'treatment' or 'care programme' but are either still under restrictions or are still considered dangerous by outside agencies, and hence cannot leave the hospital (Bowden, 1981; Gostin, 1986).

Some of these contradictions are brought out by studies which have shown length of stay in the Special Hospital to correlate with severity of offending behaviour, rather than psychological functioning (Norris, 1984). Hence the more severe the offence, the longer the treatment required. The control/treatment association has also been highlighted by Grounds (1987), who studied the transfer of inmates from prison to Special Hospital between 1960 and 1983. He noted that through the course of this period, sentenced prisoners were likely to be referred to hospital at a point increasingly nearer to their earliest date of release. This trend suggested that the control and prolonged custody of the inmates, rather than their 'care' and 'treatment' was the prime consideration amongst both the referring agents and those institutions which received them.

A similar picture is developed by Dell and Robertson (1988) in their account of 'non-psychotic'(that is, psychopathic) men in Broadmoor. Their study makes a number of salient points. First, at the time of the study, treatment appeared to be given a low priority, with only a minority of men – 35 per cent – participating in any form of psychological therapy. The authors estimated that for the majority of their time in hospital, 'non-psychotic' men were engaged in no specific treatment. Secondly, an attitude of scepticism towards treatment was elicited from Broadmoor consultants. Consultants were often unable to define the specific help required by patients which they had admitted under the psychopathic category, and in only 38 per cent of cases was it expected that the provision of psychological treatment would make more of a difference than the simple passing of time. Thirdly, despite the complexity of issues surrounding the discharge of patients from the hospital, one factor remained constant; no one detained under this category was proposed for discharge before a period of 3 years after their admission had elapsed. Dell and Robertson (1988: 116) conclude from these facts that, whilst it might be officially denied, patients admitted to Special Hospital under the psychopathic category were expected to pay back 'time for crime'. Considered together these studies suggest that clinical, treatment issues share at least an equal, if not subordinate status, to custodial and legal ones.

Discourse, identity and psychopathy in the Special Hospital

Our analysis of the category of psychopathy has so far thrown up three interrelated themes: first, the emergence of the category as a typology constructed as a form of subjectivity made possible within the modernist episteme; secondly, an uneasy relationship between 'scientific' models of psychopathy and wider social norms; and thirdly, in relation to the above, a set of scientific, clinical practices – constituting the psychopath as a definable, 'researchable' entity – and a more pragmatic, non-clinical set of applications, containing a significant legal element, and being connected with the containment and detention of psychopaths within secure regimes.

In this concluding section we will seek to integrate a number of these themes by considering an empirical example of how particular discourses are played out within the setting of the Special Hospital (an arena that we will liken to Harré's public–collective domain) and how such discourses operate, through the processes of assimilation and publication, as a linguistic resource through which individuals, who have received a diagnosis of psychopathy, make sense of themselves and others.

In the study briefly described here, an attempt was made to identify and delineate the various accounts and modes of talk about psychopathy shared amongst a staff and patient population within a Special Hospital. Accounts of psychopathy were identified primarily through the application of Q-methodology (McKeown and Thomas, 1988), a type of pattern analytic approach that purports to identify configurations of propositions within a population of interest. In this study the propositions were derived from two sources – from the theoretical literature on psychopathy and from semi-structured interviews conducted with patients and staff within the Special Hospital. Sixty-one statements about the cause, definition and treatment of psychopathy were derived from these sources and these were then sorted along a response matrix (agree/disagree) in accordance with a forced free response format. Forty participants completed the Q sort, comprising 31 professional staff, from a range of disciplines and nine patients, all of whom were detained under the legal category of psychopathy. The responses were factor analysed and the propositions, constituting the emergent factors, interpreted. The interviews from which some of these statements were derived were transcribed and provided a source of data to illustrate some of the possible ways in which both staff and patients deployed and worked with the identified accounts. These accounts were considered as a series of conceptual locations, or texts, within which individuals, subject to detention by the legal category of psychopathy, could be 'read' and 'positioned' (Davies and Harré, 1990). The results of this small study reflected a wide spectrum of descriptions of psychopathy. Analysis identified six interpretable factors and brief details of these are given below.

1 *'The treatable psychopath'*. This factor affirmed the role of adverse life experiences and environmental factors in influencing the aberrant behaviour of the psychopath. It dismissed the relevance of intrinsic, biological features or fixed psychological traits and, for these reasons, seemed to offer the hope of change through the receipt of psychological treatment and the provision of a more nurturing environment.

2 *'The autonomous psychopath'*. Deviant, anti-social behaviour is ascribed to volition and is not attributable to environmental factors. Psychopathy is located as a form of 'lifestyle' which certain individuals have elected to adopt. In a similar way psychopaths can 'will' their own recovery. Consistent with this account, one interview participant – a patient – described a critical moment in his life when he was confronted with a choice between a conventional or more anti-social lifestyle and chose the latter.

3 *'The victims of labelling'*. Psychopathy is presented as a label that makes arbitrary distinctions between groups of people. It therefore has little scientific value but survives as a legal category which is employed to regulate and detain in secure institutions unconventional, non-conforming groups or anti-social groups.

4 *'The separate population'*. This factor downplayed the causal signifi-cance of life experience and the environment to the development of psychopathy and constructed the psychopath almost as a separate species, with unique, idiosyncratic characteristics. Within this narrative the core features, or inner reality, of the psychopath were presented as immutable so that a propensity for anti-social behaviour was preserved.

5 *'Psychopaths have an appearance and a reality'*. This appealed to notions of the psychopath having an underlying 'depth-reality', which was inherently bad, evil and unchanging, and a 'surface-appearance' through which superficial conformity to social and institutional norms were affected. Illustrative of this position was one interview participant who spoke of an inmate at Grendon Underwood, whom she described as being psychopathic, as 'having a first class honours degree in Grendon language'.

6 *'Psychopathy is an objective scientific label'*. This presented a conven-tional empiricist account of psychopathy, representing it as a category that is neutrally and accurately applied to describe an already intact group of people.

The relationship between power, language and the self was implied by the fact that despite the fact that many of these accounts did not seem particularly 'user friendly' to psychopaths – appearing to express a combination of cynicism and therapeutic pessimism – here was evidence, provided in interviews with patients, of them being readily taken up. There are several possible reasons for this. One explanation might be that the accounts of psychopathy identified by Q analysis were amongst the more powerful or plausible ones in circulation within the institution and, in this sense, there were risks in failing to identify with them. Shotter (1993) has argued that everyday reasoning and discourse has a coercive quality to it, in as much that it is only by seeing and talking about things in a regimented or institutionalized way that we come to be recognized by other members of a community as responsible and competent. Barrett (1988) has indicated how this process might be augmented when it operates in psychiatric settings. He suggests that through repeated assessments and interactions with professional staff, patients increasingly come to define their experiences in relation to professional norms and categories and, as such, come to be seen as competent patients. The reverse of this, however, is that they risk rejection or discreditation through identifying with more peripheral, unorthodox forms of knowledge.

The accounts described here can also be seen as defining the boundaries of a particular conceptual universe. How we reflect upon and define ourselves is determined and constrained by the structures of knowledge available to us within that universe. As this study suggested that the above descriptions were amongst the more popular and visible, it should not be seen as surprising that they were deployed as part of peoples' everyday attempts to make sense of themselves and the world.

In interviews, the morally coercive pull of language organized through discourse was illustrated by the frustration of patients who, having initially expressed their opposition to the term 'psychopath', found themselves, during the course of the interview incorporating the term in their description of themselves and others. Here it seemed that the institutional vocabulary was so saturated with this particular lexical item that it became difficult to avoid using it. A number of interviewees expressed antipathy to the concept but then, as the interview progressed, found themselves employing the term quite readily. For example, one interviewee said:

> I mean you can channel, or perhaps . . . , you can channel your psychopathy into acceptable levels. I am conscious here that I am accepting the term psychopath but although I am constantly using it I still dispute it in a sense.

An additional feature of the discursive material identified concerned its contradictory patterns and practices. Some discourses are openly antagonistic (for example, 'The treatable psychopath' compared to 'The separate population' discourse). Whatever the explanation for this, variation must be considered highly relevant to the relationship between language and identity. Davies and Harré (1990: 46) have suggested that a proliferation of contradictory discourses allows for 'at least the possibility of notional choice' by giving to the person some freedom over which particular narrative or story to choose and engage in. Harré (1983) has argued that identity amounts to the assimilation of socially available theories and templates. Hence, by electing to be the subject or object of a particular narrative or discourse the individual can be seen as invoking the action function of language, deploying a particular account as an attempt to create a space or position within which a particular form of identity could emerge. For example, the adoption of an objectivist account of psychopathy might be associated with 'scientific' respectability, a labelling account with being 'radical', and an appearance reality account with being 'streetwise'.

The suggestion made here is that, in developing and working with particular types of contradictory narratives, interviewees were not being inconsistent, but were engaged in a form of 'identity politics', attempting to negotiate a favourable identity for themselves through the deployment of a chosen text. This perspective, which emphasizes the *action*, rather than referential function of language, allows us to see both the fluidity and multiplicity of identity. The types of psychopathic identity which we have described here can be seen as historically constructed, shifting political constructs, invoked for tactical purposes, rather than to maintain fidelity with some reified inner state. They appear as constantly shifting, momentary positions and the sense of movement which they invoke allows us a glimpse of the self as no more than a 'nexus of subjectivities' set in relation to different types of (contradictory) texts (Walkerdine, 1981).

For those who are able to grasp the action function of discourse, and are able to reflect upon themselves as the objects of a scientific discourse, there is the possibility of successfully resisting marginalization or devaluation. For such people, however, a threat is then posed by being too closely aligned with the social order and hence losing individuality. In this sense, Barrett (1988) has described how psychiatric patients, through the course of repeated assessments, come increasingly to define their experiences in accordance with a professional definition of psychiatric illness. As such they come to be seen by clinicians as 'competent' patients whose idiosyncratic qualities are swallowed up within global psychiatric categories. The task for such people, and for the patients in this study whose social identity is constructed within the narratives described above, is to retain a sense of uniqueness through resisting the oppression of dominant narratives.

The potential for such resistance is permitted by the notional choice that permits the manipulation of contradictory discursive material in accordance with the demands of the discursive context. This occurred within interviews as participants moved through a variety of different discursive positions. The following extract is fairly representative of this pattern. At an early stage in the interview the participant, a patient, appears to adopt an objectivist position:

> Erm, yes [*pause*]. Obviously on my definitions already I've shown or said about two different types of psychopath. Er, it's where you draw the line really. It's like

if you go up from the normal person to the primary psychopath, or whatever, erm [*pause*], there would be differences, yes.

At a later point the arbitrariness of diagnosis and definition is emphasized:

Erm, once again I'm gonna' come back to my personal being. I've been labelled at some stage a psychopath. Through talking to people and the relaxed atmosphere then I don't think I'm a psychopath no longer by whatever terms I was classed by in the first place.

Scientific notions of treatment were also derided when it was asked whether the provision of any kind of treatment influenced change:

Oh yes, it does, but once again it's very hard because, once again the people in authority, if someone has committed a crime to be a psychopath and then they're locked away for it erm, first of all you've got to do your time, basically. Once you've done the certain amount of time that's been set by the courts, whatever, erm, people can be a little bit over-careful. As I say it's hard for them because they've got responsibility to release somebody and not wonder whether they're going to reoffend. So they've got to be secure in their own minds, but I find it very frustrating when I know I'm alright now and trying to put that point across to the people who have responsibility.

The patient is therefore accepting the dominant discourse but combining this with a more peripheral discourse. One interpretation of this sequence is that by drawing upon this flexible repertoire the patient/psychopath is able to defend against becoming the 'model patient', the mere 'cipher at the centre of the role', by developing a position that is at variance with the established order.

Similar resistance could be offered by developing a position based upon a 'separate population' or 'surface/depth' story line, narratives which contradict and challenge the dominant discourses of objectivity and treatment. The positions adopted here might emphasize the inherent differences of the psychopath, and hence the impossibility of coopting them into the social order. Alternatively it might stress the fact that change through treatment represents only token compliance on the part of the psychopath. Underneath, the underlying personality structure remains 'intact' and hence 'individuality' is preserved.

Concluding comments

In this chapter we have sought to give further consideration to the way in which language influences our experience of self and of mental distress. We have explored this through an examination of the way in which subjectivity might emerge in relation to psychiatric texts. We have consistently avoided making the 'individual' the focus of our analysis, and have chosen instead to examine the discursive practices through which the individual – 'the dangerous man', 'the psychopath' – has been brought into being in relation to such texts.

We have noted how these texts are taken into the person, and provide types of self-knowledge and understanding. We also noted how the internalization of a particular text, or mental health category, such as 'psychopath', is associated with the practice of 'subjectification'; the subject of the text or category actively participates in a discourse that constrains and regulates their lived reality. As such, the text was always 'more than just words'. We have deconstructed notions of identity, here concentrating on psychopathic identity, to show how the self is always linked to context and must be situated in particular regimes of truth and power. We will consider further the nature of discursive power in relation to psychotic language in the following chapter.

6

Psychotic Discourse

This chapter looks at research on language, and the ways in which traditional psychiatric work on psychosis, which produces a circular argument to confirm existing labels, can be challenged. Some alternative theoretical approaches, drawing on pragmatic, psychoanalytic and narrative therapy ideas are described. Implications of each of these different ways of interpreting 'abnormal' talk are explored.

Clinical disorders in language

In previous chapters we have discussed the central role of language in the production of psychopathology. We have examined the ways in which cultural discourses enter into and inform professional narratives and have analysed how language is at the core of professional practices of diagnosis and classification and of the construction of pathological identities. We have seen how, by concealing the role that language plays in the production of clinical categories and practices, these categories and practices are naturalized and justified. In this chapter we will move from this analysis of the way language functions in constructing and justifying clinical categories to the way language is taken as the subject of clinical research. Our topic here will be research on psychopathological speech in psychiatry and clinical psychology.

This shift in perspective will allow us to complement the analysis we developed in the previous chapters with the examination of a series of new questions. First, we will use clinical research on psychopathological speech as one more example of how pathology – in this case 'pathological language' – is constructed by professional practices. We will look at the research and clinical procedures through which individuals come to be diagnosed as 'speech disordered'. Secondly, we will examine how the category of 'speech disorder' has been constructed by psychiatric research on language and speech. The argument we will pursue is that psychiatric research does not simply describe and classify characteristics of groups of individuals, but that it actively *constructs* a version of both normal and abnormal speech, which is then applied to individuals who end up being classified as normal or abnormal. Moreover, we will illustrate the mutual relation of support between clinical research and practice in reproducing clinical categories. We will see how research draws on existing clinical categories and how its results are fed back into the diagnostic systems. Thirdly, the analysis of research on pathological language will allow us to reveal assumptions about language and speech that underlie and make possible both research and practices of diagnosis and classification. We have argued in the previous chapters that language does not merely describe or explain, but that it constructs its object. Psychiatric language, embedded in research and clinical practices, constitutes the very 'pathological phenomena' it seeks to explain. Psychiatry, however, pretends to be scientific. It pretends to study and classify what is out there, in individuals' minds and bodies, in a neutral and objective way. This, we will argue in this chapter, is the effect of psychiatric denial of the constitutive role of language and of the adoption of the view that language is a neutral and transparent means of observing external reality. By looking at how psychiatric research has studied 'psychopathological speech', we will unravel assumptions about language and speech that underlie psychiatric research and practices. Finally, the criticism of these assumptions will lead us towards other theories of the nature and function of language and speech. In the second half of the chapter we will examine those theories. We will look at the way they can be applied in the study of 'psychopathological speech' and at the possibilities they offer for a non-pathologizing view of differences in language.

Although language is the main focus of this chapter – as indeed is the rest of the book – we want to point out that ours is not a fetishization of language. Language is a powerful means of constructing and maintaining 'realities'. In the case of psychiatric research on speech the realities produced involve pathologization, silencing and marginalization of the groups of individuals that fall under its authority. Since language has played a major role in this dynamic of pathologization, our aim is to use the same means to highlight it, and potentially overturn it. Our use of language is a tactical one. If psychiatric research and practice has been able to operate by leaving its underlying assumptions unarticulated and, therefore, unquestioned, our deconstructive task is to articulate those assumptions. By throwing light on them, we will be able to question them, reveal their contradictions and inadequacies, and open up the way to alternatives that would construct less pathologizing and more emancipating 'realities'. Ours is not a quest for truth, since there is no truth either in language or beyond it. If specific ways in which language is organized produce specific 'scientific truths', we aim to destabilize them and enable alternative 'truths' that will empower instead of marginalizing those individuals whose speech, experience and behaviour falls outside what has come to be defined as 'the norm'.

Our analysis of the language of psychopathology will focus on clinical research on psychotic speech. Due to the assumption in psychiatry that speech disorder is one of the main characteristics of psychosis, research on psychotic speech is much more extensive than research on the speech of any other psychopathological group. Furthermore, psychotic speech has been considered the extreme of pathological speech. Research on psychotic speech is, then, the best example for the analysis of how assumptions about normal and pathological speech are produced and how the polarity between them is constructed.

The concept of thought disorder

The study of psychotic speech dates as far back as the beginning of the century. Both Bleuler (1950 [1911]) and Kraepelin (1919) considered speech disorder one of the main characteristics of schizophrenia. This assumption is still prevalent today. Speech disorder is one of the main criteria for the diagnosis of schizophrenia and other psychotic disorders. Moreover, Bleuler and Kraepelin's claim has initiated extensive theorizing and research into the nature of psychotic thought and speech. Elucidating the mechanisms of psychotic speech has been considered a central way of understanding the nature of the cognitive and neuro-physiological factors supposedly responsible for a psychotic breakdown.

Kraepelin (1919) first established the distinction between disorder of the *content* of thought and disorder of the *form* in which thoughts are expressed. The former corresponds roughly to delusional thought, while the latter is used to describe disordered speech. The distinction has been retained to the present, with disordered speech described as formal thought disorder, or, simply, *thought disorder*. Despite claims that the term 'thought disorder' is misleading, because it equates thought and speech (Andreasen, 1979), and despite attempts to distinguish observable speech phenomena from inferred thought processes (Chaika, 1990), the term has survived to the present as one of the main criteria for the diagnosis of schizophrenia and other psychotic disorders.

Studies on *the prevalence of thought disorder* have shown that it is not a distinctive characteristic of schizophrenia, as was initially believed (Bleuler, 1950 [1911]), but that it is also present in other psychotic and non-psychotic groups and in normal speakers, especially under conditions of stress and fatigue (Andreasen et al., 1985; Harrow et al., 1987). Moreover, it has been acknowledged that not all individuals diagnosed as psychotic present thought disorder, and that the ones who do, do so only intermittently (Andreasen et al., 1985; Pavy, 1968; Rochester and Martin, 1979). Research on thought disorder has tried to address a series of problems opened up by these findings. First, the problem of why only some individuals diagnosed as psychotic present thought disorder initiated debates about whether a single underlying factor could explain both the presence and lack of thought disorder in different individuals or in the same individual. Secondly, the acknowledgement that thought disorder is prevalent in both psychotic and non-psychotic groups forced researchers to investigate whether specific groups could be differentiated by the nature and degree of thought disorder that characterizes them.

Research on thought disorder

The studies on the nature and characteristics of thought disorder can be broadly classified into three main categories: clinical, laboratory and natural language research (Harvey and Neale, 1983).

Clinical research

Clinical research emerged from the acknowledgement that the terms used to describe thought disorder in the major diagnostic systems (American Psychiatric Association, 1987; Spitzer and Endicott, 1968) – incoherence, illogical thinking, loosening of associations, impaired understandability – were too vague, and, therefore, unsuitable for valid and reliable diagnoses. The aim of the research was to operationalize the concept of thought disorder and make it more definable for research and diagnostic purposes. Data are collected from clinical interviews (Andreasen, 1979) and verbal testing sessions (Harrow and Quinlan, 1985; Johnston and Holzman, 1979), and the characteristics and degree of thought disorder are assessed by trained raters.

Andreasen (1979) opens the presentation of her 'Thought, Language and Communication Disorders Index' with the claim that thought disorder refers only to speech phenomena and that it should be carefully separated from inferred underlying thought processes. The Index she constructed, however, is supposed to measure both thought, language and communication failures. Other scales (Harrow and Quinlan, 1985; Johnston and Holzman, 1979) include even more divergent phenomena. They are designed to measure failures in the syntactical, grammatical and lexical level, failures to observe conversational rules, deviation from the rules of logic and commonsense concerns, and inappropriate affective and psychomotor behaviour. Leaving aside the question of if and how these scales measure the factors they are supposed to measure, the basic premises of such an enterprise need to be questioned. One wonders how such a variety of linguistic, communicational and behavioural phenomena can be listed under one concept, that of 'thought disorder'. The question becomes even more important in light of the fact that thought disorder is originally meant to define peculiar speech.

The scales are supposed to measure both the quality and the degree of thought disorder. For this purpose there are sub-scores, which give the measure of different groups of phenomena, as well as the total thought disorder score. Although the sub-scores have been used in some studies, it is the total score that is widely used in research and clinical work. The consequence is that individuals found to be 'thought disordered' can display a variety of speech and behaviour peculiarities. Two individuals with the same degree of thought disorder can present completely different speech and behaviour. Thought disorder has become an umbrella term under which any type of speech and behaviour peculiarity can be included.

The nature of 'disorder' is also quite problematic. Thought disorder scales are meant to measure deviance, but there is no discussion about what thought disordered individuals are supposed to deviate *from*. The norm is not the way 'normal' speakers talk. This is obvious from the fact that there is no discussion in the scales of the way that the majority of the speaking population talks. Moreover, normal speakers were also found to have mild degrees of thought disorder. The scales have been constructed with assumptions not about how talk is but rather about how talk should be. Thought disorder is, then, measured against a postulated ideal of speech and communication. We will discuss later what this ideal is.

The measurement of thought disorder based on these scales is performed by trained raters. The method of rating carries a series of assumptions. First, it presupposes that normal speakers have an intuitive knowledge of the rules of conversation and they can apply this when judging another person's speech. This seems to contradict the findings of the same studies that normal speakers can also be mildly thought disordered. Secondly, the role of the rater is supposed to be objective and neutral, and so there is no discussion of how personal, social and cultural characteristics of raters can influence their judgement and produce different scores for the same fragment (with the exception of Maher et al., 1987). Thirdly, the relation between speech and its impact on the rater is assumed to be transparent. There is no distinction between the properties of speech and the impression it creates on the listener. There is no notion that the listener's subjective understanding can mediate between the rating and the speech.

If we step back from these notions for a moment and read the oppositions that are at work here deconstructively, we will see some bizarre assumptions about the supposed nature of 'normal' speech. Here, normal speech is seen as completely pure and uncontaminated by any idiosyncrasy, as completely neutral, and as entirely transparent between speakers and listeners. Surely, we have to ask whether anyone ever speaks in that way, and to reverse the privilege given to this type of speech over the other 'abnormal' forms. Is not this version of normal speech itself very abnormal, and is it not the case that idiosyncrasy, bias and messiness are parts of 'normal' communication? The abnormal nature of this idealized 'normal' speech in the psychotic language research is all the more apparent when we turn to the way it is viewed in cognitive studies.

Laboratory research

Laboratory research was initiated by Bleuler's (1950 [1911]) claim that incoherence and abrupt or unexplained shifts of topic, which are character-istic of schizophrenic speech, are due to an intrusion of irrelevant associations in thoughts. Bleuler's model of schizophrenia was *a model of deviant cognition*: disturbed cognitive processes were held to be directly reflected in speech. Laboratory research has been trying to identify cognitive disturbances that are held to underlie deviant speech through the analysis of speech fragments produced in experimental tasks. The main areas of research are associational structures (reviewed in Schwartz, 1982), conceptual ability (reviewed in Reed, 1970), selective attention (reviewed in Maher, 1972), short-term memory (reviewed in Koh, 1978) and information processing (reviewed in Frith and Done, 1988).

The main characteristic of all these laboratory studies is the assumption that thought disorder is an effect of the failure of some cognitive or neuro-physiological mechanism of the psychotic subject. The aim is to identify that mechanism through various experimental tasks. The first problem with such an enterprise is the transparent relation that is assumed to exist between cognitive processes and speech production. Indeed, the relation between thought and speech has hardly been theorized in most of this research. The fact that there is not a one-to-one correspondence between cognitive processes and speech phenomena seems to escape researchers. The second problem has to do with the method of measuring these supposedly underlying cognitive factors. The measurement of cognitive deficits is carried out with highly structured experimental tasks which have nothing to do with actual everyday speech. The most important problem, however, is that once laboratory research has reached certain conclusions about the nature of thought disorder, laboratory task performance is often used as a method for the diagnosis of thought disorder. A full circle is, therefore, reached. Individuals with speech that is difficult to understand are diagnosed as thought disordered. Hypotheses are made about the nature of their *speech* deficit. Experimental tasks are then set up to measure that deficit, and the same tasks end up being a method for the diagnosis of thought disorder. The problem, then, is not just that 'many researchers have lost track of the fact that thought disorder was originally defined in terms of *speech* that was very difficult to understand and often nonsensical' (Harvey and Neale, 1983:174, emphasis in the original). The central problem is that a vicious circle is created where diagnosis and research encourage one another leaving their assumptions unquestioned, while maintaining the same practices.

It would be tempting, in the light of these artificial laboratory studies, to deconstruct the relationship between 'normal' and 'abnormal' speech by insisting, as we did earlier, that everyday speech is marked by just the kind of idiosyncrasy, bias and messiness that researchers pathologize, and that we should respond by privileging everyday language over the weird speech that occurs in cognitive studies. Before we take our deconstructive reading of this research any further, however, we should look carefully at what psychiatric research does when it looks at everyday 'natural' language.

Natural language research

Natural language research focuses exclusively on linguistic production. This type of research flourished out of the acknowledgement that a thorough analysis and understanding of the features of psychotic speech are prerequisites for any hypotheses concerning the nature and cause of the psychotic breakdown. The studies were set up to describe the peculiarities of psychotic speech by comparing it with that of other psychopathological groups and of 'normal' subjects. Although attempts at explanation are occasionally made, natural language research tends to be mainly descriptive. Following developments in psycholinguistics, natural language research gradually moved from the study of the word to the study of the sentence and of discourse, meaning the overall structure of speech. Research on predictability and repetition (reviewed in Barr et al., 1989; Hotchkiss and Harvey, 1986) has been gradually replaced by studies of within and between sentence syntax (Allen and Allen, 1985; Fraser et al., 1986), cohesion (Rochester and Martin, 1979) and discourse hierarchies (Hoffman et al., 1982). Consequently, the claims that psychotic speech peculiarity is due to peculiar word and sentence formation (Chaika, 1974) have been succeeded by claims that the problem lies in that linguistic and logical links between sentences are deviant (Hoffman et al., 1982) and in that conversational rules are not obeyed (Dawson et al., 1980).

Natural language studies share the obsession with objectivity and formalism that underpins the rest of the approaches mentioned above. Some of them did devise ways of analysis that appear to be neutral and to measure directly the properties of speech (for example, 'type-token ratio', reviewed in Cozolino, 1983), 'within and between sentence syntax' (Thomas et al., 1990), 'cohesion analysis' (Rochester and Martin, 1979)). For others, the claim to neutrality is clearly problematic. For example, in the 'cloze procedure' (Cozolino, 1983), the 'reconstruction method' (Rutter, 1979, 1985) and the 'discourse hierarchies measurement' (Hoffman et al., 1982), the supposedly neutral role of the rater is questionable. It is not clear whether what is measured are the properties of speech or the impression speech has on the listener. Most of these studies leave the distinction untheorized. Hoffman (Hoffman, 1986; Hoffman et al., 1982) attempts to deal with this but finds himself in a dead-end. His argument is that there should be a distinction between speech and the understanding of it. He does also consider that the understanding of speech is subjective. He argues, however, that somehow the understanding of the listener correctly reflects the properties of speech. Our claim is that as long as scientific research holds onto the discourse of neutrality, it is doomed to fall into such impasses and contradictions. A deconstruction here needs to home in on the *meaning* that is made by speakers and listeners, a meaning-making that research on thought disorder seems unable to understand.

Criticisms of research on thought disorder

Research on thought disorder reflects the tendency of psychiatry to disregard the experience of the subject and to concentrate on formal characteristics of his or her speech. It is indicative that, while initially thought disorder referred both to 'disorder of form' and 'disorder of content', it increasingly became identified only with 'formal thought disorder'. Research on psychotic speech has *focused on the form* in which thoughts are expressed. Studies of content of thought (Gottschalk and Gleser, 1979; Oxman et al., 1982) are exceptions. Considerations of content do come into Thought Disorder Scales, but even in those cases the experience of the speaker is disregarded. Content is assessed only in terms of logical inferences from one sentence to the next (termed 'illogical thinking'), deviations from common sense, and the amount of information provided (referred to as 'poverty of speech').

A main characteristic of all these types of studies is the complete *suppression of the context of interaction*. Speech is taken out of the situation in which it was produced, and it is treated as an object that can be analysed and classified. But speech is not an abstract reflection of the cognitive state of the speaker; it is the dynamic product of a situation that involves speaker and listeners interacting in a specific time and place. Or, as Sally Swartz states, 'a text cannot be said to be simply incoherent; it is incoherent to a particular listener in a specific situation' (Swartz, 1994: 32).

This points towards another problematic issue in these types of research, *the role of the listener*. In many trends of research the role of the listener – and, consequently, that of the rater and of the researcher – are treated as objective and unproblematic. In the vast majority of studies the role of the listener is completely untheorized, while some have even argued that the feelings of the listener directly reflect the problems of the text (Hoffman, 1986). Only very few researchers have pointed out that the characteristics of the listeners *influence* the understanding, and, therefore, the rating of fragments of speech (Maher et al., 1987). By systematically confusing the properties of speech with the impression it makes on the listener, and by

ignoring the fact that understanding is not a direct effect of the properties
of speech but the result of an active interpretation on the part of the
listener, research reproduces dichotomies between normal and abnormal
speech and between abnormal speakers and normal listeners.

The most important problem with research on psychotic speech in
general is its *circularity*. In both laboratory and natural language research
the speech production of different psychotic and non-psychotic groups is
compared with the aim of finding the characteristics of either speech or
cognitive mechanisms (that supposedly underlie the speech) that could
differentiate the groups. The groups are thus taken-for-granted natural
categories, and researchers then assume that they will be able to find
underlying characteristics that must distinguish them from one another.
The fact that these groups are *constructed* by diagnosis is systematically
ignored. Furthermore, the diagnosis includes speech as one of its main
components. The groups are, then, selected by, amongst other factors,
their speech production and then their speech is scrutinized in order to
arrive at conclusions about its characteristics. Even worse, the results of
research are eventually incorporated into the diagnostic procedure, either
as descriptive concepts or as diagnostic methods. We have discussed above
how laboratory task performance tends to be used as a diagnostic instead
of explanatory tool. In addition, researchers on psychotic speech often
discuss whether the type of speech analysis they have devised can be used
for diagnostic purposes (Andreasen, 1979; Morice and Ingram, 1982). As
Maher and his colleagues have put it, as long as researchers analyse the
language features of groups diagnosed as such through language, they do
nothing more than 'discover "DSM-III" ' (Maher et al., 1987: 196). Now,
presumably, they will 'discover' DSM-IV, little suspecting that they are
engaged in powerful practices which actually reconstruct it every time.

The problem of comparing groups constructed by diagnosis becomes
even more pertinent since the criteria for diagnosis are either vague or
heterogeneous. Since the diagnostic criteria for 'thought disorder' are so
heterogeneous, individuals diagnosed as thought disordered tend to
display an extreme variety of linguistic phenomena. Comparing groups
that are internally so heterogeneous is doomed to produce inconsistent
results. Furthermore, treating the groups as internally consistent and trying
to extract the mean difference between features of their speech, besides
producing a false image of homogeneity, does not contribute much to the
exploration and understanding of the variety of linguistic phenomena that
one encounters in psychotic speech. It therefore hinders instead of
enhancing a more thorough understanding of the phenomenon under
study. We will argue in the next section of the chapter that examining in a
positive way this variability has much more insight to offer into 'psychotic
speech' than sterile statistical correlation.

Once we have acknowledged the circular and constructed nature of
psychiatric diagnosis and research on psychotic speech, two questions

emerge. The first concerns the answers that such an approach might be able to give to problems that research has been trying to deal with for the past decades. The second concerns the function that circularity has in the maintenance of psychiatric practices. One of the questions that research in the past decades has attempted to answer is why not all individuals diagnosed as psychotic actually present speech disorders (Chaika, 1990; Harvey 1983; Pavy, 1968). The fact that the individuals that present speech disorder do so only intermittently has also been addressed (Andreasen, 1979; Chaika, 1990; Rochester and Martin, 1979). Researchers working on the assumption that different subtypes of psychosis are due to the breakdown of certain cognitive or neuro-physiological mechanisms are faced with the task of identifying a mechanism which would be responsible for both the absence *and* the intermittent presence of thought disorder. The task becomes even more difficult given the heterogeneity in linguistic failures performed by psychotic patients. The search for a cognitive or neuro-physiological factor that could account for such a variety of linguistic phenomena in the speech of psychotic patients has inevitably been fruitless.

The category 'psychotic patient' is constructed through diagnosis, and so, as we argued before, the answer to the problems has to be sought in the diagnostic criteria. Speech disorder is one of the main criteria for the diagnosis of schizophrenia and other psychotic disorders but not a necessary one. This explains why certain individuals diagnosed as psychotic present thought disorder while others do not. Moreover, the criteria for the diagnosis of thought disorder are heterogeneous. This explains the variety of linguistic phenomena that individuals diagnosed as thought disordered present. As for the intermittent production of disordered speech, this can be much better explained by looking at the context of linguistic production than by seeking a mechanism internal to the subject that would account for it. As to why individuals diagnosed as psychotic tend to have more deviant speech production than non-psychotic subjects, the answer has to be sought not to their 'being psychotic' with all the implications the term carries, but to a series of other factors of the subject's condition and of the context. This will be further discussed below.

But first we need to consider the question as to why psychiatry has systematically ignored the obvious fact of the construction of the categories of psychosis and of the circularity between theory and research on psychotic speech. The answer has to do with the maintenance of the academic and psychiatric power. Facts do not necessarily correspond to an external reality. Facts are constructed by associations between groups of professionals and institutions, by practices that bring them into existence and maintain them. (It is not surprising that the same names keep turning up in reviews of mainstream research. There is a short-circuit in research on thought disorder in which the same people working in the different strands keep quoting and commenting on one another.) One of the prerequisites of the creation of facts is that their constructed character should be concealed. In this way they acquire the status of self-evident representations of external reality. 'Psychosis', 'schizophrenia', 'thought disorder' have acquired the status of facts through intense clinical and academic work over decades. It is their factual self-evident character that allows researchers and practitioners to continue analysing, diagnosing and treating individuals who carry those categories. It is these 'facts', reproduced by a series of associated practices, that have allowed psychiatry and clinical psychology to keep their power for the management of human distress over the past century. Facts do not represent a pre-existing reality, but they certainly create realities. And the realities constructed by 'psychosis', 'schizophrenia', 'thought disorder' are of an all-powerful psychiatric establishment which has the exclusive right and obligation to treat 'psychotic' and 'thought disordered' individuals.

Developing and deconstructing alternatives

The closed world of mainstream research into thought disorder now needs to be opened up, and we can now turn to some alternative ways of looking at language which take context, subjectivity and contradiction seriously. We should make it clear at this point that we do not see any of the three alternative approaches that we will describe as fully formed solutions. Each contains assumptions about normality and psychopathology that are problematic. Rather than look to them to save us, we explore them now in deconstructive spirit. That is, we use them to trouble the mainstream approaches to psychotic discourse, to block a return to mainstream oppositions between normal and abnormal talk. They are our deconstructive spanners in the works of the clinical truth machine. To use them deconstructively, then, we also have to think tactically, and give up the obsession with fixed truth that drives traditional research.

Speech as action: the tradition of pragmatics

Although the relation between speech and thought has been untheorized in most of the research on psychotic speech, the underlying assumption seems to be that speech is a direct reflection of the speaker's cognitive and neurophysiological state. The model of speech used in the majority of these studies is one of *communication* in a strict (and mistaken) sense of the term. The speaker and the listener are depicted in a contextual and cultural vacuum, and a message is seen as transmitted from the one to the other. Language is considered to be just a medium through which thoughts and feelings are expressed in a direct way (cf. Easthope, 1990). The ideal subject is held to be one who has mastery over their linguistic production. She knows what she wants to say and how to say it, and the message reflects directly the intentions and ideas in the mind of the speaker. The psychotic subject in this framework is the one who has lost this fundamental mastery. Psychotic discourse is described as the result of a breakdown in the ability to monitor one's own linguistic production (Frith and Done, 1988; McGrath, 1991). This argument is supported by debates in the psychiatric literature over whether psychotic subjects consider that their speech corresponds to what they wanted to say, and whether they are aware that they fail to communicate (Chaika, 1974; Harrow et al., 1989).

With the development of 'ordinary language philosophy' linguistics discovered that messages do not only convey information but that they perform acts (Austin, 1962; Wittgenstein, 1958). The assumption that language does what the speaker intends it to do is replaced by the recognition that the force of the utterance is dependent on a variety of linguistic and non-linguistic factors of the context (Levinson, 1983). The transmission of information takes its place as just one more of the many possible effects of linguistic interactions. The acknowledgement that types of discourses that are not strictly informative have an impact and produce effects opens up the field for positive research into types of interaction that would previously simply be considered to be 'communicative failures'. In the framework of research into psychotic discourse, pragmatics allows the shift from the polarity between communicative competence or failure to the study of what different types of speech do and how they produce effects.

This pragmatic approach leads us to look at speech not as an end-product that can be isolated and analysed, but as a part of a dynamic process. Instead of looking at the message as an object it allows an analysis of the *process* of its generation in a specific *context*. An analysis of psychotic speech should focus on the relation between speech and context. It should examine the way the context is encoded in speech, the relation between features of speech and features of the context, and the way both the speaker and the listener are positioned in relation to what is being said.

Unfortunately there has not been much research on psychotic speech which follows this tradition of linguistic analysis. Van Belle (1987), as one example, analysed assertive speech acts in conversations with 'schizophrenic' subjects in order to examine how the truth of what is being said is established. In most conversations the truth of what is being said is negotiated and arrived at by consensus between the speakers. Van Belle concluded that the truth of the utterances of schizophrenic subjects is often not consensually validated and, instead, it is granted to the listener or some other external authority. Swartz and Swartz (1987) argue that it is not possible to understand speech without taking into account the participants assumptions about how talk is and how it should be. By analysing these assumptions as they are expressed in comments on the interaction in an interview with a manic patient they showed that many previously incomprehensible utterances could become clear. In a later article Swartz (1992) demonstrated that misunderstandings in conversations with psychotic patients are often due not to the unintelligibility of the patients' speech but to factors related to the assumptions of the listener and the expectations that arise from the institutional context in which the interactions take place. Alverson and Rosenberg (1990) took up Labov and Fanshel's (1977) claims that coherence is not based on relations between utterances but between actions performed by these utterances. By uncovering the pragmatic force of the utterances they managed to reconstitute the meaning of an apparently incomprehensible fragment of schizophrenic speech.

The studies mentioned above constitute a positive step in the analysis of psychotic discourse in that they take into account the context of interaction and they examine the actions and functions that speech performs. They still, however, often take for granted the categories of 'psychosis' and 'schizophrenia' as properties internal to the speakers. A sense of individual unity and intentionality underpins this trend of research. Although language is not considered transparent, and it is acknowledged that the actions speech performs are not fully controlled by the speaker, speech is still seen as a mere tool speakers use for the production of actions and effects. Moreover, meaning is still conceived in a uniform way. The assumptions about the way meaning is constructed that underlie this type of research are different from those of mainstream psychiatric research. There is still, however, an assumption about 'normal' ways through which meaning is produced. The aim of the studies mentioned above is to show that behind the apparent disorganization of 'psychotic' speech there are 'normal' messages trying to be conveyed. We will argue that, despite the good intentions of the researchers, from the moment that 'normal speech' is defined, the polarity between 'normal' and 'abnormal' is bound to be reproduced. The very idea of 'normality' is founded upon the idea of 'abnormality', of that which lies outside the definition of the norm. A truly radical approach cannot be based on redefining and expanding the notion of normality, and then arguing that 'psychotic discourse' is inherently 'normal'. A deconstructive approach aims to break down and overturn those very categories. Only if the polarity between normality and abnormality ceases to exist can non-pathologizing ways of looking at difference be employed.

The discursive construction of subjectivity: a psychoanalytic approach

Certain trends within the psychoanalytic tradition have to a certain extent escaped this reductionism and have devised ways of analysing psychotic discourse that neither take individual intentionality for granted nor assume that meaning is constructed in a linear fashion. In psychoanalysis, speech also performs acts. These acts are not, however, performed through a conscious act of will of the speaker. The speaker is also constituted as a subject through her own discourse. The subject in psychoanalytic theory is not exterior to language. Language is not just a tool that the subject uses to express herself. The subject is born into a symbolic universe organized in and through language, and it is access to this symbolic system that gives to the subject a place within the human community. Language is, then, the space within which subjectivity is constructed. In every linguistic interaction, subjectivity is at play, negotiated between two subjects, affirmed or denied, recognized or annihilated (Lacan, 1977).

Kristeva (1969) and Barthes (1981 [1973]) epitomize this view of linguistic interactions. They criticize the dominant tradition in linguistics and the human sciences which views the subject as unitary and self-sufficient, who is the generator of her own message, assumes responsibility for it and uses language to express him/herself. To this concept of 'signification' they oppose the concept of *'significance'* which views discourse as a process whereby the subject gets constituted and altered by the workings of language. Speech, as a series of linguistic interactions, is not an activity but a *signifying practice*, a dialectical interplay between the subject and language, whereby they are both reproduced and transformed. The analysis of discourse should then examine the way in which multiple forms of subjectivity are constructed in speech through the different forms of encounter between the subject and language in specific contexts. In this framework the subject who controls her linguistic production is not a prerequisite but an *effect* of certain types of signifying practices, one amongst many possible types of subjectivity constructed in and through speech. The concept of 'significance' allows a shift from the simple problematics of 'control versus lack of control' to the analysis of the ways in which different types of subjectivity are also constructed and reproduced in discourse.

Irigaray (1985), for example, analysed how the speaker and the listener are constituted in psychotic discourse through the interplay between the 'I' and 'you' in speech. Discourse is the appropriation of language by a particular speaker in the actual moment of interaction. Discourse is always addressed to someone. The 'I', then, designates the speaker in the moment of appropriation of language and the 'you' designates the person to whom discourse is addressed. According to Irigaray the 'you', the addressee, is often missing in the discourse of individuals diagnosed as 'schizophrenic'. Moreover, the 'I' does not clearly correspond to the speaker at the moment of interaction. Third person pronouns are used instead and the whole mode of speaking appears to be detached from the situation of interaction. Irigaray concludes that 'schizophrenic' speech is a speech of citations and statements about statements; it is not a practice of pragmatically converting language into discourse. The consequence is that the speaker is not constituted as a unitary subject who produces and sustains her discourse but she becomes lost behind a discourse that appears to develop on its own and is not bound to the interaction.

Consoli (1979), also working in this framework, analysed narrations of individuals diagnosed as 'schizophrenic' as responses to and descriptions of a series of drawings. Narration presupposes a distinction between the act of telling a story and the events that are being described. Moreover, it presupposes a distance between the speaker and the story she produces; the speaker is both responsible for and detached from it. In 'schizophrenic' narrations, according to Consoli, both distinctions are lost. The act of narrating and the narrated events are merged. The story would thus be presented here as happening at the same time and as being as real as the act of speaking. Alternatively, elements of the situation of interaction would become integral parts of the story. Furthermore, the story would either appear as real and objective, not a fictional product of the speaker, or merged with the preoccupations and features of the speaker.

Both Irigaray's and Consoli's studies raise two important issues: the relation between discourse and context and the constitution of the psychotic subject through her discourse. Rosenbaum and Sonne (1986) address both in a comprehensive framework and arrive at similar conclusions about these matters. They argue that the 'I' and 'you' interplay not only constitutes the speaker and the addressee of discourse, but also that it is essential in linking discourse to the situation of interaction, and they point to the *physical* co-presence of the speaker and the listener. In schizophrenic discourse the 'you' does not constitute a stable listener, while the 'I' is replaceable by other elements. Consequently, speech seems no longer produced by the speaker and addressed to the listener. Others have taken up the place of the speaker and other discourses enter speech in an unmediated way. As a result the schizophrenic subject becomes dispersed behind a discourse she cannot sustain, while the discourse becomes detached from the situation of interaction.

These alternative studies and approaches move away from the traditional paradigm of speech either as a reflection of individual cognitive or neurophysiological properties or as communication. They still, however, assume that there are 'psychotic' or 'schizophrenic' individuals whose speech can be analysed and compared to 'normal' speech. Georgaca and Gordo-López (1995) have tried to overcome this assumption. They argue that subjectivity is not something inherent to the individual, but that it is discursively constructed in linguistic interactions. Unitary or dispersed subjectivities are, thus, constructed at different moments in discourse in order to serve different rhetorical purposes. Through an analysis of interviews with individuals diagnosed as 'psychotic' they demonstrate how a range of subjective positions – from the position of the unitary subject who sustains her discourse to the position of a subjectivity dispersed in different voices – are deployed in order to pose demands, distribute responsibilities or justify actions.

Psychotic discourse in this type of study is not pathologized by being compared to a norm or other groups. Neither is it normalized by claims that behind the apparent disorganization there are 'normal' messages trying to be conveyed (Alverson and Rosenberg, 1990). Both approaches reproduce a view of speech as transparent and neutral, and reduce speech to communication. It instead explores 'difference' in a positive way by analysing the various ways of making sense, doing things with speech and producing effects. Moreover, 'psychotic discourse' is not analysed as the speech produced by 'psychotic individuals'. Psychosis is traditionally related to disorganization and fragmentation. These, nevertheless, are not viewed as properties of individuals but as properties of discourse. If the term 'psychotic' has to be retained – and this is debatable – to describe exactly those characteristics, then it does not refer to 'psychotic subjects', meaning fragmented individuals, but to 'psychotic discourses', meaning discourses that make sense and have effects that are different from what is traditionally considered meaningful or intelligible.

Individuals diagnosed as psychotic do not form a homogeneous group that shares identifiable characteristics. 'Psychotics' are a group constructed by diagnosis which includes extremely diverse criteria, and, consequently, their linguistic production is as heterogeneous as any other randomly chosen group. But, at the same time, because of the diagnostic criteria, subjects diagnosed as psychotic are more likely to produce various types of 'unusual' speech. In that sense psychosis is an exemplary case for the analysis of the multiplicity of 'non-conformist' ways of making sense. Speech should not be examined with the aim of drawing conclusions about the cognitive, emotional or neurophysiological state of the speaker. Conversations should rather be seen as signifying practices, as dynamic processes between individuals in specific contexts. The subject of analysis is not 'psychotic speech', meaning the way individuals diagnosed as psychotic speak. It is rather 'psychotic discourses', that is to say, the multiple ways in which meaning is constituted outside discourses of communication.

Theory and therapy down under: deconstruction in practice?

In the last two sections of this chapter we have described alternatives to mainstream research on 'psychotic' speech. We have critically examined their potential, as well as their drawbacks, for the analysis of 'pathological' speech. Now we will move from the field of research to the area of clinical practice. We will examine a form of therapy that takes the function of language in psychiatry into account, and tries to devise methods through which psychiatric discourses can be deconstructed in clinical practice. While the previous sections were more relevant to researchers in the field of speech, this last section uses narrative therapy as an example of how the ideas outlined above can become relevant to practitioners.

An approach has developed out of the cybernetic systems family therapy tradition in Australia and New Zealand that provides an intriguing example of deconstruction in practice. There is a double-shift in this work. The first shift is from 'First Order Cybernetics', in which the family is seen as a system which produces pathology in a member (the identified patient who is the one who is seen by the family to produce the 'psychotic discourse'), to 'Second Order Cybernetics', in which the therapist sees the family as constructing their problem, but is then also *included* in the system. The pure, neutral and transparent communication from therapist to family then unravels, for the 'expert' is now part of the problem, and it is possible to see the patient as part of the solution. The second shift is from the language of the family to the wider discourses that circulate through culture, and now it is possible to ask what functions 'expert' knowledges about psychosis serve when they categorize certain individuals. Some see this double-shift as heralding the birth of a 'postmodern' therapy (McNamee and Gergen, 1992).

The deconstructive response to this, a response that explicitly links deconstruction with Foucault's (1977, 1981) observations on surveillance and confession is to separate the person from the problem, and to move the spotlight from the individual onto the system of concepts that holds them in place, and holds them in their distress. Narrative therapy (for example, Epston and White, 1989) looks to the ways in which the objectification of diagnostic categories and of people can be turned against itself. This deconstruction of the privilege given to certain forms of knowledge, and the internal unravelling of that privilege, is rooted in material practices of scientific classification and individualization.

> In the process of externalizing problems, cultural practices of objectification are utilized against cultural practices of objectification. The problem itself is externalized so that the person is not the problem. Instead, the problem is the problem. This objectification and externalization of the problem challenges those individualizing techniques of scientific classification and other more general dividing practices. (White, 1987: 52)

The process of questioning in this framework has been developed to help those who have been labelled by the psychiatric system to explore the way the language of 'experts' defines their experience, and to be able to redefine experience by striking a critical distance from the problem. This approach looks, then, to 'organizing therapy as a context for the new' (White, 1987: 54), and in this context a different relationship is formed between the person and the 'experts' around them. The questions focus on the ways the problem can be externalized and the 'unique outcomes' that escape the expectations of the family members and professionals who, up till that moment, have pretended to know best (and have believed that they do).

White's (1987) discussion of the predicament those who have been diagnosed as 'schizophrenic' find themselves in, reframes the 'career' they have to adopt as an 'in-the-corner' lifestyle. In the examples he presents the 'problem' is externalized by questions like 'In what ways have you felt pushed into a corner by schizophrenia?', and this externalized problem is then distanced further through identifying strategies that combat it: 'How do you think such steps could weaken schizophrenia's influence on your life?'. The context may then be treated, and so made manageable by stretching it to visibility, perhaps by reframing it as a variety of 'soap opera'. Resources are identified, and these may then be addressed to deal with what is usually termed 'relapse' in more traditional clinical interventions. Here, White suggests questions such as 'How are you going to teach your impatience that you can make your own discoveries at a pace that suits you and not it?'. In one example of the application of this approach in a group setting, O'Neill and Stockell (1991) used White's (1988) discussion of 'relative influence questioning' fairly systematically to code the transcripts from 18 weekly sessions with young men who had been diagnosed 'schizophrenic'. The participants were able, in the process, to move from one name they gave to their group – 'the Losers' group – to another – 'The Worthy of Discussion' group – and this transformation in *reflective, collective self-diagnosis* had effects on the rest of the community in the centre (Tapping, 1991).

This deconstruction in practice by those who are labelled 'schizophrenic' thus reverses the priority that is given to 'expert research' on thought disorder in which clinicians define who is disordered. The 'deconstructive therapy' we have described here is a way of drawing attention to the way sets of clinical categories that fix 'schizophrenics' are themselves part of a 'psychotic discourse' (White, 1991). When the problem is 'externalized', the problem is treated as the problem rather than the person, and we can then see how that psychotic discourse operates as part of the problem. It should be pointed out that some proponents of this still sometimes tend to push away part of psychotic language into the realms of 'illness', and will turn to 'psychoeducational' work on occasion to more effectively communicate with families about the nature of the experience that the labelled family member is suffering (for example, McGorry, 1991). This also illustrates the impossibility of holding a 'pure' Epston and White approach, and ensuring that it is not taken up and applied in ways that collude with traditional psychiatric notions, especially by focusing on particular techniques. The deference to a medical frame of reference when the distress is very serious then sits uneasily with attempts to develop a new 'co-constructed view of schizophrenia' (Lee, 1992). Nevertheless, there is a serious attempt to grapple with the way 'traditional understandings' operate as 'micro-practices', and the ways in which those who are fixed in place as 'the schizophrenic' can start to speak back, and redefine the uniqueness of their experience in a supportive context.

Concluding comments

Once the opposition between normality and abnormality has been deconstructed, and once positive ways of analysing difference have been found,
it is debatable whether the term 'psychotic' should be completely abolished, or whether it should be retained with a different meaning. This
question reflects more general debates around the practice of deconstruction. Is the aim of deconstruction to abolish completely terms that mark
the polarity between normal and abnormal? Is it not more useful to
overturn the distinction and retain the previously devalued terms, but
under a different meaning? If the term 'psychotic' was abolished, another
term would creep in to take its place once the chance is given for the
polarity to be reconstructed. By retaining the term, introducing it to
another framework, and giving it a different value, the danger of collapsing
back into the same distinctions can be fended off.

In psychiatry the term 'psychotic' refers to individuals, behaviours and
practices that deviate from a postulated normality, which is posited as the
ideal. We have taken several steps to deconstruct this polarity between
'normal' and 'psychotic' speech. First, we have shown how the polarity
does not reflect any objective qualities of speech, but it is constructed by
the very processes of research which seek to describe it. Secondly, we have
argued that what is presented as 'normal' speech is not the way 'normal'
people speak in their everyday interactions, but a sterilized contextless
form of speech which psychiatric theories have taken to be the ideal.
'Normal' everyday speech is much more messy than psychiatric research
holds it to be, and, therefore, cannot be clearly distinguished from or
opposed to 'psychotic' speech. Thirdly, we have claimed that speech is not
the direct reflection of the cognitive or neuro-physiological properties of
the speaker, but a cooperative enterprise between speakers in specific
contexts. The terms 'normal' and 'psychotic' do not, therefore, refer to the
qualities of the speaker but to qualities of discourse as it unravels in specific
interactional situations.

Our deconstructive unravelling of the polarity between 'normal' and
'psychotic' speech has transformed the meaning of both 'normality' and
'speech' in such a way that the opposition between 'normal' and 'psychotic'
cannot be sustained any longer. We do, however, retain the terms within a
different framework. In the framework we proposed towards the end of
this chapter the term 'psychotic' refers to variable and multiple discourses
that produce meaning outside what has been narrowly defined as 'communication'. From the moment this narrow view of communication is
reduced to just one amongst the many ways of making sense, then
what we defined as 'psychotic discourses' are not deviant, but different
forms of speech. Their study does not compare them to a postulated
norm but analyses them as 'different' ways of making sense. Moreover,

these types of discourses are not confined to the speech of 'psychotic' individuals, but are types of speech 'normal' people use to produce meaning. It would be tempting to push this deconstruction a step further, and argue that the psychiatric system of classification is a form of 'psychotic discourse' that positions patients as the ones with the problem. The term 'psychotic' is retained, but this time acquiring positive connotations. 'Psychotic' discourses become a subject of research and clinical practice in their own right, and their study under this perspective can reveal much more about the function of language and speech than the study of 'normal' communication.

7

Radical Mental Health

This chapter covers the development of alternative mental health movements. This follows our deconstruction of traditional discourse so far, and our commitment to transforming current clinical work by prioritizing areas previously silenced in psychiatric practice. In the previous chapter we argued that our object of analysis should be 'psychotic discourse' since, rather than lying within the individual, 'psychosis' should be located in discursive practices. Here we will give the argument a further deconstructive twist, and consider 'psychosis' as a property of the (unequally shared) collective discourses of psychopathology. If this sounds strangely unfamiliar or at least distinctly uncomfortable, then our deconstruction is a practical one. It may be unfamiliar to you because you are fairly new to psychiatric terminology and because the language of psychopathology does look like a bizarre self-referring jargon. It may be uncomfortable because you are used to this way of speaking, and we are throwing something into question that it is part of your commonsense. We intend to place individual existential needs in relation to the possibilities of political change, and we also enter into the characteristic grim humour of the psychiatrized patient at the spectacle of professionals rushing to defend the power of psychiatry with each challenge to the diagnostic criteria, and at the antics of 2,000 American psychiatrists who assemble periodically to reassess the situation and the fortunes of the DSM. If this chapter has a more ironic feel to it, that may be because irony is one strategy for surviving psychiatry.

We will be addressing some of the radical responses to psychopathology (Banton et al., 1985; Sedgwick, 1982), and asking how far they build a dialogue between reason and unreason. We argue that taking 'mental illness' as a reality is a bad way of doing this, and that we need to be aware of the way in which psychiatric power insinuates itself into practices that promise, at first sight, to empower 'users'. This power is evident also in the influence of psychiatrists in many of the alternatives that have sprung up over the years. We discussed some of these in Chapter 2, and we now turn to the more radical experiments that have developed. We will first examine how alternative histories are written and lived before considering the consequences of the Trieste experiment and empowerment work, as well as the experience of direct action in Germany and the US, and then the mushrooming in the UK of the Hearing Voices Network. The lessons we draw out from these movements emphasize the importance of context, politics and experience in radical practical deconstructive work.

Reason and silence

We start with a quote from Foucault's preface to *Madness and Civilization*:

> As for a common language, there is no such thing; or rather there is no such thing any longer; the constitution of madness as mental illness, at the end of the eighteenth century, affords the evidence of a broken dialogue, posits the separation as already effected and thrusts into oblivion all those stammered, imperfect words without fixed syntax on which the exchange between madness and reason was made. The language of psychiatry, which is a monologue of reason *about* madness, has been established only on the basis of such a silence. I have not tried to write the history of that language, but rather the archaeology of that silence. (Foucault, 1971: x–xi)

In this chapter we are concerned to prioritize a story which is silenced by psychopathology and its historians. To take one example, Jones (1993) in her scholarly history of the mental health services, describes the central role of social reform in her history of the Bethlem hospital but neglects to mention that in the folklore of the 'users' movement, this history began with the Bedlam riots, with protests *against* confinement, bad material conditions and lack of food. As Boyle (1990) makes clear, whether it is Clare (1976) representing the progressive nature of psychiatry or Sedgwick (1982) siding with the patient, writers in this field are all too often united in the assumption of the existence of mental illness as the starting point of theory and practice. They continue the 'monologue of reason *about* madness'. Let us start with Sedgwick, for his review of the anti-psychiatry movement provides such a powerful starting point for radical critiques. Even Sedgwick draws back from a social constructionist, let alone a deconstructionist stance toward the notion of mental 'illness'. He argues that 'In trying to remove and reduce the concept of mental illness, the revisionist theorists have made it that bit harder for a powerful campaign of reform in the mental health services to get off the ground' (Sedgwick, 1982: 41). Sedgwick was inclined to be dismissive of Foucault's anti-psychiatric romanticism:

> a historical period in which Reason engaged in an equal dialogue with Unreason is a useful counterpoint to our way of modern ways of dismissing the insane; but is unlikely to sample any further behaviour from the past than that of an intelligentsia which has always preferred to toy with 'madness' as a literary or artistic spectacle. (Sedgwick, 1982:135)

The charge of anti-psychiatric romanticism, which is routinely made against critics of the mad doctors past and present, is a common defence by the medical doctor, and here even Sedgwick is caught nailing his banner to the door. This critique gives short shrift to the expressive activities of the pathologized when they try to break from medical discourse. At the same time we need to remind ourselves that notions of 'illness' privilege the *form* of distress over the content of the distressing experience; this is typical, for example, of the treatment of hearing voices (what psychiatrists call 'auditory hallucinations') in the diagnoses of psychotic disorders, where whether the voices are in the third person or not is treated as being of greater consequence than what the voices might *mean* to the hearer. When Sedgwick refers to illness he is, once again, treating formal properties of experience as being more important than the content. The content of experience always escapes strict formal categories, but the poor patient cannot escape. The consequence for the patient is, then, the denial of their account, and even the denial of the possibility of a 'talking cure' which the naïve patient (for good or ill) has been led to expect of the psychiatric examination. The act of 'labelling' is now an imperative and the good patient must address the *clinician's* 'problem', the pathology, and pursue a prognosis through the bizarre semantic minefield of the psychotic discourse to which she or he is subjected, with questions as to when a hallucination is in fact a 'pseudo-hallucination' and so on.

In contrast, we can recover from Foucault's words not only a critique relating to the philosophy of science but the possibility of communication through deconstructed discourse. Instead of privileging (medical) reason, we want to open up a place for that which reason excludes to be able to speak. Sometimes, what it speaks will then appear to those on the side of reason not to make sense. However it is not just Foucault's elliptical style which accounts for the lack of reference to Foucault in the everyday battle against psychopathology (and here Sedgwick is right, for that style does have a particular appeal to the intelligentsia, and to their delight in mystifying people 'outside' the way it speaks). Foucault himself can be found later rejecting some of the ambitious claims he made in *Madness and Civilization* when, as a trained clinical psychologist, he grew away from German phenomenology and the concerns of the common insane (Macey, 1994). As we shall see, the political demands of 'users' of services, of 'survivors' of psychiatry, or of voice hearers were to be firmly stamped in terms of the *ownership* of experience, a demand sitting uneasily with the later more obscure foucauldian descriptions of subjectivity and contemporary radical public policy makers, those who think that it is enough to tinker with language and piecemeal reforms, those we might call the foucauldians in high places.

Competing discourses define the history and possible practices open to activists, and in addressing psychopathology they sometimes confirm those discourses again in different ways. Thus, writing within the discourse of (psychodynamic) therapy, Banton et al. (1985: 196), whilst seeming to sense the importance of 'power' in their foucauldian description, seek to make it therapeutic: 'radicalizing mental health can mean making public what is hidden, making open and generous what is confined, and making political what has been reduced to personal, silent pain.' We need to ask, though, what this would mean in practice.

We are attending to mental health history in a tradition of deconstruction, with a suspicious eye, with an identification with the most oppressed, and we are seeking to uncover a voice which is not normally acceptable in a text book or under the psychiatrist's gaze. From the outset we have sought to argue that the prognosis of psychotic disorder cannot be traced within the individual, or even within a simple combination of the individual and society, but through the analysis of *discourses*. The course of psychosis, theoretically and practically is punctuated by politics. That is, as part of psychiatric talk, they *construct* the phenomena they claim to discover. The discourses are split, they are fragmentary, they are 'psychotic'. We can see how this works, and why the doctors are so frightened, if we look at some of the ways images of 'psychosis' are constructed in the clinical literature.

The demonology of madness in clinical discourses

It is insufficient to acknowledge, as we have, the deconstructive work on psychopathology in relation to scientific validity, genetic and biochemical research, without considering the power relations implicated in the production of knowledge. Let us examine Frosh's (1991) citations from the psychoanalysts Freud, Lacan, Bion and Rosenfeld in this light: 'If we ask ourselves what it is that gives the character of strangeness to the substitutive formation and the symptoms of schizophrenia, we eventually come to realize that it is the predominance of what has to do with words over what has to do with things' (Freud, cited in Frosh, 1991: 157).

Freud's characterization of schizophrenia as the power of words over things is taken up and exaggerated in Lacan's account. Note that language now not only is given 'predominance', but is rendered capable of 'abolition' of everything else in 'Repudiation of castration, foreclosure of its signifier – symbolic abolition of the phallus.' (Lacan, cited in Frosh, 1991: 162). While Lacan's formulations were being developed in France, equally scary descriptions were gathering pace in the UK, with Bion identifying 'Beta-elements', which 'are the objects that can be evacuated or used for a kind of thinking that depends on the manipulation of what are felt to be things in themselves as if to substitute such manipulations for words or ideas' (Bion, cited in Frosh, 1991: 174). In a bizarre 'deconstruction' of the relationship between language and objects, the psychotic subject (and, for Bion, there was a psychotic part to every subject) is able to 'manipulate' words as if they were objects. Across in the United States, Rosenfeld unwittingly captures something of the dynamic of this movement of experience into language, and the reification of mad bits of language in psychiatric discourse in his discussion of 'projective identification':

> In this form of projective identification the projection of the mad part of the self into the analyst often predominates. The analyst is then perceived as having become mad, which arouses extreme anxiety as the patient is afraid that the analyst will retaliate and force the madness back into the patient, depriving him entirely of his sanity. At such times the patient is in danger of disintegration. (Rosenfeld, cited in Frosh, 1991: 171)

Rosenfeld describes the way in which the psychiatrist is immersed in the psychotic experience, but the step he is unable to take is to see that experience as being an *effect* of the very language he has been using. Even Frosh is bewitched by the horrible imagery for mental states that he conjures up, and which he imagines simply to be describing what is going on in someone else's head when he offers a description of bionic beta-elements: 'They just sit there, great toads that they are, intermittently leaping whole into space, devouring consciousness, devouring links with others, devouring thought' (Frosh, 1991: 174).

We want to agree with Frosh's (1991: 178) conclusion that 'All this is a theory, ostensibly explaining the psychotic condition; but it is the psychotic state as well'. And if we accept psychoanalytic terminology for the moment, we might interpret the discourse and practice of psychopathology as a 'psychotic defence'. We want to argue here that the images of madness that are relayed in clinical texts *construct* a reality for the clinician that is fantastic and frightening, and that it is then no surprise that psychiatrists who write and read this stuff should be so frightened of being in the presence of someone who is 'mad'.

This type of talk, and the practice that follows from it makes it difficult for practitioners to work across the divide between reason and unreason. The demonology of psychotic experience in psychiatric texts increases the gap, and makes all the more 'other' the experience of those it talks about. Any alternative approach, such as the ones we describe in this chapter, have had to build alternative languages that render the variety of human experience in a way that makes the demands of 'users' intelligible and reasonable.

It should be noted that Frosh then steps back, however, and urges caution and responsibility in a manner reminiscent of Sedgwick's response to Foucault: 'it is crucial that this evocation does not also obscure the suffering reality of the schizophrenic condition' (Frosh, 1991: 178). Frosh associates (extreme) deconstruction with an attack on fragile selves. The condition is again, then, reified, made to seem as if it was a 'real' thing out there, outside language, outside all of the persuasive and coercive practices that brought it into being and which maintain it against the protests of so many patients. It can be discussed within the discourses of mental health provision, much as we have seen 'the psychotic' discussed in the clinical literature. We should point out that it is not our intention here to single out psychoanalysis as the only villain; clinical psychiatry and psychology, whilst short on the poetry, also take delusional forms, first when they seek to name syndromes (Boyle, 1990), and then when they measure hallucinations. Clinical diagnosis, in its most concrete practice, sets out systematically to undermine the patient's belief systems (Chadwick and Birchwood, 1994).

Three points need to be kept in mind. Each is to do with the reproduction of power in clinical practice. The first is importance of psychiatric language organized into discourse which constructs pathology in ways that mean that the doctor is genuinely frightened for the safety of the patient, and for his or her own safety. Medical power ensures that these images mark the types of experience patients are permitted to describe. The second is the importance of the doctor in framing alternative approaches. Medical power is expressed in some of the most radical 'anti-psychiatry' experiments in the way the psychiatrist as expert is still allowed to take the lead in framing the reforms (and, as we shall see, this applies to Basaglia in Trieste, Huber in Germany, and Romme in The Netherlands). The third is the importance of that power in reform programmes which promises a 'partnership' between the doctor and the patient. We are interested in building a dialogue, but we need to keep to the centre of our analysis how medical power is reproduced and how it is challenged in these types of alliances. This is crucial if we are to understand *and* deconstruct power in psychopathology. Let us turn to some of the practical ways these discourses and practices have been deconstructed, in some cases from the base up.

Three fates of resistance

Popular textbooks on the history of psychology and medicine often commence their narrative with the ancient Greeks. First year psychology undergraduates, for example, are expected to be impressed by the knowledge that the Greeks observed a relationship between hysteria and the female reproductive organ (cf. Turner, 1987). We might have preferred to commence with the equally controversial theory of the psychologist Julian Jaynes (1976) in which he argues that up to 1500 BC all the Greeks heard voices, before the lateralization of brain hemispheres and the development of consciousness. Rather than imagining the beginnings of rational civilization here, we might emphasize the way in which the Greeks in periods of crisis and decision-making listened to the voices of the gods and perhaps talked back, walking the streets without the moral panic which ensues today (even though Hippocrates was not happy with this situation). Stepping back from the 'history' of psychopathology, we now want to give it instead some of the status of mythology rather than scientific history. So, we will be guided by the first Fate, Clotho, as psychopathology is born into the world, as the gaze enters the asylum and as bedlam threatens to spill out into the community. Here we will examine the fate of 'the Trieste experiment' and mental health work combined with political action in working class communities. Then, under the eye of Lechesis, the second Fate, we look at the life of resistance, the experience of direct action in the German socialist patients collective, in the US, and in more 'social' therapy. Finally, with Atropos, we confront the inevitable, the death of psychopathology, as we examine the radical challenge of the Hearing Voices Network in The Netherlands and the UK. This is our third Fate, for now.

Clotho

In 1978 in Italy a mental health reform law ('Law 180') was passed by parliament which stipulated that mental hospitals should be phased out, and that there should be no more compulsory admissions. This Law, which came into effect in 1981, was a response to activities by a campaigning group called *Psichiatria Democratica* which had managed to collect signatures for a referendum on mental health provision. Although this movement was led by psychiatrists, the most important being Franco Basaglia, it included activists from different far Left groups, patients' groups and from the Communist Party (which at that time was on the verge of gaining power). There was, then, a context for reflection and empowerment among different marginalized groups, and Basaglia took the lead in the Northern city of Trieste to close the mental hospital San Giovanni and to provide services for a new category that he dubbed the 'emarginated'. These people included those who had been in San Giovanni, or who might have entered the psychiatric system, and any other people who might need social support. The philosophy of the 'Trieste reforms' (so-called, partly because Basaglia was the driving force in Trieste, and because other local authorities dragged their feet over the Law), was that 'illness' was an expression of social circumstances, that activists had to engage in 'deinstitutionalization' not simply dehospitalization. It was necessary to change the meanings of mental distress through festivals, exhibitions and through making San Giovanni a community resource (Basaglia, 1987).

Psychologists working in the hospital changed jobs in this new climate, with some working in San Giovanni's open community cafe and some working as gardeners. One of the distinctive features of the Trieste example is the general hostility to psychotherapy, and the emphasis was on the collective work that service users could undertake in the cooperatives (which ranged from hairdressing to furniture-moving). Medication was used only to stabilize, and not as part of a treatment regime. A network of seven Community Mental Health Centres was opened through the city (with one based at the old hospital site linked directly to the cooperative workshops, and another for the Slovenian minority community in Trieste). These centres were run through open meetings which included 'users'. (Those who had been in San Giovanni for many years, and were unable to cope outside, were called 'guests', and had rights to participate in the meetings there.)

Activists from other European countries, as well as from Latin America have travelled to Trieste to help, and participants in that experiment have travelled back in return to attempt similar experiments outside Italy. Comparisons between Italy and the situation in other countries also reveal the scale of the problems facing *Psichiatria Democratica* (Ramon, 1985; Ramon and Giannichedda, 1989), and it looks now as if political and economic forces have beaten back the Trieste reforms. Just as it is impossible for islands of socialism to survive in a capitalist world, so it is impossible for cooperative enterprises to compete in a hostile economic environment, and for mental activists to exist under an increasingly right-wing local and central government. As a World Health Organization pilot area, the services had always to be provided to those designated as suffering identifiable 'illnesses', and there has been pressure from family organizations to reintroduce hospital treatments. The hospital clinic, which is still in the grounds of San Giovanni, in addition, was always hostile to the reforms. Some commentators on community care have argued that 'in some places, the psychiatric wards in general hospitals have reproduced some of the worst features of the old mental hospitals, such as physical restraint of patients and the indiscriminate use of drugs' (Barham, 1992: 141).

These features certainly appear in the UK, where there is a greater space for resistance precisely because of the existence of the Mental Health Act. In Italy, in principle at least, the psychiatrist was empowered, released from the strait-jacket of the bureaucrats. In the UK even the most well-meaning psychiatrist has been caught in the miseries of government policy (Coleman and McLaughlin, 1994). There has been no mass movement demanding the closure of the asylums in the UK and *at the same time* building a network of local mental health centres. If nothing else, the Trieste experiment showed that in a progressive political context, massive changes could be made very fast which would provide services that were more user friendly. One of the ironies in all this, is that because the drugs bill was lower in Trieste after the closure of San Giovanni, the provision of good mental health care was actually cheaper for local and central government. We can only conclude that the biggest problem facing a radical mental health movement is not so much the balance of the budget, but the balance of power, and the extent to which that may be threatened.

It is impossible to defend islands of progressive mental health care in a hostile political and economic climate, but each sporadic attempt to empower 'users' is an example and lesson. One case in the UK which was particularly concerned with working class and women's community action was the White City project in West London. We have drawn attention to the absence of writing and action around class in the psychiatric system, and the White City project stands out in its engagement with this issue at the same time as it tackled other varieties of oppression. Some descriptions of this work lean heavily on psychoanalytic notions, but the project, which was based in Battersea and the White City, attempted to build psycho-therapy services which took seriously the interrelationship between gender, race and class in the experience of alienation and depression under capitalism (Holland, 1992; Holland and Holland, 1984).

The Italian experience is a mixture of success and failure, with signs for radicals that it is possible to dispense with large asylums, and hard political lessons about what happens when a hostile economic climate starts to press in. The activities of the White City project did not even have the benefit of a popular activist movement around to support them. What these reforms did achieve, though, was the linking of 'therapeutic' work (broadly understood) with empowerment, and social action. Each case illustrates the importance of the wider context for radical mental health work. The Trieste experiment survived so long because of a variety of forces around it that were sympathetic, while the White City project struggled to survive in a different more difficult context, and maintained itself for a brief period against the odds. We turn to some other examples of direct action next which have had to tackle problems of political context, and have tried to do so by linking with broader political movements as allies in a hostile cultural environment.

Lechesis

In Germany the *Sozialistchen Patientenkollektiv* (SPK) was founded by Wolfgang Huber at the Psychiatric and Neurological University Hospital, Heidleburg, in 1970. The SPK argued that mental and physical illness was a revolt against an insane world of capitalism, alienation, pollution and repressive sexual morals. It sought to turn illness into a weapon. While receiving letters and support from Sartre and Foucault, the group faced much resistance from student groups, the university administration and the police. The SPK disbanded in 1971, after which several members were sentenced to prison as 'terrorists'. It was falsely linked with the Red Army Fraction. While in solitary confinement in 1973, Dr Huber founded the *Patientenfront*, which has existed continuously since that time (Spandler, 1994). The SPK acted alone for the most part, and this has been an aspect of its work that has marked its activity since. Radical action always risks falling into sectarian squabbling with rival groups, and that vicious circle can only be broken by building coalitions across different campaigns.

This experience connects and constrasts directly with the advanced networking and lobbying of North American activists and the force of American pragmatism. Whilst Thomas Szasz, ironically, provides an academic marker for the liberation movement, the practice of the North American activists has fortunately assumed a life of its own, dedicated to gaining control of mental health services. Judi Chamberlin states the position: 'We must remember that terms like mental illness or schizophrenia are useful only if they help us to understand what they describe' (Chamberlin, 1988: pxvi). Chamberlin was one of the founder members of the National Alliance of Mental Patients, formed in 1985, dedicated to the abolition of involuntary psychiatric intervention and the development of user run programmes as true alternatives to the psychiatric system. It is important here that, following Szasz, the concept of 'mental illness' is questioned as an explanation of distressing human behaviour. In 1994, Chamberlin was able to report the beginning of an alliance between the disability movement and psychiatric survivors over the demand to end forced psychiatry (*Dendron News*, Summer, 1994: 5). This move not only confirms an approach to mental distress within a social constructionist framework, and drawing on the politics of disability, but also connects with another militant history, the wheelchair demonstrations in France organized by the *Comité de Lutte des Handicapes* or the occupation of Stoke Mandeville hospital in the UK by paraplegics in 1980. Sedgwick was perhaps overcome by pessimism in stating that: 'Mental patients are among the most private of citizens . . . The stigma attached still to their various disabilities and illnesses usually prevents most of them from asserting a group identity in public, for the purposes of demonstration or financial appeal' (Sedgwick, 1982: 222). Direct action in the United States shows that it is possible to organize collectively against psychiatric reason, and through 'unreasonable' actions to build an alternative community which will support those who need it.

A further development in the United States is of some significance. In contrast to the anti-collectivist legacy of Thomas Szasz and Herbert Spencer, it is based on a Marxist or at least radically humanistic reading of the Soviet psychologist Vygotsky. The Institute for Social Therapy is not only attached to a publishing and cultural centre, with its own Vygotskian 'laboratory' school, but also has its own political party. Its charismatic founder, Fred Newman, subverts from the standpoint of 'developmentalism' the primacy of explanation at the core of psychopathology. Following on from treatises on Vygotsky and anti-psychology tracts (Holzman, 1995), Newman's (1994) book *Let's Develop*, is unashamedly 'pop' psychology – 'a book that will change your life'. It is avowedly anti-psychoanalytic, whilst locking into discourses of growth and therapy, aimed at a mass public, and providing a frame of reference to those combating the pathologizing professions. Newman's practice of groups as vygotsykian zones of proximal development adds to the resources of the self-help movement in a contradictory way, not excluding the therapist (indeed, therapists are often part of the groups), nor denying an engagement in politics. Characteristically, American mental health politics are oriented towards redress under the legal system. In the case of the Newman group, attacks on their psychology project led the group to take action in the courts against the FBI in response to the charge levelled against them of cultism. This was in the context of the siege of Waco and the precedent (and the paranoia) this set for the treatment of groups who stepped outside the gaze of the institutions of psychology (and the introduction of spiritual disorder as a new category in DSM-IV, might serve to exacerbate such fears). It should be pointed out that the factional activities of the Newman group have made the rest of the Left just as wary of them (Harris, 1995; Parker, 1995b).

In the UK too, the role of the mental health charity MIND is consistently framed in terms of legal advocacy and issues of human rights. It falls to National MIND in the wake of the Blom-Cooper, Hally and Murphy (1995) report (with a wierdly Jungian title), 'The Falling Shadow', and the tabloid headlines of 'Slaughter in the Community' and the like, to report the number of deaths attributable at present to neuroleptic medication, one death a week according to MIND (Mihill, 1994b). It is to the local autonomous branches that we must look for new initiatives, and to the development of networking for their realization. Even the grassroots organizations of the pro-psychiatry National Schizophrenia Fellowship (NSF) and the 'Making Space' group which emerged following the NSF split fit this pattern despite the dedication of the national organization to biological research and the needs of carers. Some NSF local groups are more progressive than others. Planning for care in the community has led to numerous user run services, although many would see this as tokenism in the context of the cuts in National Health Service funding. 'Empowerment' is the buzzword in this context, and everywhere examples of good practice are heralded. Meanwhile, a media war has been declared around the issue of care or forced treatment in the community. Here, the mental health charity SANE has the highest profile, backed eagerly by the national press.

As well as drawing attention to the importance of context, these developments in direct action in Germany, the United States and the UK make clear the importance of some political framework for mental health movements. In this respect, activists in the UK have much to learn from developments in other countries, and a political understanding and deconstruction of psychiatry has to include an internationalist perspective and the deconstruction of parochial thinking. So far we have traced a movement dedicated to civil rights, and economic and therapeutic provision, but still predicated on the existence of mental illness. Now we turn to one of the most radical of recent challenges to clinical reason, the network of people who hear voices, who threaten to unravel psychiatric categories from the inside while carrying forward the dynamics of critique and empowerment that characterize the movements we have discussed so far.

Atropos

The Hearing Voices Network (HVN) challenges the 'reality' of mental illness, and redefines areas of experience outside the psychiatric apparatus. In this section we will focus on the development of HVN, a radical movement distinguished by its continuity with the tradition of Democratic Psychiatry and a critique of the medical model. It calls for partnership between voice hearers and allies, and it is attracting some central funding. It is popular amongst service providers and develops in parallel with a growing body of psychological research critical of the concept of schizophrenia, and it is stepping we might say into the new foucauldian history of psychiatry, a history not of diseases but of *discourses*. The history of HVN in the UK might be traced to members of the network Survivors Speak Out. However, it is precisely the status of victim which HVN tends to subvert, together with the concept of psychopathology.

The voices are seen as real. Is that, to return to Foucault's statement about the dialogue between reason and unreason, 'reasonable'? Certainly in terms of the lexicon of abnormal psychology, auditory hallucinations cannot be real. Boyle (1994: 196) points out that the question of reality and subjective reporting is a profound issue, particularly when the importance of culture is taken into account. To clinical psychologists, these dilemmas have pointed to the possibility of an alternative schizophrenia research programme focused, for example, on symptoms, rather than gross diagnoses (Bentall,1990; Boyle, 1994). Even this shift of emphasis carries its own dangers though, and although Bentall (1990), for example, takes the position that the voices are real, they are now the subject and symptom of a new pathology. Voice hearing has a definite social stigma, whether it is influenced by the fate of famous voice hearers – whether they be Jesus Christ, Mohammed, Joan of Arc, Winston Churchill or Christopher Clunis – or simply by the convention that talking to yourself or to voices is not acceptable.

For Marius Romme, the Dutch professor of Social Psychiatry who is seen as the founder of the movement, the logic of attending to the *content* of voices was not only to support the development of psychological interventions, but also to take voices out of the illness model, to see them as part of a pattern of personal growth and as a facet of human experience such as left-handedness or homosexuality. The threat to the establishment is of mass lobbies campaigning to remove voice hearing from the DSM.

Romme's encouragement to voice hearers is thus different from other radically humanistic treatments of schizophrenia, as being well outside the disease model (Jenner et al., 1993). But for Romme the conversion did not come easily; his account deserves attention.

> For some years one of my patients, a thirty year old woman, has been hearing voices in her mind. These voices give her orders or forbid her to do things and dominate her completely. She has been hospitalized several times and diagnosed as having schizophrenia. Neuroleptics have no effect on the voices, although they do reduce her anxiety. Unfortunately, these drugs also reduce her mental alertness; consequently she does not take medication over long periods, nor does she remain long as an in-patient when she is hospitalized. Nevertheless, the voices have increasingly isolated her by forbidding her to do things she had always loved.
>
> Last year she started to talk more and more frequently about suicide, and I could see her starting down a path from which there might be no return. The only positive note in our conversations at that time was provided by the theory she had developed about the nature of the voices. This theory was based on a book by the American psychologist Julien Jaynes, *The Origin of Consciousness in the Breakdown of the Bicameral Mind* (1976). She found it reassuring to read that the hearing of voices, had been regarded as a normal way of making decisions until about 1300 BC. According to Jaynes the experience of hearing voices has almost entirely disappeared and been replaced by what we now call consciousness.
>
> I began to wonder whether she might prove to be a good communicator with others who also heard voices, and whether they might find her theory acceptable or useful. I thought this might have a positive affect on her isolation, her suicidal tendencies and her feelings of dependency on her voices. Together she and I began to plan ways in which she might share some of her experiences and views.
>
> In due course we set up one-to-one meetings with others who heard voices. As I sat there listening to their conversations, I was struck by the eagerness with which they recognized one another's experience. Initially, I found it difficult to follow these conversations: to my ears the contents were bizarre and extra-ordinary, and yet all this was freely discussed as though it constituted a real world of and unto itself. (Romme and Escher, 1993: 11)

It is quite clear from this account, at least to voice hearers, that HVN had *two* founders – Professor Marius Romme and patient Patsy Hage – and from now on, there was to be two competing histories. Romme and Hage's research strategy deserves a fuller account. In the first place, they both appeared on a popular television chat show to talk about voices and psychiatry and appealed to viewers to contact them. This formed their research sample and the basis for organizing the first voice hearers' conference in Utrecht in 1987, which was attended by the Dutch minister for health. The response of the Dutch media was sympathetic, in contrast to the media in other countries. The Dutch research has been published in detail elsewhere (Romme et al., 1992), however an overview of the findings is presented here, not only because it constitutes the basis of an expanding training programme developed by HVN, but also because it poses important questions for the deconstruction of schizophrenia. This deconstruction is played out beyond the clinical journals in a growing network of self-help groups. Against a background of the failure of neuroleptic medication, the emergence of a third of Romme's sample as coping with voices without recourse to psychiatry was important. Their voices were of a form which would attract diagnoses by a psychiatrist. The responses suggested that it was possible to accept and live with the voices, and that it could be of positive value in coping with life events.

There is now a growing literature on clinical approaches to coping with voices. This evidences a particular tension between cognitive, behavioural and psychodynamic models of therapy, models which sit uneasily with the principles established in the self-help groups. Moreover, there is a vacuum of group approaches in the clinical setting, a fact which confirms the practical role of the self-help groups. There is also a tension between voice hearers in HVN and their clinical research allies, who are often enjoying funding for clinical trials by drug companies. Voice hearing is here formulated as a residual or drug resistant symptom, within the tenets of the DSM or ICD, and subjects are maintained on 'stable neuroleptic medication'. Whilst there is nothing 'stable' to the user about neuroleptic medication, the confirmation of disease status acts as a counter to the psychotherapeutic intervention. The use of 'control' subjects feels distinctly unethical, whilst for those seeking to reduce or eliminate medication nothing is on offer. Whilst the function of depression and delusional belief systems in coping with voices emerges as an experimental design problem, the form of clinical intervention often serves to reconfirm the voice hearer in the role of victimhood when the researcher aims to get rid of the voices instead of asking whether they might be an important part of the hearer's identity.

The notion of voice hearing as an aspect of growth is confirmed by a simple but powerful conceptualization of the experience moving through three phases: the startling phase, the phase of organization and coping, and the phase of stabilization and integration. The 'startling phase' is the period of onset of voices, of distress and fear; it is perhaps something that corresponds most closely to the popular and clinical picture of acute psychosis; it can last a life-time but need not. Before the talking starts the voice hearer will have developed frames of reference, the hallmark of the 'organizational phase', but these may be categorized as delusional systems. The 'stabilization phase' sees not only the integration of the voices (the symptom) but a wider change in the society of the person, and this connects with a strong political strand in HVN (which it shares with certain strands of group-oriented psychoanalysis). In practice, the work of the self-help groups develops from facilitating acceptance of the voices to being able to talk about the content of the voices, the triggers, relationships and coping strategies. Ultimately the dynamics of self-help in HVN require crossing and re-crossing the boundaries between phases. At the heart of that activity is reflection upon the nature and transcendence of victim status.

What seems most important is that forms of explanation are necessary to define coping strategies. It is in the area of explanation that the paths of voice hearers and professionals seem to diverge in a battle of discourses. Telepathy is a case in point; the DSM distinctly frowns upon it, regarding it as pathological, whereas in the Hearing Voices Network it is accepted as a valid explanation if it is helpful for the voice hearer.

The circumstances of onset were a preoccupation that formed perhaps the most controversial aspect of the research. Romme and Escher (1993) indicated that 70 per cent of voice hearing was triggered by trauma, by life events. It is also worth noting that many patients report the onset as being triggered by hospitalization or medication. Further to this, HVN trainers use a technique which simulates the experience of voice hearing, demonstrating that the secondary symptoms of schizophrenia are in fact *consequences* of the experience of hearing voices. The consequences of this are twofold. For psychiatry it indicates that large numbers of schizophrenic patients should be recategorized with 'post traumatic stress disorder'. For voice hearers it creates the opportunity to attempt to examine those life traumas.

There are a number of implications of this work to do with the relation between medicine and commonsense, a relation that the activity of HVN effectively deconstructs. The first implication would require a radical revision of psychiatric theory and practice whilst the second would require a change in the culture of psychotherapy (which is generally antagonistic to the possibility of working with 'psychotic' patients) and would raise a question for voice hearers about what kind of service they required. Like the deconstructive therapy we described in the previous chapter (White, 1987, 1991), the reality of the voices is taken seriously, and the 'symptoms' are 'externalized' so they can be addressed by the hearer as part of their reality, as harmful or helpful to them. Rather like 'queer' politics, which draws in 'normal' perversions into the range of experiences that the movement is fighting to have recognized as valid as part of the variety of humanity (Butler, 1990), so 'hearing voices' is reconceptualized as something that everyone is affected by. The very definition of what it is to 'hear' a voice is picked apart in practice by HVN as the number of different explanations for the phenomenon multiply. Whether it is seen as a variety of tinnitus or telepathy, voice hearing confuses any medical system which tries to categorize symptoms. The spotlight is then turned around, as with the queer movement, on to those who are unable to tolerate the variety and ambiguity of identity that results. It has been argued, in this deconstructive spirit, that clinicians caught up in this way of thinking may be suffering from 'Professional Thought Disorder' (Lowson, 1994). Attention is drawn to the types of discourse that insist on rigid categories for mental states, a discourse that obsessively categorizes according to a logic that pretends to be reasonable but is actually very unreasonable, a discourse that we could call 'psychotic'. HVN has so far managed to connect an attention to context and politics with a sensitivity to and engagement with experience.

Concluding comments

We have been concerned in this chapter to confront the enigma contained in Foucault's statement about the relation between reason and its 'other'. Although some writers have pointed out that the philosophical implications of Foucault's history of psychiatry and Derrida's deconstruction are different, and that deconstruction finds it difficult to locate itself in any kind of history (for example, Boyne, 1990), our task here has been to turn deconstruction into a political weapon, and for that, Foucault's work has been invaluable. In recording a history of the *practical deconstruction* of psychopathology, we do not want to reduce questions of clinical power to a simple analysis of language independent of context or to reduce the challenge to traditional psychiatry to a question of talking (or not) about the content of experience. We have theorized elsewhere in this book about the nature of communication as something social through and through, but here we are concerned with the practical relations between the pathologized and the pathologizers, with the relations of power, with politics. The lack of communication bridges between professional and client are common knowledge in mental health discourse, and the medical profession has often been held as a main culprit. There is a joke in user circles: 'Who is the psychiatrist's first patient from whom he learned his communications skills and his bedside manner?', to which the answer must be 'A dead body, in medical school'. The logic of this is psychiatrists should not be medically trained, in other words, they should not exist as they do at present. The other side to this picture is the role of psychology as a discipline which promises to repair behaviour and rebuild bridges with clients.

Recent developments in services have been characterized in terms of 'user involvement'. A useful example of this is the emergence in the UK of Survivors Speak Out. Many members are also members of HVN which is committed to a more deconstructive approach to diagnostic categorization. This not only testifies to how diversity adds to the strength of the resistance movement but it also helps set the stage for talking, an advance on the soapbox and the soap opera treatment of distress. To this process is often applied the tag of 'empowerment'. As we have noted in relation to the Italian experience we have to ask who is really being empowered. This empowerment can be evaluated in terms of amelioration of social relations but not in terms of ownership of the means of production (of psychopathology). One response to this way of conceptualizing the problem is to develop a collectivist or Marxist model of self-help (Coleman and

McLaughlin, 1995). For that we have to turn to the text. A political economy of this text, however, would have to include an account of the ways in which the forces and relations of production lead to psychopathology or allow it to be transformed (Warner, 1994). We are concerned here with deconstruction, to locate psychopathology within the text.

In expanding the notion of discourse to include practices of regulation and resistance, we are concerned with the implications of this focus for 'users' of psychiatric services. In adopting the term 'user,' as opposed to 'mental patient' or 'mental health activist' we are conscious of offering a disguise for the reality, that this 'use' often is not voluntary, and that, for the most distressed, confinement and treatment is determined by the Mental Health Act, and is subsumed in psychiatric discourse where the notion of 'informed consent' is not open to interrogation. The term 'consumer' is even worse, and is surely not the kind of identity that anyone would want stamped into them. Although people do sometimes refer themselves, and usually expect some therapeutic support, or a place of 'asylum' (a safe place for resting and reflecting), the 'consumer' is too often forced to select from a range of bad medicines. All these terms are caught in discourses that sometimes warrant and sometimes obscure oppressive practices. The discourse of 'care in the community', for example, acts so as to soften policies leading to compulsory treatment in the community and registers of those considered dangerous. The Bedlam riots indicate that changes in material conditions are the key to changes in the categorization and treatment of the mad, and the fortunes and crises of capitalism provide the defining backdrop for how mental health is noticed or ignored (Warner, 1994). Our task is to deconstruct the relationship between material forces and the meaning people give to them, to bring those processes to awareness, into the text, and to empower people to change them. Although, as Boyle (1990) points out, it lacks scientific validity, schizophrenia is still a powerful legal concept, as part of the Mental Health Act, for example. As such it is also the subject of politics and here we are concerned with the role of language, to identify the dynamics of power relations and to upset them in an act of deconstruction.

Foucault's theses on the Western asylum in relation to the rise of capitalism can be tied to the spectacle of their closure in the current period, in Italy under the auspices of *Psichiatria Democratica* and in Britain under the strictures of governmental market ideology. Similarly, with the demise of much immediate possibility of collective action (at least within the institutions) the seat of resistance seems to move discursively to policy makers. In another sense an ethos of 'partnership' (between doctor and patient) pervades mental health research and practice including the dispensing of the limited funds made available through the programme of care in the community. This can also be seen as an extension into mental health of the principle of 'participation', the role of patient groups in general practice (Richardson and Bray, 1987). Evidence of a groundswell of revulsion and resistance to the relationship between general psychiatry and the pharmaceutical industry and electroconvulsive technology is well established (Hill, 1983). We have yet to find out where this resistance might lead. We might take on board Boyle's (1990) argument that the massive scientific schizophrenia programme is 'delusional' and understand her plea (1994) for 'methodological tolerance' in developing new research; but it then needs to be made clear *who* our co-researchers should be.

We are concerned to approach what it means when a survivor speaks, when voice hearers stake a claim to owning their experience, perhaps by exposing a form of property relations within the organizations of discourse. As a 'paranoid schizophrenic' once said to one of us: 'Just because I think the psychiatrist is mad, it doesn't have to be a projective identification.' Our deconstruction in this book has been directed at the language and practice of psychopathology; our concern is to show how the 'broken dialogue' Foucault describes, the breaking of dialogue, is only successful when there is a sustained attack on spaces for resistance. A radical approach to mental health necessarily involves a defence of these spaces, and a multiplication of practical challenges to clinical power that are able to link movements in different contexts with a political awareness and attention to experience. It should be clear from the examples in this chapter that the first steps to a practical deconstruction of psychopathology have been taken many times. We see this book as providing some analysis, resources and energy to move that struggle forward.

8
Deconstructive Responses and Resources

This final chapter aims to do two things. First, we will anticipate some of the reactions to the arguments we have developed in this book. Critiques of psychiatric discourse and clinical practice always have to contend with a range of excuses and defences from those who collude with, or even actively employ, traditional notions of psychopathology. These range from tired, worn-out routines that wear down radicals in mental health to vituperative and exasperated attacks on anyone who dares to suggest that there may be anything wrong. We will be picking up some of the reactions to other critiques and trying to offer some suggestions that may be useful for those working in and against the mental health system. Secondly, we will be listing and describing some of the practical resources designed to support a critical perspective. We do not pretend to have been the first to have voiced disagreement with traditional clinical notions, and our work here would not have been possible without the active resistance of mental health groups over the years. Neither do we pretend that deconstruction is the final word in a radical perspective and practice, and we hope that for readers who move on to be involved with some of the groupings and networks we mention deconstruction will only be the first word, the first step.

Reactions and responses

What might impatient psychiatrists, world-weary clinicians and burnt-out para-medical mental health workers say about this book? We have tried to anticipate the ways in which our book might be (mis)understood. The various possible claims and complaints about it have been grouped below into worries about theoretical frameworks, the serious nature of distress, and the readership for the book.

Theoretical frameworks

We imagine that some people will have read Derrida and Foucault, and will want to demonstrate their knowledge and expertise in those ideas by pointing out where we have deviated from a correct understanding of their work. The first complaint might come in the form of general irritation that *'the book doesn't accurately characterize theoretical systems'*. According to Foucault, knowledge, theoretical and scientific, does not describe a pre-existing reality but constructs realities. Our interest lies in the realities that our use of specific theoretical systems makes possible. The focus is on the way we can use these theoretical systems in order to deconstruct the already existing systems of knowledge and practice. We look at these theories with the aim of finding what is useful to us, not using them as theories which reveal some kind of 'truth'. This does not mean that we have the right to deform and misrepresent theories. It does mean, however, that accurate characterization is not our primary aim. Theoretical concepts are not there to be kept pure and be worshipped, but to be used in ways that enable alternative understandings and practices. Our point has been to lay more emphasis on exposing contradictions in and implications of theories.

The complaint about theory might be directed more specifically, such as *'this isn't deconstruction at all, just a critical reading'*. The principle of deconstruction is that it unravels the contradictions in which polarities between terms are caught up, and overturns these polarities in favour of the less privileged term. We have followed this principle in the book. Derrida, however, is purely concerned with the deconstruction of texts. We are moving in this book between the deconstruction of texts and a more 'practical' deconstruction of power relations, and the polarities that underlie and structure them. Once we move from texts to practices, the method has necessarily to change. Consequently, we have followed basic deconstructive principles, but have also accommodated the method to the subject area of our work. And, we might ask 'who owns the definition of deconstruction'? Some readers might object that *'this is a caricature of Foucault's work'*. Well, if our work does not seem foucauldian enough, it is probably because we have not adopted much foucauldian terminology which is full of jargon and exceedingly difficult to understand. We have, however, followed the principles of Foucault's work, and his theory of the relation between knowledge, power and practice in our analysis of the psychiatric system and the way psychiatric knowledge and practices are intertwined with institutions and power.

Of course, for someone wanting a detailed exegesis of the writings of Derrida or Foucault, this book will be disappointing. This was not our task, however, and we are deliberately using deconstruction, and Foucault's historical work in a way that will open up what psychiatry and other clinical practices actually do to the person as patient. The writings of Derrida and Foucault are notoriously inaccessible (we are often told) and perhaps even more so, the critiques of them. Yet these frameworks may be seen as the radical underpinnings of a new paradigm in the social sciences and psychiatry, which has turned to the analysis of discourse. But we might find little evidence of such analyses within the politics of mental health, at least from the standpoint of the user movement. Engagements with the French thinkers have in the last generation taken place behind the veils of 'postmodernism'. The least we might want to address about this cultural trend is its tendency towards the apolitical, the simply ironical and its place within 'the end of history' syndrome. We have not simply sought to examine the academic significance of a radical re-reading of deconstruction and poststructuralism but to turn them to practical use.

Neither have we laid out definitive meanings of concepts; a complaint about this would be understandable whether coming from the lay reader or the parsimonious critic. (We provide no glossary, only resources for change.) We have avoided explaining your pathology; the point is: there has been too much of that. Whilst our leanings towards specific therapeutic interventions have emerged throughout the book, we are concerned more with the development of common theory about the operation of power. We take the distinct contributions of deconstructive, foucauldian and Marxist writers seriously, but it is also important to make the theoretical ideas from these traditions into something useful. This is why we have developed what we call a 'practical deconstruction' of psychopathology which is a pragmatic engagement with the different struggles against traditional clinical notions. We have also drawn upon arguments that have been developed out of the practice of radical mental health and feminist movements, movements for which there is no single 'party line'. In the process, we have done some conceptual violence to pure theoretical systems, in the belief that it is the *diversity* of critique that gives it strength. We need to comprehend and challenge the management of abnormality from many different directions.

We have described theoretical approaches in the book, and so some might object to this and say *'this is too theoretical, and full of unnecessary jargon'*. Perhaps at points this book is too theoretical. Located in different intellectual traditions that have made different understandings possible, the book cannot ignore these theoretical systems and terms. Theory is important to understand, because without it challenges to different knowledges and practices are not possible. We do not, however, stay only at the level of theory. We try to use theory for the construction of different practices. It is always hard to avoid using difficult theoretical concepts when questioning taken-for-granted truths and stepping out of everyday understanding. Besides would you be interested if the book simply told you what you already knew?

It will also probably be said by some that *'the book doesn't take into account recent research'*. Our work is not based on the positivist paradigm of science, according to which the accumulation of scientific research will eventually provide the correct understanding of what lies out there, in reality. We deny the myth of scientific progress, according to which the more recent the research, the closer to the truth and reality it is. Old ideas can be as useful. We are, however, aware of recent research and we do use it in this book. This charge also neglects the point that 'recent research' usually refers to new 'facts' from current dominant frameworks rather than new concepts which might interpret such 'facts' in different ways. Standard psychiatry thinks it uncovers new 'facts', but deconstruction helps us to find something very different.

We have made choices in this book, and no doubt that will annoy some readers, who may want to object with something along the lines of '*what about x (my favourite radical theorist) whose work has not been discussed?*', to which we can only say that this is just a book! We cannot include everything. Is it the case that '*this just looks like old anti-psychiatry*'? Simply because criticisms have been made before does not mean they are not still relevant. In part it is the ignoring of basic concerns that makes some of these ideas even more important today. Moreover, we are not simply repeating older critiques, and we differ from previous theorists in a number of ways, for example, in accounting for why people desire to be normal rather than looking to simple coercion or labelling theories – and we are not proposing one utopian model or therapy.

Some 'mainstream' approaches have drawn upon opposition ideas in the past, and we have no doubt that some of the critiques we have developed in this book will appear alongside clinical arguments in the future. Nothing will ever guarantee that a 'radical' critique will stay that way. We do indeed have to take seriously the recuperation, the neutralizing and assimilation of critical ideas, and we have traced both the ways in which some anti-psychiatry notions failed precisely because they were absorbed by mainstream psychiatry, and the ways in which some deconstructive therapies have been linked with traditional psychiatric practices. Again, the solution does not lie in the purity of critique, in the hope that this will make us unassailable, but rather in the flexible and tactical connection with new radical approaches that arise to replace the old ones. There is always place for hope here. We have found that it has been the attempts to grapple with the worst cases of distress and institutional abuse that have led to the most innovative ideas. We are aware of – and this connects with the second set of criticisms that might meet the book – how serious these matters are.

The seriousness of distress

We imagine that some readers will be less concerned with the niceties of theory, and rather be impatient with the high-handed way in which we seem to dismiss the seriousness of the problems we discuss. Some will say '*but what do we do with dangerous people?*' It should be pointed out that it has been consistently demonstrated that 'mentally ill' people are not more dangerous than the rest of the population. Anyway, we are not arguing that dangerous people do not exist. We are arguing against the transformation of the legal into the psychiatric, the pathologization of resistance as 'dangerousness' and the legitimation of oppressive practices on the basis of an inferred potential commitment of dangerous acts. Also, in this book we have highlighted some of the discursive elements in the issue of dangerousness. Bringing these elements into focus is not, *per se*, an argument for abandoning all forms of civil control over potentially dangerous people, rather it can be seen as a basis for considering some of the ambiguities of psychiatry's relationship to this group. The origins of this relationship and the limited claims to success in the present suggest that there is no 'natural' reason why psychiatry should assume the role in managing this group. Deal with them as offenders, not as 'mentally ill' – and here we are not wishing to romanticize conditions in either hospitals or prisons, both can be equally abusive. (Moreover, it should be pointed out that the 'mentally ill' stay in hospital longer than offenders do in prison). Perhaps we should ask why dangerousness is an issue. There is no scientific evidence that books or schizophrenics are inherently dangerous to the community; there is growing evidence that neuroleptic medication, oppression, marginalization, and silencing of patients is. We have noted in Chapter 4 that dangerousness is over-emphasized in mental illness and this serves a number of powerful interests. You are more likely to be killed by someone not mentally ill, and, as criminal statistics suggest, by someone you know, most probably an ex-partner at home or outside a pub.

Linked to the worry about the seriousness with which we take distress, the claim will no doubt be made that '*deconstruction just pulls everything down leaving those who suffer with nothing*'. Our deconstruction leaves those who suffer with a series of alternatives. Our denial that there are universal truths does not mean that there is nothing left or that anything goes. Some understandings and practices are tactically better than others, and those are the ones we are arguing for. Besides, those who suffer partly suffer because of those practitioners who claim to care for them. Some will find this book too extreme, and say something like '*it is too angry, and loses sight of the reality of practical care*'. It is exactly the reality of 'practical care' we are dealing with in this book. The book shows how this 'practical care' is linked with theories and practices that are constraining and oppressive. Practical care is not free from these elements that have constituted the suffering of those individuals who are 'cared for'. Moreover, it is different types of 'practical care' we are arguing for. And it should be pointed out that such charges are often written by reviewers who are po-faced and out of touch! We have not written in anger and if we have been concerned it is at how the system seems so overwhelming. The attribution of strong 'negative' emotions or mental distress is one strategy used by the powerful to de-legitimize critical views. In this vein we might see the patronizing lament that '*this is not much use for the registrar at midnight*'. Well, it is of use if that registrar is willing to question what he or she is doing, to ask whether it is really of use to the people they see and whether there are other ways those people can be helped. We are not pretending to give easy snap answers.

What about the charge that *'this denies the reality of mental illness'*? Yes, this is exactly what the book does. It denies the reality of mental illness, in the sense that it claims that mental illness is not something in peoples' heads but which is constructed by psychiatric theories and practices. On the other hand it does not deny the reality of mental illness, since the psychiatric construction of 'mental illness' has real effects on the people who fall into this category and it becomes their reality. Parallel to this, the book does not deny the reality of suffering of the 'mentally ill', but it argues that a considerable part of this suffering is the effect of psychiatry. We are not denying that people suffer psychological distress but that distress is always mediated and constructed. Our concern is to attend to that mediation, and to ask what interests are served by the current constructions. That last charge will also be linked in some cases to the charge that *'this is irresponsible, and appeals to vulnerable, impressionable people'*. The polarity underlying this kind of statement is that between science and rhetorics. Science deals with the facts of the world and does not try to persuade, while rhetorics is the art of persuasion, and especially of vulnerable, impressionable people. This is a polarity that needs deconstructing, and we have made some steps in this direction in the book. We have seen how science is not the neutral and objective study of the world, but is enmeshed in and maintained through practices that involve power. The persuasion of scientific knowledge does not rely on the power of its argument or on its correspondence with some kind of external reality, but on its involvement in powerful institutions.

We have been suspicious through the course of the book about the ways in which 'theories' about distress masquerade as 'Truth', and the ways in which that truth is relentlessly forced upon people who have little power to resist. We are well aware of the extent of the pain that people suffer, and our work in therapy, in psychiatric social work and clinical psychology is not an academic matter. This book is as much based on our practical and personal experience of these issues as it is based in research, and it is as much meant to be a helpful practical intervention as it is meant to be an educational text for those in the field of mental health. This point leads us on to the third set of possible complaints that might be levelled against us, that we are not sure who we are addressing.

What is the aim of the book?

We designed the book for activists, students and professionals involved in mental health work, on courses or in clinical practice, but we have not simply written this as a textbook overview of the key issues. This is a 'counter-text.' It might be claimed that *'the readership of this book is unclear'*. It is. We have tried to deconstruct the polarity between academics, students and practitioners. If traditionally academics and students read theoretical stuff, and practitioners read stuff that has to do with their practice, we have tried to avoid such distinctions and include a mixture of both categories. Academically orientated readers might find the book too practical and practitioners might find it too academic. We are deliberately appealing to a diverse audience, to break down some of the boundaries that maintain oppression: user/professional, researcher/researched, and so on. For too long books have been aimed at small separated sections of the population. Since it is aimed at many then everyone will pick holes in it: academics for it not being theoretical enough, practitioners for being too theoretical and so on.

For those already involved in the politics of mental health, it might be objected that *'this is too cautious, and won't go so far as to suggest society is mad'*. We do not suggest that society is mad, and that is because we believe that madness does not exist. Actually, we are not as cautious as others who want to retain the term madness, but just expand it to the whole of society. In contrast, we argue that the category of madness itself is nothing else than a social construction. Similar criticisms might imply that some revolutionary change is necessary. It is, but what about the people in distress waiting for the revolution? There is, then, a need for political strategies which stress diverse, not monolithic tactics.

Some might just not like the perspectives we have chosen, and say something like *'this book privileges certain theoretical orientations or frameworks over others'*. We do not claim theoretical neutrality. We do privilege those orientations which we consider most useful, but the authors share different orientations. We do not consider any of those orientations the solution to the problem, but we do acknowledge that certain orientations can provide better alternatives than others. If anything is privileged it may also be to do with the dominant discourses in which we are positioned when we talk about madness. And there might still be the lingering worry that *'it is not clearly different enough from mainstream approaches not to be assimilated by them'*. Or, from the other side, 'this is what clinicians do anyway' – clinicians could talk their way out of a paper bag to avoid change! Institutions will not want to change; change often has to be forced. Therefore institutions will go through processes of responding to calls for change: ignoring them or calling them irrelevant, saying they are dangerous (when they are a threat) and, finally, attempting to assimilate them. Responses to this book could be seen as symptomatic of reviewers' institutional positions.

Resources for change

Listed here are some groups that have an activist and campaigning focus around mental health, rather than being simply service providers. We have not been able to include everything, and there are undoubtedly many other groups that should be put in an updated list. We cannot vouch for all these groups, and we are relying in some cases on the description they give of themselves. Be warned, and take care. We have not included mainstream 'self-help' organizations that deliberately reproduce medical notions or who defer to traditional 'scientific' experts on mental distress.

Afro-Caribbean Mental Health Project

Formed in Manchester in 1989 as a direct result of concern expressed in the community about the frequency with which second generation African-Caribbean youths were admitted to psychiatric hospitals and the regional forensic unit, it focused on the way in which admissions took place, treatment, after-care and housing. It encourages mental health services to become more sensitive to the needs of the African-Caribbean community, stimulates debate between community groups, facilitates the exploration of mental heath issues, and supports the establishment of self help groups.

This project is at: Zion Community Health and Resource Centre, Zion Crescent, Hulme, Manchester, M15 5BY. There is also a national group, the **Afro-Caribbean Mental Health Association**, which can be contacted at Afro-Caribbean Mental Health Association, 35–37 Electric Avenue, Brixton, London, SW9 8JP, UK.

Alliance of Women in Psychology

This group aims 'to provide active support and a critical voice for women in psychology and women users of psychological services, to examine and raise awareness of gender distribution in psychological careers and education, to collect information about women in psychology and to act as a contact and resource centre, to liaise and work with other women workers and women's groups, and other radical groups in psychology, to counteract adverse propaganda and stereotyping of women and to counter discrimination against all women, whilst recognizing and valuing differences between women, and to encourage research in line with the aims of AWP which can be used to define and attempt to influence social policy'.

AWP can be contacted c/o Kathy Loudoun, 15 West Avenue Road, Walthamstow, London, E17 9SE, UK.

Asylum

This is a quarterly magazine 'for democratic psychiatry': 'It is a non partisan forum for debate for anyone who is in anyway involved in Mental Health . . . The *Asylum* Editorial Group believes that mental health services must be more democratic and humane. This requires effective action for change and can only emerge from democratic debate in which all sides can contribute and be heard *equally*.'

You can get details about subscribing from Professor F. A. Jenner, Manor Farm, Brightonholme Lane, Wharncliffe Side, Sheffield, S30 3DB, UK.

CAPO

The Campaign Against Psychiatric Oppression was set up in 1985, but has roots in the anti-psychiatry movement going back to 1973 and the emergence of the now defunct Mental Patients' Union and the Community Organisation for Psychiatric Emergencies. CAPO works with, and debates with, other organizations in radical mental health, and maintains one of the most radical lines of different groups.

CAPO can be contacted at 28a Edgar House, Kingsmeade Estate, Homerton Road, London E9, UK.

Changes

This publication is 'An International Journal of Psychology and Psychotherapy' which is published as an academic journal by Wiley, and also functions as the house journal of the Psychology and Psychotherapy Association. There are articles by people working in different areas of mental health, as professionals or users of services, and they say in the editorial for each issue that it is 'the only journal which values personal experience in psychological therapy above professional boundaries and doctrinal jargon . . . The result is a celebration of the humanity to be found in the best kinds of psychological therapy and a statement about the kind of world in which we live and work.' The Editor is Craig Newnes, Psychology Consultancy Services, Royal Shrewsbury Hospital, Bicton Heath, Shrewsbury, SY3 8DN, UK.

Community Psychology Network

This network compiles a community psychology directory which lists all those people who have expressed interest in the idea of community psychology in the UK, either in response to a letter in the BPS journal *The Psychologist* (June 1993) or through attendance at one of the conferences in Nottingham (1993) or in Newark (1994). As of February 1995, the network brings together 44 people who are working in community psychology.

A contact address is: Janet Bostock, Steve Melluish or Sarah Warr, Psychology Department, Linden House, 261 Beechdale Road, Aspley, Nottingham, NG8 3EY, UK.

Dulwich Centre

This centre publishes a regular newsletter which has focused on a variety of problems in professional helping (with special issues focusing on, for example, masculinity and professional abuse). The centre is the home for the Epston and White deconstructive, narrative, or postmodern therapies; White is at the Adelaide base, and Epston is in New Zealand. There is a scholarship and exchange scheme for family therapists in other countries.

The main address is: Dulwich Centre, Hutt Street, PO Box 7192, Adelaide 5000, South Australia. Dulwich Centre publications can also be contacted at: c/o Ann Epston, 25 Queens Avenue, Balmoral, Auckland 4, New Zealand; and at Yaletown Family Therapy, PO Box 34185 Station B, Vancouver BC V6J 4N1, Canada.

Family Centre

This centre at Lower Hutt in New Zealand is the base for a form of therapy, 'Just Therapy', which takes seriously the role of colonization, gender, class, poverty and spirituality in the theory and practice of professional help. The centre was originally set up as a research base, and it now operates with the help of volunteers who are trained, as they put it, to be 'sensitive listeners, with an appreciation of the way social structures, pressures and racism disadvantage people'.

The Family Centre address is: PO Box 31–050, 71 Woburn Road, Lower Hutt, New Zealand.

Hearing Voices Network

This Network (HVN), which brings together people who hear voices, has national meetings which discuss the different theories and coping strategies that have been developed. Local groups have mushroomed since the end of the 1980s, and a variety of different frameworks are discussed in the groups for coping with the voices, understanding the voices, celebrating the voices, challenging the voices, or accepting the voices.

HVN can be contacted c/o Creative Support, Fourways House, 16 Tariff Street, Manchester, M1 2EP, UK.

ECT Anonymous

They say 'We are an independent voluntary group of people who are concerned about the adverse effects of Electro-Convulsive-Therapy

(ECT). We offer sympathetic support for sufferers, their families and friends. All enquiries will be treated in the strictest confidence. We have no connection with any Health Authority or Social Services department. The group is for anyone who feels distressed about their past or present ECT treatment or any family members or friends who feel in need of support or who require more information about ECT and its after effects.'

Contact ECT Anonymous at 14 Western Avenue, Riddleston, Keighley, West Yorks, BD20 5DJ, UK.

MADNESS

'MADNESS' is an electronic action and information discussion list for people who experience mood swings, fright, voices and visions (People Who). MADNESS creates an electronic forum and distribution device for exchanging ways to change social systems that touch People Who, and for distributing any information and resources that might be useful. A basic premise of science and research is also a value of MADNESS: to share your findings with others.'

To communicate with other People Who, send e-mail messages to: 'MADNESS@sjuvm.stjohns.edu'. To subscribe, send an e-mail message to: 'listserv@sjuvm.stjohns.edu' with this command in the body of the message: 'subscribe MADNESS yourfirstname yourlastname'.

MANE

MANE (Marjorie A National Emergency) is currently being set up in the UK in response to media scare stories and campaigns to reinforce medical models of mental 'illness', patronized by the Royal Family. The British government's cynical 'care in the community' scheme has thrown many distressed people on to the streets, and sections of the psychiatric establishment have been mobilized by concerned journalists through bodies like SANE (Schizophrenia A National Emergency).

MANE can be contacted c/o HVN, Creative Support, Fourways House, 16 Tariff Street, Manchester, M1 2EP, UK.

MIND

This group was set up as the 'National Association for Mental Health', and National MIND operates as an effective lobbying and information body around issues of patient's rights and mental hospital closure, as well as a coordinating centre for a loose and politically disparate collection of local MIND organizations. It publishes a magazine called 'Open Mind' as well as useful pamphlets, and it holds an annual national conference. It is also the base for 'MINDLINK' (the National MIND Consumer Network). Some of the local groups are active around the politics of mental health as well as service provision, and their addresses can be obtained from National MIND, 22 Harley Street, London, W1N 2ED, UK.

National Association of Psychiatric Survivors

This group, based in Dakota, says 'We aim to promote the human and civil rights of people in and out of psychiatric treatment situations, with special attention to their absolute right to freedom of choice; to work toward the end of involuntary psychiatric interventions, including civil commitment and forced drugging, restraint and seclusion, holding that such intervention against one's will is not a form of treatment, but a violation of liberty and the right to control one's body and mind . . . We attempt to improve the quality of life for psychiatrically labelled people by addressing housing, employment, legal and educational needs, and combating discrimination in these areas and address the needs of homeless and poor people'.

For further details write to: NAPS, PO Box 618, Sioux Falls, South Dakota 57101, USA.

NUVUPSY: A New View of Psychology/Psychiatry

They say 'NUVUPSY is a forum to share points of view critical of the "therapeutic state" and institutional psychiatry, and those supportive of contractual psychotherapy and psychiatry. We're interested in discussions concerning the relationship between liberty and responsibility and its implications for clinical, legal, and public policy. The list will serve to promote alternative views to explaining unwanted behaviors'.

To subscribe, send the following command by e-mail to 'listserv@sjuvm.stjohns.edu': 'subscribe nuvupsy firstname lastname'.

PACE

This Project for Advice, Counselling and Education services provided by lesbians and gay men 'was established in 1985 by a small group of volunteer counsellors to address the mental health issues facing lesbians and gay men in the London area, in particular the need for a counselling and psychotherapy service that does not pathologize homosexuality'. At present they operate crisis, short-term (12 week) and long-term (up to two years) counselling services in-house for individuals and couples (free or on a sliding-scale), and they have a Private Therapists Referral Network for people able to afford a market rate for counselling or psychotherapy. The counselling staff and volunteers come from a wide range of theoretical perspectives within the analytic, existential and humanistic schools.

PACE can be contacted at 34 Hartham Road, London, N7 9JL, UK.

Patient Power

The bi-monthly magazine *Breakthrough* is 'a national bi-monthly magazine produced entirely by sufferers/survivors of mental illness/emotional distress, and carers. Its principle aims are to educate, inform, and most importantly, open up lines of communication between service users and the professional caring services. *Breakthrough* is published by Patient Power. Patient Power believes that it is vital that the views of sufferers/survivors and carers are listened to. It will seek to promote their voice through involvement in the organization, and most importantly, written material'.

For further information about Patient Power and *Breakthrough* contact Richard Marx at 13 St Anthony's House, Caldbeck Avenue, Walker, Newcastle upon Tyne, NE6 3SE, UK.

POPAN

'POPAN (Prevention of Professional Abuse Network) came into being in early 1990 in order to address the issue of sexual abuse in psychotherapy. Even without publicity it has become alarmingly clear to the co-ordinators that the whole issue of abuse in all the so-called caring professions is widespread, extremely damaging, and wherever possible swept under the carpet by professionals.' Since January 1991 'open house' network meetings have been arranged every month for those abused in therapy and in other professional relationships. The network is looking at the availability of Codes of Ethics and Practice, and Complaints Procedures.

POPAN can be contacted at Flat 1, 20 Daleham Gardens, London, NW3 5DA, UK.

Psichiatria Democratica (PD)

PD is the organization set up in Italy to support Franco Basaglia's moves to close the mental hospital in Trieste and build a system of community mental health centres as an empowering alternative to medical regimes. The Trieste example has been important in Latin America, and the work of PD is represented in the English-speaking world by the bi-lingual (English and Italian) journal *Per La Salute Mentale: Pratiche, richerche, culture dell'innovazione*. The journal *Asylum* also takes inspiration from the Trieste example, and although it covers a wider range of alternatives, it still carries the subtitle 'The Magazine of Democratic Psychiatry.'

PD and *Per La Salute Mentale* can be contacted at Via S. Cilino, 16, 34100, Trieste, Italy.

Psy-watch

Psy-watch in South Africa is a psychiatric victims' support group and consumer group based on the critique of Thomas Szasz. It is currently campaigning on behalf of detained patients in South African psychiatric hospitals and is demanding the repeal of the Mental Disorders Act.

For further details contact: Robin Edwards, Denmark House, 3 Rouwkoop Road, Rondebosch 7700, Cape Town, South Africa.

Psychology Politics Resistance (PPR)

PPR was founded in 1994 as a network of people – both psychologists and non-psychologists – who are prepared to oppose the abusive uses of psychology. This means challenging the ideas within psychology that lead to oppressive practices, supporting those who are on the receiving end, and using psychological knowledge positively to help those engaged in struggles for social justice. The group decided as its first task to build an open database designed to operate as a resource network for the organization, and for anyone who wants to call upon PPR or its different subgroupings for information or help. The database will be open on the electronic mail network as an international resource, and so it will be available to anyone who wants to contact people involved in radical psychology or wants to organize other meetings or initiatives.

PPR can be contacted via the Department of Psychology and Speech Pathology, The Manchester Metropolitan University, Hathersage Road, Manchester, M13 OJA, UK.

Psychology and Psychotherapy Association (PPA)

The PPA was founded in 1973. In their advertising they say 'The objects of the Association are to explore and specify the implications of making the person central to psychology inquiry, psychotherapeutic practice and teaching in both psychology and psychological therapies. The Association aims to provide contexts for learning, training and mutual support. Psychological and psychotherapeutic workshops and training meetings are organized and all members receive *Changes*, the PPA's journal, free of charge.'

Application forms are available from Penny Copinger Binns, The Counselling Service, Westox House, Trinity Road, Dudley, West Midlands, DY1 1JB, UK.

Schizophrenia Media Agency (Northwest)

The Schizophrenia Media Agency (SMA) was launched in December 1994 'to make it morally unacceptable to portray people with schizophrenia as violent and dangerous on the one hand or pathetic and pitiable on the other. It publishes a booklet "Freed to Kill" which details coverage at the height of recent press attacks on people with schizophrenia . . . SMA will also encourage and facilitate the press and media to report issues concerning schizophrenia in different and more interesting ways that reflect the actual experience of people with the diagnosis.' It has produced a leaflet with guidelines on reporting, and can be contacted via Nigel Rose, Manchester MIND, 23 New Mount Street, Manchester, M4 4DE, UK.

Support Coalition International

Support Coalition International brings together a wide variety of activist groups – 28 at present – around mental health and publishes the 6,000 copy circulation quarterly newspaper *Dendron* which has been going since 1988. '*Dendron* is an independent non-profit service for the global psychiatric survivors movement, and our allies.' This newspaper, with its slogan 'Madness Network News', is a quarterly 20 page broadsheet; it is active in building links with the disability, women's and anti-racist movements, campaigning against 'forced electroshock, forced psychiatric drugging and racism in psychiatry'. It promotes itself as the 'Greenpeace of mental health'. In the next period the development of electronic mail will undoubtedly expand the influence and subversiveness of the network. Membership of Support Coalition International includes a year's subscription to *Dendron*, and it can be contacted at: Dendron, PO Box 11284, Eugene, OR 97440, USA.

Survivors Speak Out (SSO)

At their conference in September 1987, SSO agreed a 15 point 'Charter of Needs and Demands', which includes: valuing of first hand experience of emotional distress, provision of refuge, counselling and choice of services and resources, a government review and adequate funding, representation of users and ex-users of services on statutory bodies, access to personal medical records and legal protection, the rights of staff to refuse to administer any treatment and the phasing out of ECT and psycho-surgery, independent monitoring of drug use and provision of information on treatments, and an end to discrimination against people who receive, or who have received, psychiatric services.

SSO can be contacted c/o Peter Campbell, 33 Lichfield Road, London, NW2 2RG, UK.

UKAN

The United Kingdom Advocacy Network is the Federation of User-Run Patients' Councils, Support Groups, Advocacy Projects and User Forums which are involved or intend to be involved in the planning, monitoring and running of mental health services of all kinds with the key aim of empowering the people who use those services.

Contact UKAN at Premier House, 14 Cross Burgess Street, Sheffield, S1 2HG, UK.

WISH

Women In Special Hospitals is a registered charity that works on behalf of women either in, or released from, Special Hospitals, Regional Secure Units and prison psychiatric units. Its broad aim is the reform of psychiatric provision for women by raising awareness and initiating relevant research. Additionally, it serves an advisory function for women who are in-patients and seeks to empower women who have been discharged from psychiatric containment.

WISH can be contacted at the following address: WISH (Women in Special Hospitals and Secure Psychiatric Units), 25 Horsell Road, London, N5 1XL, UK.

VAK

VAK stands for 'Voimavarasuuntautuneen asiaskastyon kehittamiskeskus' (which means 'Centre for Resource-Oriented Client Work'). This centre in Helsinki is an example of an attempt to develop good practice in therapy as an alternative to mainstream psychodynamic approaches in Finland. It mixes solution-focused models with the Epston and White work: 'We talk of respectful conversations turning to respectful and imaginative/playful conversations'. It also has a training programme in 'Resource-Oriented Client Work', and runs short meetings to discuss therapeutic, resource and empowerment issues.

VAK can be contacted via Eero Riikonen, VAK, Ruusulankatu 10, 02600 Helsinki, Finland.

References

Abramowitz, C.V. and Dokecki, P.R. (1977) 'The politics of clinical judgment: early empirical returns', *Psychological Bulletin*, 84: 460–476.

Allen, H. (1987) *Justice Unbalanced: Gender, Psychiatry and Judicial Decisions*. Buckingham: Open University Press.

Allen, H.A. and Allen, D.S. (1985) 'Positive symptoms and the organisation within and between ideas in schizophrenic speech', *Psychological Medicine*, 15(1): 71–80.

Allwood, R. (1995) 'The social construction of depression'. Paper presented at 'Understanding the Social World' conference, Huddersfield, July.

Alverson, H. and Rosenberg, S. (1990) 'Discourse analysis of schizophrenic speech: a critique and proposal', *Applied Psycholinguistics*, 11: 167–184.

American Psychiatric Association (1987) *Diagnostic and Statistical Manual of Mental Disorders*, 3rd rev. edn. Washington, DC: American Psychiatric Association.

American Psychiatric Association (1994) *Diagnostic and Statistical Manual of Mental Disorders (DSM-IV™)*, 4th edn. Washington, DC: American Psychiatric Association.

Andersen, T. (1987) 'The reflecting team', *Family Process*, 26: 415–428.

Andreasen, N.C. (1979) 'Thought, language and communication disorders: I. Clinical assessment, definition of terms and evaluation of their reliability', *Archives of General Psychiatry*, 36: 1315–1321.

Andreasen, N.C., Hoffman, R.E. and Grove, W.M. (1985) 'Mapping abnormalities in language and cognition', in M. Alpert (ed.), *Controversies in Schizophrenia: Changes and Constancies*. New York: Guildford Press, pp. 199–226.

Appleyard, B. (1993) 'Bryan Appleyard on paranoia', *The Independent Magazine*, 15 May, 16–17.

Austin, J.L. (1962) *How To Do Things With Words*. Oxford: Oxford University Press.

Azrin, N.H. and Holz, W.C. (1966) 'Punishment', in W.K. Honig (ed.), *Operant Behavior*. New York: Appleton-Century-Crofts.

Banton, R., Clifford, P., Frosh, S., Lousada, J. and Rosenthall, J. (1985) *The Politics of Mental Health*. London: Macmillan.

Barham, P. (1992) *Closing the Asylum: The Mental Patient in Modern Society*. Harmondsworth: Penguin.

Barker, A. (1992) 'Cries and whispers: what is a paranoia movie?, asks Adam Barker, looking at work from Coppola to "JFK" ', *Sight and Sound*, 1: 24–25.

Barnes, M. and Berke, J. (1973) *Mary Barnes: Two Accounts of a Journey Through Madness*. Harmondsworth: Penguin.

Barnes, P. (1986) *Shrink Rap: Punch on the Analyst's Couch*. London: Grafton.

Barr, W.B., Bilder, R.M., Goldberg, E., Kaplan, E. and Mukherjee, S. (1989) 'The neuropsychology of schizophrenic speech', *Journal of Communication Disorders*, 22: 327–349.

Barrett, R.J. (1988) 'Clinical writing and the documentary construction of schizophrenia', *Culture, Medicine and Psychiatry*, 12: 265–299.

Barrett, R.J. (1991) 'Psychiatric practice and the definition of schizophrenia', *Dulwich Centre Newsletter*, 4: 5–11.

Barthes, R. (1981 [1973]) 'Theory of the text', in R. Young (ed.), *Untying the Text*. London: Routledge. pp. 31–47.

Basaglia, F. (1987) *Psychiatry Inside Out: Selected Writings of Franco Basaglia*. New York: Columbia University Press.

Bateson, G. (1972) *Steps to an Ecology of Mind*. New York: Ballantine.

Beck, A.T. (1976) *Cognitive Therapy and the Emotional Disorders*. New York: International Universities Press.

Bentall, R.P. (ed.) (1990) *Reconstructing Schizophrenia*. London: Routledge.

Bentall, R.P. (1992a) 'Reconstructing psychopathology', *The Psychologist: Bulletin of the British Psychological Society*, February, 61–65.

Bentall, R.P. (1992b) 'A proposal to classify happiness as a psychiatric disorder', *Journal of Medical Ethics*, 18: 94–98.

Bentall, R.P., Jackson, H.F. and Pilgrim, D. (1988) 'Abandoning the concept of schizophrenia: some implications of validity arguments for psychological research into psychotic phenomena', *British Journal of Clinical Psychology*, 27: 303–324.

Berrios, G.E. (1988) 'Historical background to abnormal psychology', in E. Miller and P.J. Cooper (eds), *Adult Abnormal Psychology*. Edinburgh: Churchill Livingstone.

Bettelheim, B. (1986) *Freud and Man's Soul*. London: Flamingo.

Billig, M. (1991) *Ideology and Opinions: Studies in Rhetorical Psychology*. London: Sage.

Birchwood, M. and Tarrier, N. (1992) *Innovations in the Psychological Management of Schizophrenia*. Chichester: Wiley.

Black Health Workers and Patients Group (1983) 'Psychiatry and the corporate state', *Race and Class*, 25 (2): 49–64.

Blackburn, R. (1988) 'On moral judgements and personality disorders: the myth of psychopathic disorder revisited', *British Journal of Psychiatry*, 153: 505–512.

Blackburn, R. (1990) 'Treatment of the psychopathic offender, clinical approaches to working with mentally disordered and sexual offenders', in K. Howells and R. Hollins (eds), *Issues in Criminological and Legal Psychology*. Leicester: British Psychological Society.

Bleuler, E. (1950 [1911]) *Dementia Praecox: or the Group of Schizophrenias*. trans. J. Zinkin. New York: International Universities Press.

Blom-Cooper, L., Hally, M. and Murphy, J. (1995) *The Falling Shadow*. London: HMSO.

Bourdieu, P. (1984) *Distinction: a Social Critique of the Judgement of Taste*, trans. R. Nice. London: Routledge and Kegan Paul.

Bowden, P. (1981) 'What happens to patients released from Special Hospitals?', *British Journal of Psychiatry*, 138: 340–345.

Bowers, J. (1988) 'Review essay on *Discourse and Social Psychology: Beyond Attitudes and Behaviour*', *British Journal of Social Psychology*, 27: 185–192.

Boyers, R. and Orrill, R. (eds) (1971) *R. D. Laing and Anti-Psychiatry*. Harmondsworth: Penguin.

Boyle, M. (1990) *Schizophrenia: a Scientific Delusion?* London: Routledge.

Boyle, M. (1994) 'Schizophrenia and the art of the soluble', *The Psychologist*, 7 (9): 399–404.

Boyne, R. (1990) *Foucault and Derrida: the Other Side of Reason*. London: Unwin Hyman.

Breggin, P. (1991) *Toxic Psychiatry*. London: Harper Collins.

Bromley, E. (1993) 'Social class and psychotherapy revisited'. Paper presented at British Psychological Society Annual Conference, Brighton, March.

Brown, G.W. and Harris, T.O. (1978) *Social Origins of Depression*. London: Tavistock.

Bulhan, H.A. (1980) 'Frantz Fanon: the revolutionary psychiatrist', *Race and Class*, 21 (3): 251–271.

Burkitt, I. (1991) *Social Selves: Theories of the Social Formation of Personality*. London: Sage.

Burman, E. (1995) 'Identification, subjectivity and power in Feminist psychotherapy', in J. Siegfried (ed.), *Therapeutic and Everyday Discourse as Behavior Change: Towards a Micro-Analysis in Therapeutic Process Research*. New York: Ablex, pp. 469–489.

Burns, J. and Newnes, C. (eds) (1994) *Homosexuality, Psychotherapy and Society*, Special Issue, *Changes: an International Journal of Psychology and Psychotherapy*, 12 (4).

Butler, J. (1990) *Gender Trouble*. London: Routledge.

Calman, M. (1979) *Dr Calman's Dictionary of Psychoanalysis*. London: W. H. Allen.

Campbell, D. and Connor, S. (1986) *On the Record: Surveillance, Computers and Privacy – the Inside Story*. London: Michael Joseph.

Casement, P. (1985) *On Learning from the Patient*. London: Routledge.

Castel, F., Castel, R. and Lovell, A. (1979) *The Psychiatric Society*. New York: Columbia Free Press.

Cecchin, G., Lane, G. and Ray, W.A. (1993) 'From strategizing to non-intervention: toward irreverence in systemic practice', *Journal of Marital and Family Therapy*, 19: 125–136.

Chadwick, P. and Birchwood, M. (1994) 'The omnipotence of voices: a cognitive approach to auditory hallucinations', *British Journal of Psychiatry*, 164: 190–201.

Chaika, E.O. (1974) 'A linguist looks at schizophrenic language', *Brain and Language*, 1: 257–276.

Chaika, E.O. (1990) *Understanding Psychotic Speech: Beyond Freud and Chomsky*. Springfield, IL: Charles C. Thomas.

Chamberlin, J. (1988) *On Our Own: Patient Controlled Alternatives to the Mental Health System*, London: MIND.

Chaplin, J. (1988) *Feminist Counselling in Action*. London: Sage.

Chesler, P. (1973) *Women and Madness*. London: Allen Lane.

Cixous, H. (1975) 'Sorties', in E. Marks and I. de Courtivon (eds), *New French Feminisms*. Hassocks, Sussex: Harvester.

Clare, A. (1976) *Psychiatry in Dissent: Controversial Issues in Thought and Practice*, London: Tavistock.

Cleckley, H. (1964) *The Mask of Sanity*. St Louis, MO: Mosby.

Coleman, R. and McLaughlin, T. (1994) 'I'm back! In support of resisting treatment', *Asylum*, 8 (2): 26–28.

Coleman, R. and McLaughlin, T. (1995) 'A collectivist model of self help', *Asylum*.

Collier, A. (1977) *R. D. Laing: the Philosophy and Politics of Psychotherapy*. Hassocks, Sussex: Harvester.

Collins, P. (1991) 'The treatability of psychopaths', *Journal of Forensic Psychiatry*, 2 (1): 103–110.

Consoli, S. (1979) 'Le récit du psychotique', in J.M. Ribettes (ed.), *Vérité et vraisemblance du texte psychotique*. Paris: Seuil. pp. 36–76.

Cooper, D. (1972) *The Death of the Family*. Harmondsworth: Penguin.

Cope, R. and Ndegwa, D. (1990) 'Ethnic differences in admission to a Regional Secure Unit', *Journal of Forensic Psychiatry*, 1 (3): 365–378.

Cozolino, L.G. (1983) 'The oral and written productions of schizophrenic patients', *Progress in Experimental Personality Research*, 12: 101–152.

Curt, B. (1994) *Textuality and Tectonics: Troubling Social and Psychological Science*. Buckingham: Open University Press.

D'Amico, R. (1984) 'Text and Context: Derrida and Foucault on Descartes', in J. Fekete (ed.), *The Structural Allegory: Reconstructive Encounters with the New French Thought*. Manchester: Manchester University Press.

Danziger, K. (1990) 'Generative metaphor and the history of psychological discourse', in D.E. Leary (ed.), *Metaphors in the History of Psychology*. New York: Cambridge University Press.

Davies, B. and Harré, R. (1990) 'Positioning: the discursive production of selves', *Journal for the Theory of Social Behaviour*, 20: 43–63.

Dawson, F.L., Bartolucci, G. and Blum, H.M. (1980) 'Language and schizophrenia: towards a synthesis', *Comprehensive Psychiatry*, 211: 81–90.

de Shazer (1985) *Keys to Solution in Brief Therapy*. London: Norton.

Deleuze, G. and Guattari, F. (1977) *Anti-Oedipus*. New York: Athlone Press.

Dell, S. and Robertson, G. (1988), *Sentenced to Hospital: Offenders in Broadmoor*. Oxford: Oxford University Press.

Department of Health and Social Security (1977) *The Role of Psychologists in the Health Service (The Trethowan Report)*. London: HMSO.

Derrida, J. (1973) *Speech and Phenomena, and Other Essays on Husserl's Theory of Signs*. Evanston, IL: Northwestern University Press.

Derrida, J. (1976) *Of Grammatology*. Baltimore and London: Johns Hopkins University Press.

Derrida, J. (1978) *Writing and Difference*. London: Routledge and Kegan Paul.

Dolan, B. and Coid, J. (1993) *Psychopathic and Anti-Social Personality Disorders: Treatment and Research Issues*. London: Gaskell.

Easthope, A. (1990) ' "I gotta use words when I talk to you": deconstructing the theory of communication', in I. Parker and J. Shotter (eds), *Deconstructing Social Psychology*. London: Routledge. pp. 76–90.

Edelman, M. (1977) *Political Language: Words that Succeed and Policies that Fail*. London: Academic Press.

Edwards, D. and Potter, J. (1992) *Discursive Psychology*. London: Sage.

Epston, D. and White, M. (1989) *Literate Means to Therapeutic Ends*. Adelaide: Dulwich Centre Publications.

Erickson, M. and Rossi, E.L. (1979) *Hypnotherapy: an Exploratory Casebook*. New York: Irvington.

Ernst, S. and Maguire, M. (eds) (1987) *Living with the Sphinx: Papers from the Women's Therapy Centre*. London: Women's Press.

Eysenck, H.J. and Eysenck, S.B.G. (1978) 'Pyschopathy, personality and genetics', in R.D. Hare and D. Schalling (eds), *Psychopathic Behaviour: Approaches to Research*. Chichester: John Wiley.

Eysenck, H.J. and Rachman, S. (1964) *The Causes and Cures of Neurosis*. London: Routledge and Kegan Paul.

Faulk, P. (1990) 'Her Majesties Prison, Grendon Underwood', in R. Bluglass and P. Bowden (eds), *Principles and Practice of Forensic Psychiatry*. London: Churchill Livingstone.

Fernando, S. (1993) 'Psychiatry and racism', *Changes: an International Journal of Psychology and Psychotherapy*, 10: 46–58.

Forrester, J. (1980) *Language and the Origins of Psychoanalysis*. London: Macmillan.

Forshaw, D. and Rollin, H. (1990) 'The history of forensic psychiatry in England', in R. Bluglass and P. Bowden (eds), *Principles and Practice of Forensic Psychiatry*. London: Churchill Livingstone.

Foucault, M. (1971) *Madness and Civilization*. London: Tavistock Press.

Foucault, M. (1977) *Discipline and Punish: the Birth of the Prison*. London: Allen Lane.

Foucault, M. (1978) 'About the concept of the "Dangerous Individual" in 19th-century legal psychiatry', *International Journal of Law and Psychiatry*, 1: 1–18.

Foucault, M. (1980) *Power/knowledge. Selected Interviews and Other Writings 1972–1977*. Brighton: Harvester Press.

Foucault, M. (1981) *The History of Sexuality*, vol. 1. Harmondsworth: Penguin.

Fowler, D., Garety, P. and Kuipers, L. (1994) *Cognitive Behaviour Therapy for Psychosis: Theory and Practice*. Chichester: Wiley.

Fraser, W.I., King, K.M., Thomas, P. and Kendell, R.E. (1986) 'The diagnosis of schizophrenia by language analysis', *British Journal of Psychiatry*, 148: 275–278.

Freud, S. (1979 [1911]) Psycho-analytic notes on an autobiographical account of a case of paranoia (dementia paranoides). in A. Richards (ed.), *Freud Pelican Library, vol. 9, Case Histories II*. Harmondsworth: Penguin.

Freud, S. (1984 [1915]) 'The Unconscious', in A. Richards, *Freud Pelican Library*, vol. 11, *On Metapsychology*. Harmondsworth: Penguin.

Freud, S. (1973 [1933]) 'New Introductory Lectures on Psychoanalysis', in A. Richards, *Freud Pelican Library*, vol. 2, *New Introductory Lectures on Psychoanalysis*. Harmondsworth: Penguin.

Frith, C.D. and Done, D.J. (1988) 'Towards a neuropsychology of schizophrenia', *British Journal of Psychiatry*, 153: 437–443.

Frosh, S. (1991) *Identity Crisis: Modernity, Psychoanalysis and the Self*. London: Macmillan.

Gaines, A.D. (1992) 'From DSM-I to III-R; voices of self, mastery and the other: A cultural constructivist reading of US psychiatric classification', *Social Science and Medicine*, 35: 3–24.

Gandy Jr, O. H. (1993) *The Panoptic Sort: a Political Economy of Personal Information*. Oxford: Westview Press.

Georgaca, E. and Gordo-López, A.J. (1995) 'Subjectivity and "psychotic" discourses: a preliminary study', in M. Sullivan (ed.), *Psychoanalytic Seminars, 1991–1994*. London: THERIP.

Gilbert, G.N. and Mulkay, M. (1984) *Opening Pandora's Box: a Sociological Study of Scientists' Discourse*. Cambridge: Cambridge University Press.

Gleeson, K. (1991) 'Out of Our Minds: the deconstruction and reconstruction of madness'. PhD dissertation, University of Reading.

Glenn, M.L. (1967) 'Press of freedom', *Village Voice*, 14 September.

Goldberg, D. and Huxley, P. (1992) *Common Mental Disorders: a Bio-Social Model*. London: Tavistock/Routledge.

Goldner, V. (1993) 'Power and hierarchy: let's talk about it', *Family Process*, 32: 157–162.

Gordon, C. (1990) '*Histoire de la folie*: an unknown book by Michel Foucault', *History of the Human Sciences*, 3 (1): 3–26.

Gostin, L. (1986) *Institutions Observed: Towards a New Concept of Secure Provision in Mental Health*. London: King Edward's Hospital Fund for London.

Gottschalk, L.A. and Gleser, G.C. (1979) *Content Analysis of Verbal Behaviour*. New York: Medical and Scientific Books.

Graumann, C.F. and Moscovici, S. (eds) (1987) *Changing Conceptions of Conspiracy*. New York: Springer-Verlag.

Greenslade, L. (1993) 'Na daoine gan aird: Irish people and mental health services', *Changes: an International Journal of Psychology and Psychotherapy*, 11: 127–137.

Grosz, E. (1990) *Jacques Lacan: a feminist introduction*. London: Routledge.

Grounds, A. (1987) 'Detention of "psychopathic disorder" patients in Special Hospitals: critical issues', *British Journal of Psychiatry*, 151: 474–478.

Guattari, F. (1984) *Molecular Revolution: Psychiatry and Politics*. Harmondsworth: Peregrine.

Hak, T. (1989) 'Constructing a psychiatric case', in B. Torode (ed.) *Text and Talk as Social Practice*. Dordrecht, Holland: Foris Publications.

Haley, J. (1963) *Strategies of Psychotherapy*. New York: Grune and Stratton.

Hallam, R.S. (1994) 'Some constructionist observations on "anxiety" and its history', in T.R. Sarbin and J.I. Kitsuse (eds), *Constructing the Social*. London: Sage.

Hamilton, K. (1990) 'Special hospitals and the state hospital', in R. Bluglass and P. Bowden (eds) *Principles and Practice of Forensic Psychiatry*. London: Churchill Livingstone.

Handy, J.A. (1987) 'Psychology and social context', *Bulletin of the British Psychological Society*, 40: 161–167.

Hare, R.D. (1980) 'A research scale for the assessment of psychopathy in criminal populations'. *Personality and Individual Differences*, 1: 111–117.

Harper, D.J. (1993) 'Discourses of conspiracy, suspicion and mistrust: "Paranoia" and its cultural significance'. Unpublished manuscript.

Harper, D.J. (1994a) 'Histories of suspicion in a time of conspiracy: a reflection on Aubrey Lewis' history of paranoia', *History of the Human Sciences*, 7: 89–109.

Harper, D.J. (1994b) 'The professional construction of "paranoia" and the discursive use of diagnostic criteria', *British Journal of Medical Psychology*, 67: 131–143.

Harper, D.J. (in press) 'Deconstructing "paranoia": towards a discursive understanding of apparently unwarranted suspicion', *Theory and Psychology*.

Harré, R. (1983) *Personal Being*. Oxford: Basil Blackwell.

Harris, B. (1995) 'Psychology and Marxist politics in America', in I. Parker and R. Spears (eds), *Psychology and Marxism: Coexistence and Contradiction*. London: Pluto Press.

Harrow, M. and Quinlan, D.M. (1985) *Disordered Thinking and Schizophrenic Psychopathology*. New York: Gardner Press.

Harrow, M., Marengo, J. and Pogue-Geile, D.M. (1987) 'Positive thought disorder in schizophrenia: its importance, its longitudinal course and impaired perspective as a contributing factor', in P.D. Harvey and E.F. Walker (eds), *Positive and Negative Symptoms in Psychosis: Description, Research and Future Directions*. Hillsdale, NJ: Lawrence Erlbaum Associates. pp. 155–196.

Harrow, M., Lanin-Kettering, I. and Miller, J.G. (1989) 'Impaired perspective and thought pathology in schizophrenic and psychotic disorders', *Schizophrenia Bulletin*, 15: 605–623.

Hartmann, H. (1958) *Ego Psychology and the Problem of Adaptation*. New York: International Universities Press.

Harvey, P.D. (1983) 'Speech competence in manic and schizophrenic psychoses: the association between clinically rated thought disorder and cohesion and reference performance', *Journal of Abnormal Psychology*, 92: 368–377.

Harvey, P.D. and Neale, J.M. (1983) 'The specificity of thought disorder to schizophrenia: research methods in their historical perspective', *Progress in Experimental Personality Research*, 12: 153–180.

Hepworth, J. (1994) 'Qualitative analysis and eating disorders: discourse analytic research on anorexia nervosa', *International Journal of Eating Disorders*, 15: 179–185.

Hepworth, J. and Griffin, C. (1990) 'The "discovery" of anorexia nervosa: discourses of the late 19th century', *Text*, 10: 321–338.

Hill, D. (1983) *The Politics of Schizophrenia: Psychiatric Oppression in the United States*. London: University Press of America.

HMSO (1983) *The Mental Health Act, 1983*. London: HMSO.

Hobson, R. (1986) *Forms of Feeling: the Heart of Psychotherapy*. London: Tavistock.

Hoffman, R.E. (1986) 'Tree structures, the work of listening and schizophrenic discourse: a reply to Beveridge and Brown', *Brain and Language*, 27: 385–392.

Hoffman, R.E., Kirstein, L., Stopek, S. and Cicchetti, D.V. (1982) 'Apprehending schizophrenic discourse: a structural analysis of the listener's task', *Brain and Language*, 15(2): 207–233.

Holland, S. (1992) 'From social abuse to social action: a neighbourhood psychotherapy and social action project for women', *Changes: an International Journal of Psychology and Psychotherapy*, 10 (2): 146–153.

Holland, S. and Holland, R. (1984) 'Depressed women: outposts of empire and castles of skin', in B. Richards (ed.), *Capitalism and Infancy: Essays on Psychoanalysis and Politics*. London: Free Association Books.

Hollingshead, A.B. and Redlich, F.A. (1958) *Social Class and Mental Illness*. New York: Wiley.

Holzman, L. (1995) 'Newman's practice of method completes Vygotsksy', in I. Parker and R. Spears (eds), *Psychology and Marxism: Coexistence and Contradiction*. London: Pluto Press.

Hotchkiss, A.P. and Harvey, P.D. (1986) 'Linguistic analysis of speech disorder in psychosis', *Clinical Psychology Review*, 6(2): 155–175.

Howe, D. (1994) 'Modernity, post-modernity and social work', *British Journal of Social Work*, 24: 513–532.

Illich, I. (1976) *Limits to Medicine: The Expropriation of Health*. Harmondsworth: Penguin.

Irigaray, L. (1985) *Parler n'est jamais neutre*. Paris: Minuit.

Jaynes, J. (1976) *The Origin of Consciousness in the Breakdown of the Bicameral Mind*. Boston: Houghton-Mifflin.

Jenkins, H. and Asen, K. (1992) 'Family therapy without the family: a framework for systemic practice', *Journal of Family Therapy*, 14: 1–14.

Jenner, F.A., Monteiro, A.C.D., Zagalo-Cardoso, J.A. and Cunha-Oliveira, J.A. (1993) *Schizophrenia: a Disease or Some Ways of Being Human*. Sheffield: Sheffield University Press.

Johnstone, L. (1989) *Users and Abusers of Psychiatry*. London: Routledge.

Johnston, M.H. and Holzman, P.S. (1979) *Assessing Schizophrenic Thinking: a Clinical and Research Instrument for Measuring Thought Disorder*. San Francisco: Jossey-Bass.

Jones, K. (1993) *Asylums and After: a Revised History of the Mental Health Services, from the Early 18th Century to the 1990s*. London: Athlone Press.

Jones, G. and Berry, M. (1984) 'Regional Secure Units: the emerging picture', in G. Edwards (ed.), *Current Issues in Clinical Psychology*, vol. 4. London: Plenum. pp. 111–119.

Kendler, K.S. (1982) 'Demography of paranoid psychosis (delusional disorder): a review and comparison with schizophrenia and affective illness'. *Archives of General Psychiatry*, 39: 890–902.

Kiev, A. (1972) *Transcultural Psychiatry*. New York: Free Press.

Kirk, S.A. and Kutchins, H. (1992) *The Selling of DSM: The Rhetoric of Science in Psychiatry*. New York: Aldine de Gruyter.

Kitzinger, C. and Stainton Rogers, R. (1985) 'A Q-methodological study of lesbian identities', *European Journal of Social Psychology*, 15: 167–187.

Koh, S.D. (1978) 'Remembering of verbal materials by schizophrenic young adults', in S. Schwartz (ed.), *Language and Cognition in Schizophrenia*, Hillsdale, NJ: Lawrence Erlbaum Associates. pp. 55–99.

Kraepelin, E. (1919) *Dementia Praecox and Paraphrenia*, trans. R.M. Barclay. Edinburgh: Livingstone.

Kramer, H. and Sprenger, J. (1971) *Malleus Maleficarum*. London: Arrow Books.

Kristeva, J. (1969) Σημειωτικη: Récherches pour une sémanalyse. Paris: Seuil.

Kvale, S. (ed.) (1992) *Psychology and Postmodernism*. London: Sage.

Labov, W. and Fanshel, D. (1977) *Therapeutic Discourse: Psychotherapy as Conversation*. New York: Academic Press.

Lacan, J. (1977) *Écrits: a Selection*, trans. A. Sheridan. London: Tavistock.

Laing, R.D. (1965) *The Divided Self: an Existential Study in Sanity and Madness*. Harmondsworth: Penguin.

Laing, R.D. (1986) 'Sanity, madness and the psychiatric profession: an interview', *Asylum*, 1: 13–21.

Laing, R.D. and Esterson, A. (1964) *Sanity, Madness and the Family: Families of Schizophrenics*. London: Tavistock.

Lakoff, G. and Johnson, M. (1980) *Metaphors We Live By*. Chicago: University of Chicago Press.

Lee, M. (1992) 'Schizophrenia: from the inside out', *Dulwich Centre Newsletter*, 1: 18–24.

Levenson, M.R. (1992) 'Rethinking psychopathy', *Theory and Psychology*, 2 (1): 51–71.

Levinson, S.C. (1983) *Pragmatics*. Cambridge: Cambridge University Press.

Lewis, A. (1970) 'Paranoia and paranoid: a historical perspective', *Psychological Medicine*, 1: 2–12.

Lewis, A. (1979) *The Later Papers of Sir Aubrey Lewis*. Oxford: Oxford University Press.

Lidz, T. (1963) *The Family and Human Adaptation*. New York: Harper and Row.

Littlewood, R. and Lipsedge, M. (1989) *Aliens and Alienists: Ethnic Minorities and Psychiatry*, 2nd edn. London: Unwin Hyman.

Livingstone, S. and Lunt, P. (1994) Psychologists on television. *The Psychologist*, 7, 207–211.

Lomas, P. (1987) *The Limits of Interpretation: What's Wrong with Psychoanalysis?* Harmondsworth: Penguin.

Lovie, A.D. (1983) Attention and behaviourism – fact and fiction. *British Journal of Psychology*. 74, 301–310.

Lovlie, L. (1992), 'Postmodernism and subjectivity', in S. Kvale (ed.) *Psychology and Postmodernism*. London: Sage.

Lowson, D. (1994) 'Understanding professional thought disorder: a guide for service users and a challenge for professionals', *Asylum*, 8 (2): 29–30.

MacDonald, M. (1981) *Mystical Bedlam; Madness and Healing in Seventeenth-Century England*. Cambridge: Cambridge University Press.

McCord, J. (1982) *The Psychopath and Milieu Therapy: a Longitudinal Study*. New York: Academic Press.

McGorry, P.D. (1991) 'The schizophrenia concept in first episode psychosis: does it fit and is it harmful? Aspects of psychoeducational work in the first episode', *Dulwich Centre Newsletter*, 4: 40–44.

McGrath, J. (1991) 'Ordering thoughts on thought disorder', *British Journal of Psychiatry*, 158: 307–316.

McKeown, B. and Thomas, D. (1988) 'O Methodology', *QASS Vol. 66*. London: Sage.

McKinnon, L. and Miller, D. (1987) 'The new epistemology and the Milan approach: feminist and socio-political considerations', *Journal of Marital and Family Therapy*, 13: 139–155.

McNamee, S. and Gergen, K.J. (1992) *Therapy as Social Construction*. London: Sage.

Macey, D. (1988) *Lacan in Contexts*. London: Verso.

Macey, D. (1994) *The Lives of Michel Foucault*. London: Vintage.

Maher, B.A. (1972) 'The language of schizophrenia: a review and interpretation', *British Journal of Psychiatry*, 120: 3–17.

Maher, B.A., Manschreck, T.C., Hoover, T.H. and Weisstein, C.C. (1987) 'Thought disorder and measured features of language production in schizophrenia', in P.D. Harvey and E.F. Walker (eds), *Positive and Negative Symptoms in Psychosis: Description, Research and Future Directions*. Hillsdale, NJ: Lawrence Erlbaum Associates. pp. 195–215.

Mair, M. (1989) *Between Psychology and Psychotherapy: a Poetics of Experience*. London: Routledge.

Malcolm, J. (1984) *In the Freud Archives*. London: Flamingo.

Marks, I., Hallam, R., Connolly, J. and Philpott, R. (1977) *Nursing in Behavioural Psychotherapy*. London: Royal College of Nursing.

Masson, J. M. (1984) *The Assault on Truth: Freud's Abandonment of the Seduction Theory*. London: Harmondsworth.

Maturana, H.R. and Varela, F.J. (1980) *Autopoiesis and Cognition: the Realisation of the Living*. Dordrecht: D. Reidel.

Méndez, C.L., Coddou, F. and Maturana, H.R. (1988) 'The bringing forth of pathology', *Irish Journal of Psychology*, 9: 144–172.

Mercer, K. (1986) 'Racism and transcultural psychiatry', in P. Miller and N. Rose (eds), *The Power of Psychiatry*. Cambridge: Polity Press.

Middleton, P. (1992) *The Inward Gaze: Masculinity and Subjectivity in Modern Culture*. London: Routledge.

Mihill, C. (1994a) 'Warning signs given by mental patients who killed', *Guardian*, 17 August: p. 5.

Mihill, C. (1994b) 'Tranquilizers "kill one a week" ', *Guardian*, 27 August: p. 4.

Miles, R. (1989) *Racism*. London: Routledge.

Miller, P (1986) 'Psychotherapy of work and unemployment', in N. Rose and P. Miller (eds), *The Power of Psychiatry*. Cambridge: Polity Press.

Miller, P. and Rose, N. (eds) (1986) *The Power of Psychiatry*. Cambridge: Polity Press.

Millett, K. (1977) *Sexual Politics*. London: Virago.

Minuchin, S. (1974) *Families and Family Therapy*. London: Tavistock Press.

Mitchell, J. (1974) *Psychoanalysis and Feminism*. Harmondsworth: Penguin.

Morice, P. and Ingram, J.C.L. (1982) 'Language analysis in schizophrenia: diagnostic implications', *Australian and New Zealand Journal of Psychiatry*, 16: 11–21.

Moscovici, S. (1976) *La Psychanalyse: Son image et son public*, 2nd edn. Paris: Presses Universitaire de France.

NACRO Briefing (1991) *Race and Criminal Justice*. London.

Newman, F. (1994) *Let's Develop! A Guide to Continuous Personal Growth*. New York: Castillo International Inc.

Newson, J. and Shotter, J. (1974) 'How babies communicate', *New Statesman and Society*, 29: 345–347.

Norris, M. (1984) *Integration of Special Hospital Patients into the Community*. Aldershot: Gower.

Nuckolls, C.W. (1992) 'Introduction. Reckless driving, casual sex and shoplifting: what psychiatric categories, culture and history reveal about each other', *Social Science and Medicine*, 35: 1–2.

O'Donnell, P. (1992) 'Engendering paranoia in contemporary narrative', *Boundary 2: An International Journal of Literature and Culture*, 19: 181–204.

O'Neill, M. and Stockell, G. (1991) 'Worthy of discussion: collaborative group therapy', *Australia and New Zealand Journal of Family Therapy*, 12 (4): 201–206.

Owen, D. (1991) 'Foucault, psychiatry and the spectre of dangerousness', *Journal of Forensic Psychiatry*, 2 (3): 238–241.

Oxman, T.E., Rosenberg, S.D. and Tucker, G.J. (1982) 'The language of paranoia', *American Journal of Psychiatry*, 139(3): 275–282.

Padel, R. (1981) 'Madness in fifth-century (B.C.) Athenian tragedy', in P. Heelas and A. Lock (eds), *Indigenous Psychologies: the Anthropology of the Self*. London: Academic Press.

Parker, I. (1992) *Discourse Dynamics: Critical Analysis for Social and Individual Psychology*. London: Routledge.

Parker, I. (1995a) 'Michel Foucault, psychologist', *The Psychologist*, 8 (11): 214–216.

Parker, I. (1995b) ' "Right" said Fred "I'm too sexy for bourgeois group therapy": the case of the Institute for Social Therapy', *Changes: an International Journal of Psychology and Psychotherapy*, 13 (1): 1–22.

Parker, I. and Shotter, J. (eds) (1990) *Deconstructing Social Psychology*. London: Routledge.

Parker, I. and Spears, R. (eds) (1995) *Psychology and Marxism: Coexistence and Contradiction*. London: Pluto Press.

Pavy, D. (1968) 'Verbal behaviour in schizophrenia: a review of recent studies', *Psychological Bulletin*, 70: 164–178.

Pepper, (1942) *World Hypotheses*. Berkeley, CA: University of California Press.

Perls, F. (1969) *Gestalt Therapy Verbatim*. Lafayette, CA: Real People Press.

Philo, G. (1994) 'Media images and popular belief', *Psychiatric Bulletin*, 18: 173–174.

Pichot, P. (1978) 'Psychopathic behaviour: a historical overview', in R.D. Hare and D. Schalling (eds), *Psychopathic Behaviour: Approaches to Research*. Chichester: John Wiley.

Pilgrim, D. and Rogers, A. (1993) *A Sociology of Mental Health and Illness*. Buckingham: Open University Press.

Pilgrim, D. and Treacher, A. (1992) *Clinical Psychology Observed*. London: Routledge.

Poster, M. (1978) *Critical Theory of the Family*. London: Pluto Press.

Purdie, S. (1993) *Comedy: the Mastery of Discourse*. London: Harvester Wheatsheaf.

Rabinow, P. (ed.) (1984) *The Foucault Reader*. Harmondsworth: Penguin.

Rack, P. (1982) *Race, Culture and Mental Disorder*. London: Tavistock Press.

Ramon, S. (1985) 'The Italian psychiatric reform', in S. Mangen (ed.), *Mental Health Care in the European Community*. Beckenham, Kent: Croom Helm.

Ramon, S. (1986) 'The category of psychopathy: its professional and social context in Britain', in N. Rose and P. Miller (eds), *The Power of Psychiatry*. Cambridge: Polity Press.

Ramon, S. and Giannichedda, M. (eds) (1989) *Psychiatry in Transition: the British and Italian Experiences*. London: Pluto Press.

Reed, J.L. (1970) 'Schizophrenic thought disorder: a review and hypotheses', *Comprehensive Psychiatry*, 11: 403–432.

Richardson, A. and Bray, C. (1987) *Promoting Health Through Participation: Experience of Groups for Patient Participation in General Practice*. London: Policy Studies Institute.

Richman, J. and Mason, T. (1992) 'Quo Vadis the Special Hospital', in F. Scott, G. Williams, S. Platt and H. Thomas (eds), *Private Risks and Public Dangers*. Aldershot: Avebury.

Rochester, S.R. and Martin, J.R. (1979) *Crazy Talk: a Study of the Discourse of Schizophrenic Speakers*. New York: Plenum.

Rogers, A. (1990) 'Policing mental disorder: controversies, myths and realities', *Social Policy and Administration*, 24: 226–237.

Rogers, C.R. (1961) *On Becoming a Person*. Boston: Houghton Mifflin.

Romme, M. and Escher, A. (1993) *Accepting Voices*. London: MIND.

Romme, M., Honig, A., Noorthoorn, E. and Escher, A. (1992) 'Coping with hearing voices: an emancipatory approach', *British Journal of Psychiatry*, 161: 99–103.

Rose, N. (1986) 'Psychiatry: the discipline of mental health', in P. Miller and N. Rose (eds), *The Power of Psychiatry*. Cambridge: Polity Press.

Rose, N. (1989) *Governing the Soul: Technologies of Human Subjectivity*. London: Routledge.

Rose, N. (1990) 'Psychology as a "social" science', in I. Parker and J. Shotter (eds), *Deconstructing Social Psychology*. London: Routledge.

Rosenbaum, B. and Sonne, H. (1986) *The Language of Psychosis*. New York: New York University Press.

Rosenhan, D.L. (1973) 'On being sane in insane places', *Science*, 179: 250–258.

Rosenhan, D.L. (1975) 'The contextual nature of psychiatric diagnosis', *Journal of Abnormal Psychology*, 84: 462–474.

Rosnow, R.L. and Fine, G.A. (1976) *Rumor and Gossip: the Social Psychology of Hearsay*. New York: Elsevier.

Roth, M. (1990) 'Psychopathic (sociopathic) personality disorder', in R. Bluglass and P. Bowden (eds), *Principles and Practice of Forensic Psychiatry*. London: Churchill Livingstone.

Roth, M. and Kroll, J. (1986) *The Reality of Mental Illness*. Cambridge: Cambridge University Press.

Roudinesco, E. (1990) *Jacques Lacan & Co.: a History of Psychoanalysis in France, 1925–1985*. London: Free Association Books.

Rush, F. (1984) 'The Freudian Cover-Up', *Trouble and Strife*, 4: 29–38.

Rutter, D.R. (1979) 'The reconstruction of schizophrenic speech', *British Journal of Psychiatry*, 134: 356–359.

Rutter, D.R. (1985) 'Language in schizophrenia: the structure of monologues and conversations', *British Journal of Psychiatry*, 146: 399–404.

Ryle, A. (1990) *Cognitive-Analytic Therapy: Active Participation in Change*. Chichester: Wiley.

Sacks, O. (1984) *The Man who Mistook his Wife for a Hat*. London: Duckworth.

Sampson, E.E. (1993a) 'Identity politics: challenges to psychology's understanding', *American Psychologist*, 48: 1219–1230.

Sampson, E.E. (1993b) *Celebrating the Other: a Dialogic Account of Human Nature*. Hemel Hempstead: Harvester Wheatsheaf.

Sarason, I.G. and Sarason, B.R. (1987) *Abnormal Psychology: the Problem of Maladaptive Behavior*. New York: Prentice-Hall.

Sartre, J.-P. (1969) *Being and Nothingness: an Essay on Phenomenological Ontology*. London: Methuen.

Sartre, J.-P. (1974) *Between Existentialism and Marxism*. London: New Left Books.

Schwartz, S. (1982) 'Is there a schizophrenic language?', *The Behavioural and Brain Sciences*, 5: 579–626.

Scott, J. (1994) 'What the papers say', *Psychiatric Bulletin*, 18: 489–491.

Sedgwick, P. (1982) *Psychopolitics*. London: Pluto Press.

Selvini Palazzoli, M., Boscolo, L., Cecchin, G. and Prata, G. (1978) *Paradox and Counter-Paradox*. New York: Jason Aronson.

Selvini Palazzoli, M., Boscolo, L. Cecchin, G. and Prata, G. (1980) 'Hypothesizing-circularity-neutrality: three guidelines for the conductor of the session', *Family Process*, 19: 3–12.

Shelton, G./Rip Off Press (1985) *Freak Brothers, No. 0*. London: Knockabout Comics.

Shotter, J. (1993) *Cultural Politics of Everyday Life: Social Constructionism, Rhetoric and Knowing of the Third Kind*. Buckingham: Open University Press.

Showalter, E. (1987) *Women, Madness and English Culture, 1830–1980*. London: Virago.

Siegler, M. and Osmond, H. (1977) *Models of Madness, Models of Medicine*. London: Macmillan.

Sinason, V. (1989) 'The psycholinguistics of discrimination', in B. Richards (ed.), *Crises of the Self: Further Essays on Psychoanalysis and Politics*. London: Free Association Books. pp. 217–227.

Skynner, R. and Cleese, J. (1983) *Families, and How to Survive Them*. London: Methuen.

Smail, D.J. (1984) *Illusion and Reality: the Meaning of Anxiety*. London: Dent.

Smail, D.J. (1987) *Taking Care: an Alternative to Therapy*. London: Dent.

Smail, D.J. (1993) *The Origins of Unhappiness: a New Understanding of Personal Distress*. London: Harper Collins.

Smith, D. (1978) 'K is mentally ill: the anatomy of a factual account', *Sociology*, 12: 23–53.

Smith, R. (1988) 'Does the history of psychology have a subject?', *History of the Human Sciences*, 1: 147–177.

Socialist Health Association (1987) *Goodbye to All That? Re-thinking the Politics of Mental Health*. London: Socialist Health Association.

Spandler, H. (1994) 'To Make an Army out of Illness', *Asylum*, 6 (4): 5–15.

Spitzer, R.L. and Endicott, J. (1968) *Research Diagnostic Criteria*. New York: New York State Psychiatric Institute.

Stainton Rogers, W. (1991) *Explaining Health and Illness: an Exploration of Diversity*. Hemel Hempstead: Harvester Wheatsheaf.

Stenner, P. (1993) Discoursing jealousy, in E. Burman and I. Parker (eds), *Discourse Analytic Research: Repertoires and Readings of Texts in Action*. London: Routledge.

Stowell-Smith, M. (1995) 'Race, psychopathy and subjectivity'. Post-graduate work in progress, Manchester Metropolitan University.

Swartz, S. (1992) 'Sources of misunderstanding in interviews with psychiatric patients', *Professional Psychology: Research and Practice*, 1: 24–29.

Swartz, S. (1994) 'Some methodological issues in the analysis of psychotic speech', *Journal of Psycholinguistic Research*, 23(1): 24–9.

Swartz, S. and Swartz, L. (1987) 'Talk about talk: metacommentary and context in the analysis of psychotic discourse', *Culture, Medicine and Psychiatry*, 11: 395–416.

Szasz, T. (1961) *The Myth of Mental Illness*. New York: Harper and Row.

Szasz, T. (1976) 'Anti-Psychiatry: the Paradigm of the Plundered Mind', *The New Review*, 3: 3–14.

Szasz, T. (1979) 'Sigmund Freud: the Jewish Avenger', in *The Myth of Psychotherapy: Mental Healing as Religion, Rhetoric, and Repression*. Oxford: Oxford University Press.

Tapping, C. (1991) 'Challenging the dominant story: behind the "worthy of discussion" groups', *Dulwich Centre Newsletter*, 4: 35–39.

Thomas, P., King, K., Fraser, W.I. and Kendell, R.E. (1990) 'Linguistic performance in schizophrenia: a comparison of acute and chronic patients', *British Journal of Psychiatry*, 156: 204–210.

Timpanaro, S. (1976) *The Freudian Slip: Psychoanalysis and Textual Criticism*. London: New Left Books.

Tomm, K. (1990) 'A critique of the DSM', *Dulwich Centre Newsletter*, 3: 5–8.

Turkle, S. (1981) 'French anti-psychiatry', in D. Ingleby (ed.), *Critical Psychiatry*. Harmondsworth: Penguin.

Turner, B. (1987) *Medical Power and Social Knowledge*. London: Sage.

Ussher, J. (1991) *Women's Madness: Misogyny or Mental Illness?* Hemel Hempstead: Harvester Wheatsheaf.

Van Belle, W. (1987) 'Assertive speech acts in psychotic discourse', in R. Wodak and P. Van de Craen (eds), *Neurotic and Psychotic Language Behaviour*. Clevedon: Multilingual Matters. pp. 332–345.

Walkerdine, V. (1981) 'Sex, power and pedagogy', *Screen Education*, 38: 14–24.

Walter, G. (1992) 'The psychiatrist in American cartoons 1941–1990', *Acta Psychiatrica Scandinavica*, 85: 167–172.

Warner, R. (1994) *Recovery from Schizophrenia: Psychiatry and Political Economy, 2nd edn*. London: Routledge.

Wetherell, M. and Potter, J. (1992) *Mapping the Language of Racism: Discourse and the Legitimation of Exploitation*. Hemel Hempstead: Harvester Wheatsheaf.

White, M. (1987) 'Family therapy and schizophrenia: addressing the "in-the-corner" lifestyle', reprinted in M. White (1989), *Selected Papers*. Adelaide: Dulwich Centre Publications, pp. 47–57.

White, M. (1988) 'The process of questioning: a therapy of literary merit?', reprinted in M. White (1989), *Selected Papers*. Adelaide: Dulwich Centre Publications. pp. 37–46.

White, M. (1991) 'Deconstruction and therapy', *Dulwich Centre Newsletter*. 3: 21–40.

White, M. and Epston, D. (1990) *Narrative Means to Therapeutic Ends*. Adelaide: Dulwich Centre Press.

Wiener, M. and Marcus, D. (1994) 'A sociocultural construction of "depressions" ', in T.R. Sarbin and J.I. Kitsuse (eds), *Constructing the Social*. London: Sage.

Wilson, M. (1993) 'DSM-III and the transformation of American Psychiatry: a history', *American Journal of Psychiatry*, 150: 399–410.

Wittgenstein, L. (1958) *Philosophical Investigations*, Oxford: Basil Blackwell.

Wolpe, J. (1958) *Psychotherapy by Reciprocal Inhibition*. Stanford, CA: Stanford University Press.

World Health Organization (1992) *The ICD-10 Classification of Mental and Behavioural Disorders*. Geneva: World Health Organzsation.

Wurtzel, E. (1995) *Prozac Nation*. London: Quartet.

Young, H.S. (1988) 'Practising RET with lower-class clients', in W. Dryden and P. Trower (eds), *Developments in Rational Emotive Therapy*. Milton Keynes: Open University Press/ Taylor and Francis.

Index